MW00439944

THE

T E A C H E R ' S

BODY

THE

TEACHER'S

BODY

Embodiment, Authority,
and Identity in the Academy

Edited by

DIANE P. FREEDMAN

and

MARTHA STODDARD HOLMES

STATE UNIVERSITY OF NEW YORK PRESS

Published by
STATE UNIVERSITY OF NEW YORK PRESS
ALBANY

© 2003 State University of New York

All rights reserved

Printed in the United States of America

No part of this book may be used or reproduced in any manner whatsoever
without written permission. No part of this book may be stored in a retrieval
system or transmitted in any form or by any means including electronic,
electrostatic, magnetic tape, mechanical, photocopying, recording, or otherwise
without the prior permission in writing of the publisher.

For information, address
State University of New York Press,
90 State Street, Suite 700, Albany, NY 12207

Production, Laurie Searl
Marketing, Anne M. Valentine

Library of Congress Cataloging-in-Publication Data

The teacher's body : embodiment, authority, and identity in the academy / edited by Diane
P. Freedman and Martha Stoddard Holmes.
    p. cm.
Includes bibliographical references and index.
ISBN 0-7914-5765-6 — ISBN 0-7914-5766-4 (pbk.)
    1. College teaching—Social aspects—United States. 2. Teachers with disabilities—United
States—Psychology. 3. Teacher-student relationships—United States. I. Freedman, Diane
P. II. Stoddard Holmes, Martha.

LB2331.T317 2003
378.1'2—dc21
                                                                    2003040472

10 9 8 7 6 5 4 3 2 1

For our sons,

Abraham Brody McWilliams

and

Joshua Stoddard Holmes

Contents

Foreword:
Bodies Enter the Classroom

Rosemarie Garland-Thomson

Body criticism is surging. Witness just a few recent "body" titles: *Body Thoughts, Body Matters, Body Talk, Bodylore, The Female Body, The Male Body, The Rejected Body, The Consuming Body, The Perfectible Body, Leaky Bodies, Recovering Bodies, Extraordinary Bodies, Building Bodies, Flexible Bodies, Foreign Bodies, Volatile Bodies, Deviant Bodies, Imaginary Bodies, Posthuman Bodies, American Bodies, Bodily Discursions, Technologies of the Gendered Body,* and *Disembodying Women.* Although this list verges on parody, the explanatory subtitles of these as well as the many other critical studies about the body indicate the remarkable depth and breadth of this vital new field of inquiry. The consistent use in these titles of the noun "body" or "bodies" qualified by an adjective or a phrase implies that this plethora of inquiries investigates how bodies are marked by culture and how they are imagined to diverge from a generic "body."

What I am calling "body criticism" analyzes representational systems such as race, gender, ethnicity, and disability as discourses that explain and give significance to bodily particularities and the differences among bodies. Body criticism questions our collective understandings of bodily traits, forms, functions, behaviors, perspectives, and experiences as natural and inevitable. Body criticism asserts that the metaphors, tropes, images, portrayals, stereotypes, caricatures, and other ideological frames through which a society represents people affect their lives. Body criticism, then, has both the impulse and the potential to revise oppressive cultural narratives and to reveal liberatory ones.

But often even the critical studies seemingly most focused on the lived body veer off into the abstract or founder in the discursive, eluding the materiality and lived experience of actual bodies in specific situations. Such studies frequently overlook particular bodies embedded in social relations and history to comment on a theoretical body—"the" body rather than situated bodies. *The Teacher's Body: Embodiment, Authority, and Identity in the Academy* avoids this problem. Indeed, the introduction and the chapters collected here are exemplary in their insistence not just that bodies are always located in individual moments and places, but that bodies themselves are always singular. This volume recognizes that it is the status not of the body in general but of the particularized body that is most pertinent as we try to understand who we are and how we relate to one another.

The Teacher's Body addresses the distinctiveness that leaps out of the generalized, invisible, and unobtrusive body. The authors here situate their analyses in the dynamically relational, interactive spaces of the classroom. They center on bodies that call attention to their own particularities and that refuse the polite anonymity and disembodied equanimity that has traditionally characterized educational settings. *The Teacher's Body* does this by focusing on the remarkable bodies we don't expect in the public sphere. Here we scrutinize encounters between student bodies understood to be normative and therefore neutral and teacher's bodies that are paradoxically considered at once extraordinary and invested with the authority of the profession. The disabled body, the racialized body, the pregnant body, the foreign body, the queer body, and the female body occupy the stage in these analyses. These chapters compel as such bodies boldly announce with their exceptional presence the singularities that would typically exclude them from the authority that their positioning endows. What results is a robust critical inquiry into the operations of identity and authority in the classroom, the traditional arena where supposedly disembodied minds engage.

The Teacher's Body addresses a range of embodied identities usually disguised, muted, or excluded from the role of the classroom teacher. What is provocative and insightful about the volume is that it introduces into its critical settings a number of bodies that significantly depart from the expected teacher's body. Women, people of color, gays and lesbians, and ethnic minorities are becoming more commonly accepted and expected as classroom teachers and in pedagogical studies. A critical inquiry into the dynamics that unfold when the bodies of people with dwarfism, cancer, paraplegia, deafness, and blindness are present in the classroom, however, is quite innovative. Disability as a category of analysis yields subtle and complex examinations of identity—relations that might not be as apparent as those found in the usual studies that focus on the usual triumvirate of diversity—gender, race, and class. By attending critically to the bodies imagined as most incompatible with the duties and authority of teaching, *The Teacher's Body* critically opens questions of the body not often addressed even in the plethora of books that is emerging. The major issue this volume confronts, then, is how teachers with bodies marked by society as inferior, inappropriate, private, and embarrassingly exposed in their embodiment negotiate that space of authority that is the classroom. By evoking bodies that society takes to be woefully and often extravagantly divergent from the normative, anonymous scholarly body that we imagine to head the classroom, *The Teacher's Body* does the critical work of challenging oppressive representations and accessing liberatory narratives. Exposing how these classroom dynamics operate thus contributes to the cultural work of transforming the way we think about and act within the world.

Acknowledgments

The editors' collaboration dates back to our student days, when we gave poetry readings together, read one another's papers on modern British fiction, and cooked up recipes out of *The Moosewood Cookbook* or *Diet for a Small Planet* to feed to our cooperative household of seven students and two dogs. This book is thus a collaboration of our always-remembered student lives and our teaching and family lives as well as one with all of our book's contributors, whom we thank for their patience, dedication, and inspiration and join in thanking the sources we all cite.

We also thank our respective departments and colleges, the Department of English, and the College of Liberal Arts at the University of New Hampshire, which supported the book with funds for copying and postage and the provision of a new computer at a crucial time, and the Department of Literature and Writing Studies at California State University, San Marcos.

We thank our students.

Finally, we thank the various favorite teachers of our lives, including teachers of writing, riding, and karate; teachers of literature and the arts; and our parents and grandparents, especially our grandmothers.

Introduction

Diane P. Freedman
and
Martha Stoddard Holmes

That our world increasingly concerns the body should come as no surprise. In the United States, at least, we see television advertisements probably once considered in bad taste for products we are now willing to admit or think we need: Depends undergarments or Detrol pills for incontinence, Viagra for erectile dysfunction, SSRIs for depression/shyness/anxiety, nicotine patches for quitting smoking, Pravachol for cholesterol, and the "Little Rascal" for getting around without walking. More patients and more payers mean more visible treatments or devices advertised for hearing loss, osteoporosis, osteoarthritis, diabetes, heart disease, and the effects of aging, illness, and/or catastrophe. And more money and worries mean more public-interest or paid announcements about "just saying no" to sex or drugs. Medicine and psychiatry are no longer privately discussed doctor to patient but are dependent upon what HMOs do or must cover—infertility treatments along with Viagra, and Ritalin for the young. There are more weight-loss clinics and products, tattoos and tummy tucks, hair and

1

skincare products available than ever before. "Infomercials" flood the airways. And let us not forget the rubber gloves, gas masks, and Cipro being hawked in the wake of recent biological and chemical-warfare scares. For the first time, coffins too are for sale on TV, advertised at a discount.

On the other hand, teacher-student disclosures and discussions of the needs and effects of the body, except perhaps in the "health classes" mandated in the 1970s or in the most theoretical terms, move along more slowly. Although we remember thinking frequently about the body when we were students, we can't quite imagine having learned, as our own children have, that a fourth-grade teacher was facing a heart-valve replacement operation; a piano teacher required a hysterectomy and summer recovery; a violin teacher had painful bursitis in her shoulder; and a riding instructor had a rib broken by a kicking horse. Perhaps it's only that our children are more out there, bodily, in ways we couldn't afford to be or weren't encouraged to be. Teachers and students no longer leave school if pregnant or ill, and access to learning and work for all and to realms formerly mostly for the male student body—whether sports or auto mechanics and shop—is a right.

In an earlier time, we noticed our teachers and studied them, but we didn't know much that wasn't either spoken or visible. What we did know, however, were things like these:

Diane loved her third-grade teacher. Not only did she make Diane feel smart, but she also let her sit on her lap and in winter helped her to pull on her stubborn snow pants. Diane learned that she could be little and somewhat coddled and still be smart. And the teacher—funny, big, and loud—could be maternal and more. Diane also loved her sixth-grade teacher, who was both her homeroom teacher and her sixth-grade science teacher. She was pregnant and left before the end of the school year to have her baby. She taught Diane that someone who was visibly a woman and mother-to-be could be smart in the ways mostly only boys were then considered smart. She had a short haircut and a no-nonsense sense of style and speech, but she, too, Diane could tell, respected Diane's mind. That was also why she was so disappointed (as was Diane) when she discovered Diane had written test answers on her hand during a trip to the bathroom.

No teacher's body went unobserved by Diane, though hers was ignored or maligned by some of them. The best learning situations, however, were those in which teacher and student acknowledged and approved of one another's bodies and minds. Diane disliked or was made anxious by her seventh-grade history teacher because he called her "mouse," making fun of her small size relative to her classmates, and because he collected and then mistreated animals and students—sometimes by punishing students with a detention during which they'd have to watch him feed white mice to the class snakes. He also claimed at times that animals had been lost in transit, as when the promised African monkeys failed to arrive and he used that as the excuse for not returning the essays on which some students had worked hard (he claimed the monkeys had gotten sick over the essays). At other times he stamped "bull" or "circular file" on their papers with his collection of custom stamps. And Diane noted the crooked teeth of her tenth-grade English teacher and was bothered by them but probably only because he seemed unfriendly and distant and rocked back and forth in his chair as he spoke, never minding that the chair leg repeatedly came down on one of his feet or that his toes got pinched by the drawer slide at the back of his desk drawer. It's probably no coincidence that the book Diane most remembers from that class is William Golding's *Lord of the Flies,* a novel about boys who turn on and eventually decide to eat one other when stranded on a desert island.

Diane now finds herself wanting to argue that, far from today's injunctions that teachers not hug students and that little boys and girls refrain from kissing one another, learning in school and loving and thriving in school require that teachers and students notice—and respect—their own and others' bodies.

When Diane became a teacher herself, she was reminded on several occasions that students often think teachers are and must be disembodied, though they are usually extremely relieved when they find out differently, after which classes and learning go much better. Her eighth-grade students needed to try on her clogs and admire her earrings and once even see her turn a cartwheel to be fully convinced she could be their friend and mentor. This extraordinary comradeship was necessary, she thinks, because she was teaching at a boarding school, and the girls and boys were lonely for their families. Diane's teaching had to have something of the family way about it even though she was not yet a mother herself.

When Diane was in graduate school and working as a writing teacher year after year to pay her way, her best semester (in terms of student evaluations) was the one in which she was quite unhappy and most likely showed her pervasive sadness on her face and in her posture. There seems to have been a connection between Diane's apparent emotional—and bodily—vulnerability and her winning a coveted teaching award that year.

Her students (when she was a new assistant professor some years later) remarked on how surprised they were to see her shopping, as they were, at a campus bazaar in the student union, querying her incredulously, "Was that you we saw buying earrings in the union on Saturday?!"

On the other hand, Diane once hadn't wanted to live in the town where she'd taught college lest a student spot her engaging in one of her then-favorite pastimes, swimming nude in the local (and legally off-limits) reservoir. So of course she'd sensed that there were limits to this otherwise necessary bodily interaction, just as there were limits to the heady times when such swimming habits and the wild dancing she used to do were possible.

In his collection *Confessions of the Critics,* H. Aram Veeser notes that "students are always shocked when they come upon their teachers out of school:

incredible! The teachers actually have a life apart from the classroom!" (ix). He quotes Rachel Brownstein's contribution to the collection, a chapter that asks us "to remember 'the delight and mischief and disbelief you first felt when your third-grade teacher turned up in a two-piece bathing suit at the beach. Why that's Mrs. Fisher—out from behind the desk, in a body!'" (Diane published an essay in that collection devoted to the still-new practice of autobiographical or "personal" scholarship, an interest and practice that for her clearly grow out of her conviction about the necessarily embodied nature of knowledge and pedagogy.) Veeser makes the general claim, one to which we accede, that these days teachers (and academic writers in general) increasingly "have come to appreciate the attention they suddenly command as soon as they slip into a body" (ix).

Again, when Diane was pregnant but not-quite-showing while teaching at Skidmore College, her students asked her why she was pulling hard-boiled eggs out of her jumper pockets and choking down too-dry granola bars while they spoke. Eventually Diane's pregnancy, via her hunger, couldn't be denied. And it actually gave her some extra authority if not solicitous attention. (On the other hand, a year before, Diane had lost a baby before she began to "show," and that loss went unmarked and unmentioned, though her sadness had surely helped shape classroom dynamics then just as her pregnancy did a year later.)

At the institution where Diane has been teaching for the last ten years, her female colleagues also report increased tolerance and solicitation as their own pregnancies visibly developed. However, a colleague who adopted rather than bore a child and did so after classes ended fall term got no such extra interest or support either from her colleagues or from the institution. Although campus policies include adoptive as well as birth parents in their "parental leaves," if no one notices you and if you are trying not to achieve a certain kind of notice (in preference to others), such as when you are applying for tenure, you don't even get the time off, let alone the time of day from colleagues, students, and administrators.

For many years of teaching, Martha's overall, comforting premise was that she was a mind attached to an apparatus, the body, whose purpose was simply to transport her ideas and intelligence to the classroom. The body didn't really matter except in service of this mind, the thing she had fallen back on all through her life when her body did not, for various reasons and in various contexts, suit. To talk or even think about the body (as she did, of course) seemed unprofessional.

The shift from unmarked to marked body happened without warning, such as when a large and distressed student spoke threateningly to her in an empty community college classroom and she remembered how small she was. Martha remembers that after that encounter she made herself demonstrate her physical bravery (teacherly authority) by giving the student a ride home; it was, after all, a winter night in northern Vermont and was well below freezing. After she dropped the student off with a calm and cheery "good night, see you next week," Martha cried and swore all the way home.

Even though Martha's students did not have to be at the front of the room (that "front" that follows the teacher's body wherever she moves), they had fewer tools to change the marked status of their bodies. Not only were they more relevant to each other as bodies than Martha was, but they were also more vulnerable to notice as particular kinds of bodies, especially in those situations in which they read and talked about gender, race, sexualities, and ability, in which certain bodies seemed to light up for other students as representative and be asked, to Martha's deep discomfort and perplexity, "What does a man think about this? What does a Chicana think about this? What does a person with a disability think about this?" The focus of the text on certain bodies seemed unbearable to Martha at times, and she longed for the unmarked realm of literature, generated by minds unattached to bodies. It has even become a pleasure for Martha to age out of the realm of relevance, where she can now comment on sexuality in a text without it seeming to adhere to her at all; to many of these students, whose parents are her age or younger, sexuality is simply not a country Martha or the students' parents inhabit.

When Martha finally got to teach about the body and the mesh of words, images, and practices that make and remake its meanings, the question of marking became much more complicated. In bringing the body to the foreground of class discussion, making it the text, the focus fell on everyone, although not on all equally. The classroom bodies were all under scrutiny, even when the class talked about bodies, disabilities, or differences as concepts. Many discussions were unintentionally painful in their association with the bodies the discussants lived in outside of the classroom, bodies that were stared at, rejected, obstructed from access to bathrooms and classrooms, diagnosed and classified, loved for the wrong reasons, photographed, written about, beaten, as well as treated kindly, loved, soothed, and delighted. Such conversations invited, not always with student or teacher consent, those bodies that considered and had abortions, gave birth, despaired, binged, purged, felt alien and were marked alien by others, as well as those bodies that loved, married, enjoyed, read, and learned.

In *Wit*, a play by Margaret Edson, the protagonist, a professor of seventeenth-century English literature with stage-four ovarian cancer, notes the irony in having for so long taught others about books but now having *her body* read "like a book" by medical personnel. Now she is the one and the thing being taught—both as an audience and as an object/subject matter. We accept the idea that the teacher's body should be read, though not cordoned off, as the protagonist of *Wit* seems to be. But more commonly, teachers can become ill and still be teachers. For this, we need engaged and critical analysis of how experience and classroom relate to one another; we do not need a dismissal or elevation of the teacher's body as (a) heroically and tragically ill (if ill or disabled), (b) miraculous and inspiring in its overcoming disability or illness, (c) all well, (d) a mistake or irrelevancy, or (e) something we should not talk about because (g) it is not subject matter related to our work. The essayists represented here are unflinching in their complex portrayals of embodied experience in the classroom.

We maintain that regardless of whether we or our students, singly or multiply, have physical or other health challenges and changes in evidence; whether our research and course offerings make explicit the physical contours of our subjects; or whether they include field and site work where the body is perhaps more clearly in play, we are inevitably, ineluctably inspired, limited, plagued, and aided by—given the growing state of discourse about the body, disability, and "selfhood"—our increasingly self-conscious bodies (and by the bodies around us). We need more books this like one that powerfully insist upon here-and-now stories of teaching in académe.

The bodily reality of the college teacher may include cancer—and/or cartwheels and body piercing, ED, pregnancy, miscarriage, aging, youth, beauty, arthritis, depression, AIDS, heart disease, physical intimidation, diabetes, infertility, sleep deprivation, mobility impairment, paralysis, deafness, blindness, posttraumatic stress, rape, anorexia—many situations seen and unseen and many situations beyond those described in this volume.

Recent collections in a wide range of fields have renewed attention to the body—even, for example, *Our Monica, Ourselves* (2001), which, according to reviewer Micaela di Leonardo, reminds readers—like the Monica Lewinsky-Clinton episodes themselves and however "embarrassingly"—that the president of the United States has a body. The events, the book, and the theories and contemporary academic preoccupations on which the book is based emphasize "the classed, raced and gendered nature of embodiment in contemporary America" (9). A flier for the National Women's Studies Association 2002 Conference solicited papers for a plenary topic on the subject of "body politics" and the notion that "for more than a century, feminists have been responding to the platitude 'anatomy is destiny' and the drive both to curtail the forces of anatomy and social construction/socialization and to attend to the real needs and desires of women rooted in real bodies" (2). One of our contributors, Kimberly Wallace-Sanders, reports receiving a call for papers for a Canadian conference on "Teaching Motherhood, Being a Mother-Teacher and Doing Maternal Pedagogy." Clearly, as several contributors note, feminist scholars are at the forefront of unabashed discourse about the body. The chapters we present here thus enter an important moment of review and reenactment of the body's various meanings and employment in the college classroom.

As we well know, student bodies often command most of the attention in college classrooms. Young or old, pierced or tattooed, sleeping or rapt, these bodies dominate the room and seem to justify its existence. The body of the often-parodied professor, in contrast, is (to the students and increasingly to administrators) both present and irrelevant, disembodied by discreet or dowdy dress and, most hurried mornings, by a face unredeemed by cosmetics or careful coif. Even the battered briefcase expresses disregard for anything but the life of the mind and the practicalities of scholarship. One stereotype has the professor displaying the intellect without shame but keeping the body out of speech, sight, and investigation.

In order not to stuff all college faculty into one battered briefcase and to counter the demotion of college and university professors and teaching assistants, *The Teacher's Body* presents new essays exploring the palpable moments of discomfort, disempowerment, and/or enlightenment that emerge when we discard the fiction that the teacher (like the U.S. president) has no body. Many of these essays in fact portray the moments of embodied pedagogy as unexpected teaching opportunities. Visible and/or invisible, the body can transform both the teacher's experience and classroom dynamics. When students think the teacher's body is clearly marked by ethnicity, race, disability, size, gender, sexuality, illness, age, pregnancy, class, linguistic and geographic origins, or some combination of these, both the mode and the content of education can change. Other, less visible, aspects of a teacher's body, such as depression or a history of sexual assault, can have an equally powerful impact on how we teach and learn.

In personal and accessible prose informed by contemporary performance, disability, queer, feminist, psychoanalytical, and autobiographical theory, *The Teacher's Body* presents teaching bodies in a range of academic settings, examining their apparent effect on educational dynamics of power, authority, desire, friendship, open-mindedness, and resistance. The contributors, ranging in professional status from graduate students to full professors, teach at research institutions, small liberal arts colleges, and professional schools in the fields of composition and literature, sociology, oceanography, ESL, medicine, education, performance studies, American studies, African American studies, and women's studies.

Although this volume is unique in the range of disciplines its contributors represent and its focus on the implications of many kinds of teachers' bodies in the classroom, it continues a conversation that currently includes other thoughtful and successful volumes such as *Teaching What You're Not; This Fine Place So Far from Home: Voices of Academics from the Working Class; Calling: Essays on Teaching in the Mother Tongue; Never a Dull Moment: Teaching and the Art of Performance; A Life in School; Pedagogy: The Question of Impersonation;* and *Passing and Pedagogy: The Dynamics of Responsibility*, not to mention *Claiming Disability: Knowledge and Identity; Enhancing Diversity: Educators with Disabilities; Disability Studies: Enabling the Humanities; Staring Back: The Disability Experience from the Inside Out; Inside the Academy and Out:*

Lesbian/Gay/Queer Studies and Social Action; and *Coming Out of the Classroom Closet: Gay and Lesbian Students, Teachers, and Curricula,* among others.

A note about organization: The chapters that follow reveal so many connections even in their variety that there is no satisfactory arrangement of them into familiar limited sections. They enlighten and delight however they are encountered.

The volume opens with a chapter by Betty Smith Franklin, Professor of Curriculum, Foundations, and Research, in which she describes her changing awareness and practice of bodily engagement in the classroom experience. A prevalent theme and situation is that of eating disorders, plaguing students and faculty alike. Franklin ultimately acts inside and outside the classroom to alter the climate of female self-degradation and denial. All teachers and students, she argues, and the production of art, in fact, benefit from attention to embodied teaching reality in the classroom.

Explicitly framed by experiences of medicalization, the next three chapters are dramatic. A recollected scene of medical instruction opens Scott Smith's "On the Desk: Dwarfism, Teaching, and the Body," as "a man points at [his] hips, knees, ankles with a silver pen." Smith, now a university teacher with a critical consciousness of how medical and other cultures construct our bodies and our disabilities, argues that the body may be "the most telling text of the course, the one our students will . . . respond to in deciding what kind of teacher we will be for them."

Cortney Davis's "Body Teaching," which also begins with the clinical, provides an alternate perspective. As a medical educator, Davis knows possibly the most important part of health professionals' education occurs in examining rooms, literally hands-on, as patients' bodies, needs, voices, and various modes of being in the world merge with, deepen, and complicate the conceptual bodies of texts and lectures. The marked body is the patient's body, but what about the bodies of the teacher and learner who depend on her? As Davis elucidates, "I am keenly aware that I am a woman teaching a man [about women's bodies], and, in a role reversal even more volatile, a nurse teaching a doctor whose authority will be, ultimately, more respected than mine. Most of all, I am a female guide who must step out of her body, casting off any suggestions of sensuality or privilege, when it is precisely my body that allows me to excel at teaching this intimate exam."

Carolyn DiPalma's "Teaching Women's Studies/E-Mailing Cancer" examines the body moving in one time frame between academic and medical culture, theory and practice. "I . . . knew much about gendered body image, the signification of the breast and its (problematic) relationship to the social construction of 'femaleness' and 'femininity,'" she writes. What was more challenging was "weaving this knowledge usefully" into the experience of being diagnosed and treated for breast cancer and then bringing that weave of theory and practice into a women's studies classroom. Apprehensive both about encountering the medical model and being constructed in troubling new ways by colleagues and students, DiPalma instead found her healthcare encounters "appropriate, appealing, and personalized" and her students, in particular, ready to engage and support her experience. They clearly expressed in various ways that "[they] were going through an ill-defined and important process together—one at which [they] were all willing to work."

Teaching contemporary critical theory, which many of us do with a sense of its liberatory possibilities, often produces a scene of unnoticed and unattended distancing from the body, even when the theory itself engages embodiment. Diane Price Herndl's "Johnny Mnemonic" asks the difficult question of what it would mean to teach the postmodern subject with less of that safe distance if, for example, rather than celebrating the rhizomatic subject while passing as a Cartesian one, we actually acknowledged that our lives are fractured or that we feel, for example, like "bimbo professors" in the face of contemporary life. Further complicating a critique that is both assiduous and playful, Price Herndl's epilogue takes us beyond the bimbo professor to the ways her pedagogy changed when the body she brought to class was diagnosed with breast cancer, underwent chemotherapy and mastectomy, and eventually had the cancer go into remission.

If the teacher's body fades from awareness in the course of many classes, it always shows up on the first day of school, an opportunity sociology professor Rod Michalko uses to launch his students' first engagement with the basics of his discipline; from day one they learn Sociology 101 and "blindness," as he relates in "'I've Got a Blind Prof': The Place of Blindness in the Academy." But what is the Butlerian "scenography" of the entry of blindness into the university classroom, an event to which many students react with surprise? Michalko's investigation is both local, focused on the particular social organization of the university classroom, and applicable to many other scenes in which disability enters a social frame but is already framed by and even integrated into its most basic assumptions about bodies and knowledge.

As academic culture frames and places disabled bodies, attitudinal and physical environments can be mutually reinforcing, especially when the discipline and its research modes are both inscribed as "physical." Richard Radtke in "My Body, Myself: A Quadriplegic's Perception of and Approach to Teaching" narrates how academic culture narrowly defines both the "appropriate" physical and professional space of a quadriplegic oceanography professor and—in practical detail—his daily work within this space, work that increasingly stretches its boundaries.

The teacher's body often achieves presence by virtue of its difference from the context. In "The Day the Foreign Devil Came to Class," Pam Whitfield writes about the four years she spent teaching in Zhangzhou province in Southern China and of the realization that "my body would have to assimilate too," a public and private process in which Whitfield's negotiations of her distance from Chinese norms—not just of appearance and language but also of those "stylized, repetitive social acts" that constituted femininity in her new home— both obscured and clarified her ambitious goals as a teacher.

By probing the effectiveness or noneffectiveness of debating race and racial issues in the classroom, Simone A. James Alexander's "Walking on Thin Ice: The Il/legitimacy of Race and Racial Issues in the Classroom" examines how race, gender, and class determine classroom dynamics and course content. Alexander, a teacher of African American studies, addresses the responsibilities that both students and the institution expect the teacher to shoulder and how these expectations change when the teacher is of color. Although the head of her class, the teacher, ironically, not only suffers bodily containment in the enclosed classroom but tailors her discourse to suit the needs of her students and the institution. Moreover, the students, governed by race- and gender-restricted discourses, similarly suffer great discomfort. To negotiate this uncomfortable situation, Alexander challenges her students by teaching texts that celebrate differences and otherness.

Dance is both figure and practice for Petra Kuppers and Brenda Daly, in two very different chapters about dance as the enactment of learning. In "Moving Bodies," Kuppers demonstrates how contact improvisations and specifically the tactical use of the teacher's body (in a wheelchair) can allow students to engage difference physically and conceptually when the teacher sets up the dance classroom as a place where students can experience differences between nondisabled and disabled people, among nondisabled people, and within the self.

In Daly's "Dancing Revolution," an impromptu jig performed to rouse a somnolent student involves the whole class in the unclouded pleasure of overturning the academic dictum to "leave the body behind." "Dancing Revolution" sustains its exploration of dance as literary trope, pedagogic metaphor, and embodied experience for several more turns by reflecting on the different rhythms and crises of the dancing body through the combined life cycles of the teacher herself and the changing academic culture in which she teaches.

The nexus of professional development, bodily transformation, and theory forms the core of Ray Pence's "Enforcing Diversity and Living with Disability: Learning from My First Teaching Year," which explores his experiences of "change and convergence" initiated by the concurrence of his first year of graduate school, teaching, and living with chronic illness. Pence's experiences in the classrooms where he taught, seminar rooms where he learned about new epistemologies, and clinical spaces where he was defined as a psoriatic arthritis patient provide the raw material for these reflections. He locates his narrative within disability studies and American studies, disciplines that continue to shape his perceptions of identities: his own and those of people with whom he interacts as a teacher and scholar.

The idea that a teacher's body and sexuality must be both remembered and forgotten to produce effective teaching is part of Jonathan Alexander's "A 'Sisterly Camaraderie' and Other Queer Friendships: A Gay Teacher Interacting with Straight Students." Writing around and through his students' correspondence with him about who he was to them before and after he disclosed his sexuality, Alexander affirms "that there are multiple pedagogical advantages to 'coming out' in the classroom. . . . [I]n marking our sexual orientation, we encourage straight students (and faculty) to mark their sexual orientations and become aware of the ways in which sexuality is labeled, codified, and politicized in our society. At the simplest level, we postulate that, if the unexamined life is not worth living, then the unexamined heterosexual life, with latent homophobic attitudes left intact, could be lethal—as it has been, for instance, for Matthew Shepard and many other gays and lesbians." What complicates the value of disclosure, Alexander asserts, is the reality that "[his] embodiment and authority as a teacher more often than not depend on [his] students' actively suppressing 'knowledge' of [his] sexuality."

Amy Spangler Gerald writes about similar dilemmas in "Teaching Pregnant: A Case for Holistic Pedagogy," one of several chapters taking up perhaps the most common changed-body experience that occurs in the college classroom setting and thus deserves serious attention. Gerald here reflects on a composition class in which she assiduously kept her visible pregnancy out of the discussion, thinking that keeping her body out of the conversation would be an important professionalizing gesture. In fact, although it may have conferred more professional authority, keeping silent about pregnancy seems to have taken away another kind of teaching credit in the realm of the intimacy and nurturing that students expect disproportionately of women teachers.

Kimberly Wallace-Sanders also writes, in "A Vessel of Possibilities: Teaching through the Expectant Body," of the complications and undermining of authority that may arise when a teacher, because visibly pregnant, is inevitably seen by her students as both sexual and maternal, doubled (because revealed as "more than a whole body") and "fragmented" ("the emphasized abdomen obscures the rest of the body"). But even though pregnancy may thus compound what "faculty of color, and female faculty of color in particular," like herself, already experience—an acute awareness of their bodies in the classroom—it is also, for this teacher of women's studies and African American material culture, a "vessel of pedagogical possibilities."

In her own chapter on teaching pregnant, "At Home at Work: Confining and Defining Pregnancy in the Academy," literary scholar Allison Giffen addresses the institutional "confinement" of the pregnant professor. She proposes that although she may have found something liberatory (and salutary educationally) occurring in the classroom, we need to ask to what extent "baby talk" might "further codif[y] the legitimizing centrality of heterosexuality within the classroom and the university, and consequently exclud[e] queer identities, or even those men and women for whom having children was either not an option or not a desirable option."

The conversation about the pedagogical and political value of coming out, "making visible an identity that has been largely invisible, discredited, or actively ignored in the academy," has engaged the academy for several years now. As Brenda Jo Brueggemann and Debra A. Moddelmog discuss in "Coming Out Pedagogy: Risking Identity in Language and Literature Classrooms," when teachers claim "historically abject" identities (e.g., disabled person, queer), "knowledge, discourse, affirmation, recognition, and a political context" are produced in the interlinked realms of scholarship and the classroom. Brueggemann and Moddelmog's chapter powerfully interweaves two narratives of coming out (or, in the frame of Pamela Caughie, changing what they "pass" as) in the classroom, deepening and complicating what it means to pass as able bodied/heterosexual and then come out as disabled/homosexual. As the two authors, who teach together, illustrate with examples from their course, changing or "troubling" our performed identities in the presence of our students has powerful effects on teaching, learning, and notions of the body and identity.

The power of disclosing truths about the body is partly contingent on the vulnerability such disclosures produce in the classroom community. As Michelle Cox and Katherine E. Tirabassi observe, the small size of composition classes and their emphasis on first-person writing often generate student disclosures with their mixed harvest of pain and power, and composition teachers often wonder how to respond. Their "Dangerous Responses," however, looks at a different dynamic, narrating and analyzing how two classes' uncritical responses to an essay on date rape produced successive levels of vulnerability and personal and professional critique within their teachers. Feeling vulnerable can be particularly uncomfortable for us as teachers, while at the same time it creates the potential for an intensely ethical classroom encounter, one in which personal experience is tendered with the intent of giving a voice to silenced students. Cox and Tirabassi's collaborative narrative and analysis unravels exactly how complicated decisions about disclosure can be and offers an alternate scenario to teacher-class disclosure.

Finally, educational theorist Madeleine R. Grumet provides an afterword, "*My* Teacher's Body," on the dual nature of every body, the body as object and subject. Grumet herself moves between a discussion of "the teacher's body" and "*my* teacher's body [her own body or the body of the person who teaches her]," as she sums up some of the ways a teacher's subjectivity is first erased and then restored, both in this volume and in pedagogical history. Grumet celebrates "a curriculum at every level of education that acknowledges the existential realities of its teachers and students" and the contributors here, who "make themselves present so that their students may be present as well," integrated and educated.

Martha's most memorable experience of teaching and the body came during an NEH Summer Seminar on Disability Studies co-led by Rosemarie Garland-Thomson and Paul Longmore at San Francisco State University. The participants' differences included gender, age, ethnicity, academic discipline, and a wide range of disabilities. As the leaders may have predicted, the key text for many weeks became none of the cutting-edge essays and books assigned but rather the dynamics with which the group—and all their differences—came together in a seminar space.

As they worked with space, place, time, body, and communication, words such as "access" and "reasonable accommodation" acquired mass, dimension, texture, and tenor in ways that they can only if people with disabilities are present, seen and/or heard, and recognized in the interaction. This process of working out how to be together in conversation, in their different bodies, in that room, transformed every discussion the group had that summer.

It wasn't always easy or comfortable. A free-flowing sentence had to be interrupted: "Can you please use the microphone?" "You need to use the mike." "Do I have to use the mike?" "You have to use the mike." "Can you please identify yourself before you speak?" "Can you please move this chair?" A recurrent text was who was heard and who was not; who could come to the table and who did not have access. The group talked about what it felt like to have to keep asking for what you needed, even if you asked yesterday; what it felt like to forget what someone needed; and what it felt like, finally, not to need to ask and not to forget—to be able to converse because we had worked out, at least temporarily, these crucial (and reasonable) basics.

The group also talked about the academic conversations that took place and would take place again outside the seminar. What did it mean to disclose disability during a job search? If tenure committees had certain equations in mind for a body in motion toward tenure, what would it mean when a surgery needed to happen within that time? Would disability and pregnancy be viewed as parallel delays to the tenure clock, and did you have to pick one? How could disabled students have better access to our disability studies classes?

These conversations had more of an impact on the process of communication and collegiality—on scenes of teaching—than any of the content texts, convincing the group that discussions of the concept and history of difference, as important as they are, have significant limits. Visible, audible, tactile spaces of clear diversity, on the other hand, have remarkable power that doesn't often get realized. We all need to learn more about the real dimensions of access and about the many modes in which we invite or exclude conversation if we want to make our classrooms places where difference is really welcome.

Every teacher, even the distance-learning teacher, has a body (virtual or imagined though it may be) and needs to negotiate its place in the classroom, possibly transforming what cannot be made invisible into a sign of authority or, if she is particularly courageous, an acknowledged element of the learning process, as many of the writers in this collection have done. The body is already in the classroom, but how to acknowledge this and work with it is the question many of these writers explore. The focus is explicitly on the teacher's body and on a wide range of experiences of embodiment and pedagogy: what it's like to suddenly be a marked body, how that experience changes over time, how we engage those changes in powerful and productive and curious ways, how we change the meanings of our bodies and our students' bodies in the real time of the classroom and in the spaces of writing that attach to it.

One of the things this collection explores implicitly is this profession's interesting geography, the spaces in which our bodies exist and profess. As Simone James Alexander points out, the real time of the classroom is only one such space; for her, as for several of the other writers in this collection, the space of the essay is a place in which what happened there is unpacked and worked out, eventually to return to a new teaching space. Our students, similarly, work through the classroom time in their assignments, e-mails, office-hour visits, course evaluations, and nowadays in Internet discussion lists as well. Our bodies are diffused across many such sites of expression and interaction. But what many of these chapters remind us of is the power of presence and particularly the power of diversity in that presence: the difference that having a class in which the teacher and most of the students have visible or otherwise articulated and explored differences can make to our scenes of learning.

WORKS CITED AND FOR FURTHER READING

Brueggemann, Brenda Jo, Rosemarie Garland-Thomson, and Sharon Snyder, eds. *Disability Studies: Enabling the Humanities*. New York: MLA, 2002.

Dews, C. L., Barney and Carolyn Leste Law, eds. *This Fine Place So Far from Home: Voices of Academics from the Working Class*. Philadelphia: Temple UP, 1995.

Felman, Jyl Lynn. *Never a Dull Moment: Teaching and the Art of Performance*. New York: Routledge, 2001.

Fries, Kenny, ed. *Staring Back: The Disability Experience from the Inside Out*. New York: Plume, 1987.

Gallop, Jane, ed. *Pedagogy: The Question of Impersonation*. Bloomington: U of Indiana P, 1995.

Griffin, Gail. *Calling: Essays on Teaching in the Mother Tongue*. Pasadena: Trilogy, 1992.

Leonardo, Micaela di. Rev. of *Our Monica, Ourselves*, ed. Lauren Berlant. *Women's Review of Books* 18.12 (Sept. 2001): 8–9.

Mayberry, Katherine, ed. *Teaching What You're Not*. New York: New York UP, 1996.

Veeser, H. Aram. Introduction: "The Case for Confessional Criticism." *Confessions of the Critics*. New York: Routledge, 1996. ix–xxvii.

The Teacher's Body

Betty Smith Franklin

"Miz Franklin, how come you don't eat candy bars?"

She is in the doorway—skinny, eighteen years old, wide-eyed about most everything. She has ventured into college and is looking at all the strange people there—people who don't act like the ones she sees everyday in her little town. I look up from my desk, smile, and try to focus and think of a good reply.

"Well," I say, "I like food that is crunchy, good tasting, and good for me. And I want to eat things that I think are a good example for my children. Want an apple?"

"Yes," she says and sits down. She watches me, wondering about being a woman in the wider world, a world way past vending machine niches where a diet Coke and a candy bar pass for breakfast.

I remembered the event, but I didn't think much about it for years. I was clueless about teaching with the body—my body—in action in 1974. Back then, I gave right answers. I made a lot of handouts and mimeographed them. I had charts and graphs, topic-related articles from popular magazines—a bit of Margaret Mead from *Redbook*. I knew that gaps between the world of schooling and the everyday world of living had to be bridged for education to work. I believed in observation and reflection. Lots of it. But I did not see how closely I was being observed, nor did I reflect on what I was teaching with my body, voice, and passions.

By 1994 I had caught on. I was better able to "read the world" in the Freirean sense. I made fewer handouts. (More trees lived.) I was more often able to see myself, my living being, in the educational milieu. Gradually I had become less embedded in the teacher role—I could see it and stand alongside it. I read. As bell hooks had reminded us, teaching was a performative act. Madeleine Grumet had made parallels between teaching and mothering—that complex physical relationship with its mutual shaping of mind and body. Parker Palmer made the connection between every curriculum decision and our tacit commitments to ways of knowing and being.

I observed. In a new teaching setting in a culture rampant with eating disorders, I noticed that faculty women were not eating, certainly not eating in a pleasurable, relaxed, or entitled way. So I consciously began to have lunch in a public place, unhurried, in good company with good food and without the normative chat about food and guilt. Next I institutionalized the practice. I posted times and sign-up sheets for group conferences in the student center at lunchtime twice a week. Students signed up. We talked, we ate, we laughed, and we did some planning for group projects. We were redefining "what grown women do" by establishing a setting for a pleasurable, embodied mix of work and play. We were not performing self-abnegation, self-neglect, or self-punishment in order to belong to the popular club of long-suffering, painfully thin faculty and students. Early in the next semester, two young women came to my office with a request. They wanted me to join their academic dance class as a student. "Come," they said. "People are making terrible comments about their bodies in class every day. They won't do it if you are there. This is a political action." So I enrolled in Beginning Modern. And the discourse of the class changed.

The students watched me, wondering about being a woman in the wider world. They noted the body in action—not the one caught in the static gaze and theorized about. They wanted an ally in resisting the common verbal current of disparagement. They wanted someone to actively stand by but not too close, not as an intruder or explainer. They wanted someone who witnessed their realm and shared in aspects of their identity—woman, learner, physical presence—someone to come into the embodied culture the way Freire described himself—with "epistemological curiosity and affection."

I watched them. The young women wondered aloud what parts of themselves might survive their education and professional acculturation—what parts might have to be given up. They spoke in my classes of "poses," false selves that enabled them to get by, and they wondered whether even small patches of authenticity in their student and social roles were too dangerous to tread. I learned more and more to be quiet, to wait, to watch, to think about the embodied differences in our generation and gender roles.

I planned classes on the basis of what I was learning. I offered thoughts and readings that showed how other people had struggled with the themes I was witnessing. Most effectively, I offered my students connections with living others. I included expressive life writing and poetry in every text selection and collaborative projects into every term. I built into the curriculum opportunities to go together to campus events and to meet the speakers and performers and watch them "off camera." I invited guests to class and set the pace so that people could connect with each other—somebody to somebody. I asked students to write at the end of term about one or two things in our work together that were really important to them. A young man wrote that the class visit from a lifelong activist was the most important thing that had happened for him. He said, "People always tell me that it is alright to be an idealist when you are young, but that you have to give it up as you grow older. When I met her, I knew that was wrong. I can be who I am my whole life."

I created opportunities for collaborative research that engaged students in rethinking their own knowledge and power. One social psychology class event, later named "The Body Project," became a critical event for the class, the college, and me. As a method of teaching qualitative research, specifically, the organization of data, I assigned the class members the job of listening to what people were saying about their bodies at different locations on campus for a twenty-four-hour period. That first evening the students took Post-It notes for recording the talk and decided how to code the interactions. They chose to code by gender of speaker and listener, audience size, time, and place. They mapped the campus and organized their stations ranging from the dorm to classrooms, the gym, and the administration building. In the next class session when the data came in, we took the yellow patches with samples of "body talk" and gave them to small groups who would then develop schemes for analysis. Nearly all of the recorded comments were negative and disparaging to the speaker. We were on to something. The work took fire. In Freirean terms, we had found a generative theme.

For a month, the data, their analysis, and the interventions the class groups developed to respond to their learning were the subject of campus newspaper articles, angry graffiti, and hundreds of conversations. One group came to theorize women's continuous negative talk about their bodies as an element of a "ritual of belonging," parallel to men's military or fraternity hazing.

The class groups planned interventions. A group of women focused on ways to change their own internal dialogues about bodies that blocked their insights and their potential for change. They practiced alternatives aloud and logged their daily responses. Another group of men and women took on the task of disrupting public dialogues by first rehearsing systematic alternatives to the normative negative body talk and then using them in the informal conversations they encountered. A third research group took the literal words and phrases overheard on campus and made from them a reader's theater piece called "I'm So Fat," which they audiotaped and played over and over in the campus gathering place near the post office. We had uncovered a silent ritual and created ways to represent it in science and in the arts.

I was learning that as a teacher, my body is always on the line in the activist sense. I had already learned and taught about the presence of the researcher in his or her work. There is no researcher distance untouched by presence, Fran Markowitz and Michael Ashkenazi remind us. Even the physicist Gell-Mann writes, "Any definition of complexity is necessarily context-dependent, even subjective"; furthermore, "it depends on the observer or the observing equipment" (33). Michelle Fine helps us to see farther and to know that the relationship is mutual—we shape the "data" and they shape us. And of course for the teacher/researcher, one who is attuned to and learning from the teaching experience, the relationship extends. Just as the researcher is the instrument, the teacher is the medium for knowing and teaching.

We know each other and ourselves through our bodies. As I listen to someone's powerful story, the hair on my arms stands up. When I am held captive in a meeting listening to the droning of endless cover stories, I feel a deadening tension in my lower back. As I hear and see the creation of ideas and networks that release the power of knowing, I am filled with the deep breathing of excitement and at the same time quieted by awe and solemnity. I experience the world.

So it is no surprise that I am drawn to the arts, where the body and the senses more often "leave the page." The imagination that we release, says Maxine Greene, opens in the body through sound, sight, and movement. The school home that Jane Roland Martin theorizes about and describes (1992) is rich in embodied, integrated, relational, and passionate action. It resists the sensory disconnection that is privileged as a higher form of schooling.

I find less of what I need to navigate my experience of teaching in the current theoretical writing about "the body." As Kathy Davis says, "The body may be back but the new body theory is just as . . . disembodied as it ever was. . . . Postmodern theorizing about the body has all too often been a cerebral, esoteric, and ultimately disembodied activity" (14). In *Coming of Age in Academe* (50), Jane Roland Martin helps us frame this position of discourse as "aerial distance," a way of seeing that enables the removal of oneself from traditionally disparaged women's concerns to the distant scholarly enclaves. In order to ascend the pyramid of status, scholars may leave behind real, sensory, physically located bodies.

Yet I am deeply moved by the history of education. I have to stop and breathe deeply as I read the accounts of complex lives that reveal the conscious and unconscious intentions shaping our past and present. The letters and diaries of teachers in each historical era illustrate the paradox of freedom and bondage within teachers' lives. The living/dying bodies tell the stories. For example, Joel Spring's account of Indian education reveals that many of the very young women, girls really, who went west to teach were often orphans with few prospects. After 1820 these young women, sent from the East by the missionary board to teach among the Choctaw, "labored for a stipend of twelve to fifteen dollars monthly. Invariably they succumbed to the unhealthful climate in which they labored, and suffered through long sieges of illness, and often their emaciated bodies were interred in the malarial soil of the far off wilderness" (124). Oklahoma teachers' journals described physical and mental debility. One young missionary teacher, Eliza Cleaver, "was found wandering over the prairies with mind so disordered as to make her return home imperative" (124).

Martyrdom, one of the themes that shrouds our understanding of teaching, is revealed in our bodies as well as in those teachers' bodies in historic accounts. Do we dissipate our selves in hostile conditions as a way of bringing heroic significance to our work? Does commitment to the life of the mind and spirit necessitate denial of our physical and emotional needs? In hostile academic conditions, do we allow essential bits of ourselves to dissipate in service to some higher, purer, scholarly end? And, if so, does this then not mirror the relational aspects of women's and girls' lives, wherein, according to Gilligan, "womanhood" requires a "dissociative split between experience and what is generally taken to be reality" (xxi)? That is, the experience of education, a disembodied education, for women especially, is much like their initiation into adulthood—a process of instruction during which they learn that they must take themselves *out* of relationship (to their bodies and to others) in order paradoxically to be *in* relationship. Be less to be more. Shut down to be open. Attend but not to this context, this time and place, or these bodies.

The pain of these contradictions can bring us to such a yearning for a disembodied certainty that we deny ourselves a richness of purpose and surrender others to an epistemology of expediency. We know the pain in our bodies, just as we know the glory. We see the pain of being shut down; its evidence is apparent in the defensive hunches of gathered bodies at faculty meetings and conferences where we anxiously pile up the modern-day cyberequivalents of mimeographed handouts.

As George Eliot writes in *Middlemarch:*

It is an uneasy lot at best, to be what we call highly taught and yet not to enjoy; to be present at this great spectacle of life and never to be fully possessed of the glory we behold, never to have our consciousness rapturously transformed into the vividness of a thought, the ardor of passion, the energy of action. (206–207)

So to be possessed of glory in the dynamics of teaching and learning is to be embodied and to honor the embodiment of others. That is why the arts are connected to school achievement. That is what attention to race, class, and gender—embodied realities—is all about. That is why the current issues in education are all about who counts and who serves in the present, who is honored, and who has been dishonored in the past. Michelle Fine—whose energy and moral courage are evidenced in all of her work—the topics, the methods, the public engagements—looks fierce as she addresses the camera!

We are complex organisms—as full of contradictions as our education system. Knowing and finding embodied well-being has not been a large part of our curriculum, yet we are learning from our pain. We have written much of this experiential knowledge into novels and biographies, displacedly pouring into such favorite forms all of the familiar, compelling struggles we experience as we journey toward knowing—implicitly understanding that such embodied knowledge has no place in our academic writing or, more important, in our academic lives.

Unconvinced, we search for and find new ways to know and be ourselves, embodied, located in stories. Jane Tompkins's *A Life in School*, Annie Ernaux's *A Frozen Woman*, Joan Weimer's *Back Talk: Teaching Lost Selves to Speak*, and Eavan Boland's *Object Lessons* all account for the move from a disconnected to an embodied life. Nancy Mairs evokes the internal world of disabled and aging bodies from her wheelchair in *Waist-High in the World*. (When I heard her speak I was so powerfully moved that I had to flee the auditorium. Two women, strangers, attuned to my embodied response, followed me to make sure I was all right. They were not there to shut down my response but to witness it.)

If our educations have been rich and continuous, we make art—art that presses us to look at our living/dying selves and at our dangers and illusions. We make art that helps us to communicate and to "know what we know and know what we don't know." Notably, Judy Chicago's Homeplace installation at the University of Kentucky, Margaret Edson's *Wit*, and Eve Ensler's *The Vagina Monologues* have in this decade drawn our eyes to the body, not as an object of analysis but as a mortal dwelling for each of our souls. We do not live on paper or "on the line," as my mother calls cyberspace. "I don't see how people can get in so much trouble 'on the line,' " she says. My imagination flies to the clothesline in her backyard with people pinned up by the hands, the wind blowing and moving them in a wave, trapped and staring blankly.

I am thinking more in images these days. Since that first Beginning Modern class where I was recruited to "embody," I have had eight years of study, and my understanding of space and movement has grown. I have added eight years of Boal work, a theater genre that uses among other methods "image theater," designed to help us see what we are looking at and to listen to what we are hearing and to feel what we are touching. This year I have begun yoga classes, joining young student athletes who are groaning beside me on Tuesday evenings on the gym floor. (We only know each other through our audible struggles with stretching, our moans and groans. We are friends.)

So the teacher's body (our bodies) enters our consciousness through our direct sensory awareness, through literature and the arts, through our long ventures in illness and health, and through our "othered" appearances. We have come a ways since pregnant teachers were routinely dismissed from schools so that their embodied sexuality would not influence students. We have a ways to go to honor our embodied lives in all their dynamics. This volume is a good place to start the discussions that will take us into a richer, more embodied future.

WORKS CITED

Boal, Augusto. *The Rainbow of Desire*. London and New York: Routledge, 1995.

Boland, Eavan. *Object Lessons: The Life of the Woman and the Poet in Our Time*. New York and London: Norton, 1995.

Davies, Bronwyn. *(in)scribing body/landscape relations*. New York: Altamira, 2000.

Davis, Kathy. "Embody-ing Theory: Beyond Modernist and Post Modernist Readings of the Body." *Embodied Practices: Feminist Perspectives on the Body*. Ed. Kathy Davis. London: Sage, 1997. 1–23.

Eliot, George. *Middlemarch*. 1872. Boston: Houghton Miflin, 1956.

Ernaux, Annie. *A Frozen Woman*. New York: Seven Stories, 1995.

Ensler, Eve. *The Vagina Monologues*. New York: Random, 2001.

Fine, Michelle. "Working the Hyphens: Reinventing Self and Other in Qualitative Research." *The Handbook of Qualitative Research*. Eds. Norman Denzin and Yvonne Lincoln. Thousand Oaks, Calif.: Sage, 1994.

Fine, Michelle, Bernadette Anand, Markie Hancock, Carlton Jordan, and Dana Sherman. *Off Track: Classroom Privilege for All Teachers*. Videocassette. Teacher's College P, 1998. 70–82.

Freire, Paulo. *Pedagogy of the Oppressed*. New York: Continuum, 1970.

Gell-Mann, Murray. *The Quark and the Jaguar*. New York: Freeman, 1994.

Gilligan, Carol. *In a Different Voice*. Cambridge: Harvard UP, 1982/1983.

Greene, Maxine. *Releasing the Imagination*. San Francisco: Jossey-Bass, 1995.

Grumet, Madeleine. *Bitter Milk: Women and Teaching*. Amherst: U of Massachusetts P, 1990.

hooks, bell. *Teaching to Transgress*. New York: Routledge, 1994.

Mairs, Nancy. *Waist-High in the World: A Life among the Nondisabled*. Boston: Beacon, 1996.

Markowitz, Fran, and Michael Ashkenazi, eds. *Sex, Sexuality and the Anthropologist*. Urbana and Chicago: U of Illinois P, 1999.

Martin, Jane Roland. *The Schoolhome: Rethinking Schools for Changing Families*. Cambridge: Harvard UP, 1992.

———. *Coming of Age in Academe*. New York: Routledge, 2000.

Palmer, Parker. *To Know as We Are Known*. San Francisco: Harper, 1983.

Spring, Joel. *The Cultural Transformation of a Native American Family and Its Tribe 1763–1995*. Mahwah, N.J.: Erlbaum, 1996.

Tompkins, Jane. *A Life in School*. New York: Addison-Wesley, 1996.

Weimer, Joan. *Back Talk: Teaching Lost Selves to Speak*. New York: Random, 1994.

On the Desk:
Dwarfism, Teaching, and the Body

Scott Andrew Smith

Come, said my Soul,
Such verses for my Body let us write,
    (for we are one)
          —Walt Whitman

What I recall about that day was that the desk was curved, black, and cold on my bare feet. Everything else around me was white: the white paper on the desk bearing black symbols and words I did not understand, the white jackets of the thirty-some others facing me, the white briefs that were my only clothing. I was seven. Or eight. I recall the standing being difficult. Standing for me, then, was something done for only five minutes or so until the pain in my knees forced me to sit down or face the pain of weight on my bowing and bending legs. I recall the pain during this ten- to fifteen-minute stretch of standing all but erasing any interest I might have had in the words uttered by a man pointing at my hips, knees, and ankles with a silver pen. I recall that pen, cold, sliding softly down the sides of legs that would be scarred years later by a cold, silver scalpel.

I was alone as my parents waited in the hallway. I was taller than I had ever been or ever would be. I felt a bit of uneasiness at this height—the same uneasiness when I would stand on chairs to reach for a bowl for cereal or a glass for water, an act I still resort to regularly at thirty-three years of age. It was the same uneasiness I would (and still) feel when climbing onto counter-tops to get a plate from the top shelf, wondering how anyone over six feet tall maintained his balance and equilibrium.

On that day, on that table, when my "condition" was discussed, I became aware that I was truly physically different from other boys. I knew this already, as evidenced by the leather and steel braces, the skipping of recess games, the extra time I was given at the end of each day to walk the hallway alone and be lifted onto the bus. But on this day that difference was as striking as the white jacket of the presenter and the black desk on top of which he stood me. None of my friends stood on desks like this; instead, they were sitting at desks at Plain Center Elementary School in Canton, Ohio, scrawling math problems on blue-lined notebook paper. They were fully dressed in sneakers and jeans and T-shirts. None of them stood in underwear before white-jacketed doctors taking notes and nodding when a man with a silver pen traced the angles of his or her own legs and hips, talking of "dwarfism" and its effects on the body—my body.

On that day I was diagnosed as suffering from slowed growth in my long bones, weak ligaments, and subsequently deformed legs. My right knee bent so badly that it came to rest almost directly underneath my crotch, my thigh angling into it, shin and calf moving back out to my right foot; my left knee bowed outward to a similar degree. A significant angle was formed by these legs, like the angles my friends back in school were sketching onto paper as I stood there, my feet aching and the angle of bending and bowing increasing ever so slightly each time I put weight on my legs when out of the braces. "Windswept" legs, they would later be called, as if some gust had left its mark on me but passed by others. The one house on the block mysteriously ruined by the storm.

I recall wanting to be outside of this room and with my parents, wanting to be dressed and seated so as to relieve the pain that came when my weight bore down on my misshapen legs. Most of all I wanted the looking to stop. That moment finally came after much nodding of heads and discussion by those in white jackets, but in a way it has never come. Years later, even after my dwarfed body has been more "normalized" by reconstructed and realigned hips and knees, bystanders frequently stare at and whisper about me. You develop a sixth sense for this and can feel, almost like some superhero, stares from behind your back. You can sense it, the way a good cop can tell when someone is aiming a gun at his head or a parent can hear, from the upstairs bedroom, a child sneaking into the house after curfew. With each stare I am aware that I am, above all else, a physical being, someone who is constantly on display at the front of the room. In fact, I have a career that demands it.

Some fifteen years after that day, I walked into a classroom, pulled a chair up to the long and lone desk at the front of a classroom at Kansas State University, and vaulted myself upward to a seated position. I was twenty-three.

I let my feet rest on this chair and began to read my first syllabus for Freshman Composition. I do not recall any whispers. No one leaned over to a classmate to say anything. My students were attentive and respectful, something true since I began this work. I had decided to teach as a means of getting a degree in creative writing, a sudden shift from what I had spent four years pursuing at Ohio University.

My undergraduate work in Ohio was in public relations. The reasons for my career choice were many: an executive position offering power and money, the chance to wear custom-made suits and have a corner office, and my love of public speaking and debating, in which I have the chance to spin an issue in the direction I want it to go and to argue to win. And, like so much of my life, the decision was based on physicality. I was aware that part of public relations was being visible, being a sort of corporate front man. I figured that my physicality would help in this area, perhaps even being the extra edge in job interviews on my way up to work with larger companies. I could imagine myself saying to some vice-president that who would be better as the guy everyone had to find at a press conference than the one standing only four feet seven inches tall? My height was the step that would lead to success when I had worked hard and done well. It was that little something extra that set me apart. And although I apply what I learned in PR every day in the classroom—my emphasis on dressing professionally (teaching in a tie, slacks, dress shirt, and dress shoes) and being organized via my love of paperwork, from typed conference sign-up sheets and schedules to typed comments on everything from paper proposals to the performance of students in discussion to final copies of papers—that career was never to be.

Heading into my final summer before graduation I had served as a public relations intern with a minor-league baseball team in my hometown. I assumed that this internship would involve much office work, something much kinder to my legs than any job involving regular standing. I was wrong. Twelve-hour days often began with a call to come to the stadium to pull tarp—a physical task of rolling or unrolling the tarp on the field with only a few other interns to help—and ended with standing throughout the entire

game to sell hot dogs and beer. Despite the fact that four reconstructive surgeries—surgeries that made walking easier and erased, via straightened legs, the
need for braces—were five years in the past, I still found it hard to stand for
even short periods of time, and so each night ended with sore legs and stiff
ankles. One morning, upon being told to wipe down the seats (all seven thousand of them) in the stadium by myself, I asked my boss if he could find me
some other, less physical, work for me to do. I explained the pain. The surgeries and months of physical therapy. And he laughed. Fifteen minutes later I
was in the car, headed for a summer not of pulling tarp and pouring beer but
of sitting on a rooftop, pen in hand, writing things I had never put to paper,
and reading endlessly.

I began with Jim Morrison of the music group "The Doors." In him I
found not only a drive to live intensely but also the focus on an inner life—
often quite sad and distressing—that I was becoming aware of. I found in him
a sexual being, so much like the one I felt but could never feel comfortable
expressing due to a shyness born of a "deformed" body. He, along with a
healthy dose of Walt Whitman's poetry of the body and Thoreau's admonition
that we live life deliberately, provided the catalyst for me finally to express
myself physically. To express my frustration with my body. My anger at having suffered so much pain and having not been able to play in the way my
friends did. My disappointment—and often rage—at feeling incredibly full of
lust and a desire for love but sensing that no woman would be interested in
me due to my height and deformed legs.

After coming down from the roof that summer with a handful of filled
journals, I went back to Athens and eventually finished my public relations and
advertising degree at Ohio University, immediately abandoning it for graduate
school and literature. And so on that first day at Kansas State University, I
began to teach. I began to ask questions and I was expected to answer the questions my students posed. Yet on that first day not one question came about my
size. Not one "What happened to you?" or "Why are you so short?" or "Why
do you waddle when you walk?" No one asked and no one ever has. Ever.

These two moments on tables at the front of the room stand at opposite
poles in my life. I have chosen a life work that demands that I stand (standing is easier for me now, though standing still for more than twenty minutes
causes pain) before others two to three times a week, fifteen weeks a semester. Sixty new faces each term. Unlike that day when I was there before doctors with clipboards writing notes as frantically as my students do on certain
days, unlike that day when so many questions were asked about my body, I
have found that my physicality exists in a void of silence in the classroom. I
have walked into the classroom hundreds of times—having taught some seven
hundred students in the course of nine years (two and a half years at Kansas
State, five years of teaching composition and creative writing at Kent State
while completing my doctorate, and now my second year of teaching junior-

and senior-level writing at the University of Southern California). Yet I have never been asked why I am, physically, who I am. This silence speaks loudly not only about disability but also about the emphasis on the *mind* in academic life. Beyond this, I have discovered that to be me requires a body that screams for explanation but one that often exists, for others, in a realm of silence. A realm in which I too existed from an early age.

I did not hear the words "little person" until I was fourteen years old. I was used to "midget" or "shorty" or "shrimp," but little person (or the parallel term "dwarf") was something clinical, something scientific, something politically correct. Or something nonexistent. Until I heard the word at fourteen, I lived in a world of normality and what would later be called, in academia, mainstreaming. My parents made every effort to treat me (and have me treated) as others my age. I participated in little leagues (though only as a bat boy or equipment manager) and was expected to do chores at home. When my father put up a basketball hoop in response to my asking for one, it stood at regulation height—ten feet. I was used to kids taller than I and not at all to anyone my own size. Not until I was fourteen.

I had gone to Johns Hopkins Hospital in Baltimore to finally meet a man known as a miracle worker among those with dwarfed bodies and twisted limbs. Until that day when I first met Dr. Steven Kopits, my parents had spent over ten years trying to find a way to solve the riddle of deformity that affected me more and more each year as my growth slowed and my legs warped underneath me. I had never heard the term "pseudoachondroplasia," but it was applied to me that day as a way of explaining my condition. Until then I had been under the care of a doctor who tried to correct the bending and bowing via surgery (at age five) and then, unsuccessful in that approach, tried nine years of bracing that pushed my knees into a locked and straight position. In the end the bracing caused more harm than good because it forced my knees into alignment without moving the tendons and ligaments out of their previously unnatural position. This created a sort of slow grinding and deterioration that was unknown and perhaps unknowable in the 1970s, when Kopits's work was still developing. And so on that day the silence of ten years of unknowing and the way to resolve the deformities was broken by a man who said, simply, "I can fix him." Perhaps, though, the silence was something I chose, albeit unconsciously. I do not recall being that interested in my case as it was explained and questioned over years of hospital visits. At some point my life simply became a series of regular visits to the doctor and bracemaker. When nothing changed I suppose I stopped listening. Even now, in writing these lines, I struggle to find a way to give a detailed account of my dwarfism. If I had to write a paper on my disorder, I'd be at a loss and would have to write a research paper like the ones my students write each term.

I know that my long bones did not grow and my ligaments are weak and that this—along with the weight put on my legs as a normal part of walking—

caused the severe deformities and instability. I know that I began life bow-legged but that at some point my right knee turned inward, curving underneath my body while my left continued to bow.

I know that my syndrome is genetic but not something inherited. I know that I have three sisters, all of normal height with healthy, straight legs. I know that my parents are both tall, my father standing over six feet (as opposed to my four feet seven inches), and both have strong, straight legs. I know that I have no family history of dwarfism and that my case, as often happens in various ways in the mysterious creation of a child, is a sort of misfire in the genetic code of father and mother. Something akin to a couple who bump heads during a passionate first kiss—something that just doesn't fit, some awkwardness or miscommunication that results in a slight bruise during an otherwise perfect moment.

After years of my searching for an answer and finding none, Dr. Kopits's explanations came at my parents and me with lightning speed. Genetic studies and examinations and descriptions of surgery. Things I forgot almost as soon as I heard them, for I cared only about shedding the braces and pain, having straight legs that would carry me at least a few blocks before I had to sit, and having legs that would not someday collapse beneath the weight of pounds and age. How that happened or why it was needed in the first place was something that, at fourteen, was low on my list of priorities. After four reconstructive surgeries by Dr. Kopits—ranging in length from four to nine hours each—four months in a cast from my rib cage to my toes, and eight months of physical therapy, all of these things came to fruition by my seventeenth year. And still I cannot say much beyond the clinical basics about what it was like to go through the experience, though emotionally and personally I could fill volumes. The medical knowledge is something that, except in a general sense, escapes me. Maybe I have deliberately escaped it.

For years as a child, when the occasionally brave classmate willing to confront my body asked me what I was called, I simply responded "Scott." I knew that the classmate was really asking why I was who I was physically, but I had no idea how to answer the question. I am in a world of adults now, a world in which only good friends ask these types of questions, ones that children would (and do) ask of me regardless of whether I knew them. Even when I had to confront other little people—something that was also new to me with the first visit to Dr. Kopits—I did not ask questions.

One of my most vivid memories of a moment such as this came when the doctor decided to show my parents and me the "before and after" photo album of cases of dwarfism he had treated. The first patient in the album was naked, and when I saw his enlarged torso, his stunted arms and legs, I laughed. Just slightly but I laughed. He seemed comical to me, standing there exposed for the camera. I stifled the laugh as soon as it came out of my mouth, sure that this was not the right response. What escaped me then—

disguised as my adolescent sense that I was laughing at seeing another man naked—was the fact that I was looking in a mirror, and because this fact escaped me or I did not want to face it, I laughed. The man looked funny to me, a sort of clownish figure exposed in the center ring. I was seeing something I was not yet ready to see but had seen for years. I was seeing the body behind my name, and no matter how many times I had said, "No, I'm just Scott," I knew on that day that I would have to face up to being something other than that.

No one laughed that first day of teaching at Kansas State in '93. No one ever has, and my sincere sense is that no one ever will. There is something about the classroom, now that I am at the head of it and not seated in rows with others my age, that erases that urge. Or at least stifles it. As a grade-school student, I found that each new year (or the occasion of an incoming new student) brought occasional whispers from a classmate, whispers that soon vanished once a self-appointed gang of friends took aside the boy (and it was always a boy) who was teasing me. I never heard the content of those conversations, but I know that the teasing always stopped at that point. I suppose it was a sort of childhood mafia, with me as the silent godfather who never really asked for protection but got it anyway. I didn't ask any questions, they didn't give me any answers. But the teasers left me alone.

With my students the gang is no longer needed, its presence replaced by maturity, respect, a title, and the university setting. Or perhaps I have overcome the body that I carry (friends have often said to me, "I just don't see you as a short person") and simply realize that my work in the classroom is about the mind and not the body. Even though I am still relatively new to teaching, I am aware of the age-old stereotype of the teacher as a mind first and foremost. I suppose, as a professor and a dwarf, I exemplify this idea in the classroom more than the lecturer in a tattered blazer with worn elbow patches. I suppose my students, though they may have questions of me physically, see the mind as the realm in which we exist together.

And yet I know it is not just this. I know that, as Whitman preaches, my body and soul are one. This entity defines who I am, and who I am defines how I carry my body. There is an intensity in me—pointed out often by others—that is born of the struggle between this body and the internal drive to endure that it demands. An intensity that I feel when I push my body to stay in shape, a task made even more difficult by a history of weight problems (in the last five years, my weight has been as high as 148 and as low as 107). An intensity quite visible on my face. When a woman I later dated for nearly four years first saw me in Kent, Ohio at a bus stop, she said, "It looked like you were on your way to kick someone's ass." And, recently, a photographer friend of mine who was snapping a few photos of me kept saying, "Not so intense, Scott, not so intense." So my position in the classroom is that of a mind that has realized that a stern and intense gaze represents who I am because the years of bracing and surgery and stares demanded such intensity. It is a silent intensity, but it is there in my face every day.

Perhaps, then, we all—teachers and students—exist in this silence about the body. The question becomes whether this silence really doesn't speak after all.

While working on my dissertation, a project that took on the male body in American poetry and in my own physical experience, I came across a transcript of a conversation between Allen Ginsberg and some undergraduates at the University of Kansas. He had spent time there working with them on their writing, and someone asked whether he felt that he had come to know them in their time together. He said that he had but then admitted that since he had not "slept" with any of the students there was a level of knowing they had not explored. I find the same thing to be true, not in terms of sex and sexuality, but simply in terms of the fact that each semester rooms all over campus are loaded with bodies that never find articulation except through the muted voice of clothing choices and body language. I do not feel this muted attitude is a problem, except in cases where we *forget* our physical selves in the course of our intellectual pursuits. Sometimes, in fact, I think introducing the body is a way not to forget this.

I teach a course called "Writing 340" at USC, where I came after receiving my doctorate two summers ago. Each semester I have three classrooms of twenty students each. The course content is geared toward broad divisions such as "arts and humanities," "health sciences," and "social sciences." My aim is to develop course content and writing assignments appropriate to the divisions and thus to the students' interests and majors.

I had decided that since the course was to teach a skill (and not so much content, as a lecture class might), I would try something new and use images instead of texts to do that. My sense was that students might have an easier time interpreting images than other texts, and so the focus was on photography and art. I took a cultural studies direction, with my aim being a discussion—in writing—of the significance of the images that surround us. For example, I asked my students to use visual evidence from an image to make an argument about what that image has to teach about us. One example of this came in the "retrospect" assignment. Each student presented a collection of images, using them as evidence of some cultural shift over time. One student looked at the progression of Johnson and Johnson's baby powder advertisements, tracking the company's increased marketing to men over time, thus suggesting a cultural shift in our notion of gender roles. Similar projects looked at the U.S. Army's advertising campaign, the progression of advertising techniques used by alcohol manufacturers, and changes in style and fashion as seen on the covers of magazines such as *Vogue*.

The course also included a section on "the body." Here I asked students to take photographs of friends, relatives, and strangers and bring them to class. We then exchanged photographs and talked about how one might make assumptions based on the physical evidence of another person. This led to some very clever papers in which students explored, via interviews with friends, what we expect of the body and what the body can mean. In the course of this work one student, Karl, brought in a photo of a man and woman heading out for the evening. The man was dressed in his Navy "dress whites," and the woman wore a full-length, white, silk gown. She stood some six to eight inches taller than he. As my students worked in small groups with the photos, Karl showed me the picture and asked what I thought. "It reminds me," I said, "of all the photos I took with Rebecca and Linda, the two women I dated over the past ten years—both of whom were well over five feet tall." That was the end of the conversation, as Karl gave an understanding nod even though he stands nearly six feet tall. It was as if he had asked a question about my body but pulled back, not out of shyness or awkwardness but simply out of respect that this topic—the professor's body—might not have been appropriate in a classroom setting.

I always ask my students for more. If they mention a rich passage from a book we have been reading, I ask them to quote the passage, to work through it, and to analyze it. If, in discussion, they say they hated the reading I ask them why. I prod them into giving me a clear sense of what they are responding to. If they make a claim in a paper, I demand that they give me as much evidence as possible. I ask them to push themselves to be clear and detailed. I suppose anyone who teaches writing does the same, yet those demands never come back to me in terms of physicality. No student in my nine years of being on that table at the head of the class has ever asked me to explain the paragraphs of my legs or the thesis statement of my dwarfism. There have been moments, like the one in Karl's question, but they have been brief. No one has yet to break that silence fully and completely, and I am not sure I want it broken any more than I want students to ask me about my holiday plans or what I do for fun on a Friday night.

And yet I *am* my body—it has shaped my personhood more than any other single factor in my life. I carry my body with each word in class. I speak with a confidence that comes of having walked on braced legs for years, a confidence that comes of having had to learn how to walk again at age seventeen when my legs were so rebuilt that my mind did not know how to move them. I also work with a compassion for my students born of years of uncompassionate stares and the kind hands of my parents, my three sisters, nurses, doctors, and physical therapists. As my students struggle to write, as they face that fear of failure in a task so many of them hate, *I need only respond as my body has taught me to:* by encouraging patience but intense resolve, by pushing them but not without praising them. My body has created who I am in the classroom. I often joke, when asked by friends what I am like as a teacher, that I am a standard "good cop—bad cop." I am both stern and strict in terms of having high standards, but I am also, sometimes to a fault, willing to give the benefit of the doubt and to listen to a student who wants to spend office hours discussing a personal problem. Without my body, I doubt I would be this kind of teacher.

As a graduate student I vowed that my greatest accomplishment when walking across the stage to receive my Master's and Ph.D. degrees would be not what I'd achieved with my mind but what I'd achieved with my body. I vowed that I would be in the best shape of my life on those days. This work began, not coincidentally, when I went to Kansas State to pursue literature and my own writing. I was seeking self-knowledge and self-improvement through literature and writing, and caring for my body in ways that braces and surgeries had previously prevented seemed to fit with this desire. My legs had been too fragile to allow me to play or engage in sports, but the surgeries allowed much more freedom to exercise and play, cautiously, but without braces. This began slowly, with short trips to the gym to row on a rowing machine or lift weights. It ended with completing a "sprint" triathlon in Cleveland (a half-mile swim, a fifteen-mile bicycle ride, and a three-mile run—which I had to walk because running is still too hard on my legs) just two years before getting my doctorate. Even now, the first thing I do each term is renew my locker at USC's swim center, where I spend an hour turning laps in the afternoon sun between classes. On my days away from school, my mornings begin with stretching and road cycling for hours on the streets of Venice and Santa Monica and into the canyons of Southern California.

At this point in my life I continue to enjoy—and need—my fitness regime (which covers six days a week and ranges from an hour to two-plus hours a day, including weight lifting, bicycling, swimming, stretching, and meditating, in addition to making homemade juices every day). Although I certainly put in long hours and enjoy doing so (conferencing with each student, for example, on each paper—spending ten to fifteen minutes with all sixty of them, individually, four times a semester—and typing a full, single-spaced sheet of comments for each of them on each essay written during the term), I am committed to never letting my work overwhelm my friendships and my outside pursuits—the chief of which is my body's health. This is a genuine outgrowth of my belief in the interplay of mind and body. I see no use in developing my mind and soul without bringing my body along for the ride—after all, it was my body and its pain (and now moments of the bliss born of fitness) that led me to be who the person I am today—and I wonder, as did Whitman, how a separation of brain and breath, muscle and mind can possibly occur. To me, the two are always and forever yoked, one and the same.

So perhaps our bodies, for all their silence, do have something to say. Perhaps what we carry into the classroom physically—our way of carrying ourselves but also the ways in which our bodies have carried us or let us down—is just as important as the books and syllabi that we carry in our hands and the theories and ideas we carry in our heads. Perhaps the body, as it has been for many of us in the study of our own lives, is the most important text of the course. Its struggles are things we can (and should) recall when our students face adversity and failure and when they are able to transcend these fears and shortcomings and succeed.

In the classroom my physical history is just as important as my intellectual one, and even though these histories may stay silent among my students, they speak every day when I walk into the room. They are on the desk for all to see, clothed but still there. What I am and how I work is not simply something I learned in a classroom but also something born of leg braces, stumbles, scalpels, stitches, stares, and the struggle to celebrate a body that was once constrained and bound. To forget this would be to forget myself, and though I never speak of my body in the classroom this is a forgetting I will never allow.

Body Teaching

Cortney Davis

I've been working as a nurse practitioner in a busy women's health clinic, alongside eight OB-GYN residents, for ten years. Last summer, one of the new interns who joined our team was male; otherwise, all our care providers are female. Because our clinic is located in a teaching hospital, there's also a stream of students passing through regularly. Medical residents spend a mandatory week or two with us, usually grudgingly, to sharpen their pelvic-exam skills, and nervous medical students in short white coats do six-week rotations. About sixty percent of these students are male. They plan to become orthopods, pediatricians, or internists—rarely do they want to pursue OB-GYN. They say it's becoming a female-dominated field. If, after his weeks with us, a male student does say he might consider OB-GYN, he usually says it's because he likes the combination of surgery and medicine.

Well versed in syndromes, lab values, and auscultation of the heart, these students come to our clinic and find themselves suddenly disoriented and humbled. Here they can't hide behind shifting sodium values or unstable hemaglobins. In our world students must touch a woman's breasts and probe her vagina. They must learn to delineate the uterus, invisible beneath a woman's skin, and they must perfect the maneuvers that cause her ovaries to slip between their examining hands. Here they must come face to face with the flesh and all its implications: fecundity and longing, sexuality and pain. Here their fingertips must become as sensitive as a safecracker's.

The choice, the entire rotation, seems more natural for our female students. Although they can be just as anxious about performing their first pelvic exams, they've often had Pap tests and internals themselves. It's easier to teach them; they share an intuitive common world with our patients, and they enjoy caring for other women. But I'd rather supervise the men. They're the ones who are the most uncomfortable and who must acquire a facility that goes beyond the mere perfection of the exam. Teaching them, I try to utilize the insights that arise from my multiple roles: a woman who has also been a patient; a nurse as well as a nurse practitioner. I am keenly aware that I am a woman teaching a man and, in a role reversal even more volatile, a nurse teaching a doctor, whose authority will ultimately be more respected than mine. Most of all, I am a female guide who must step out of her body, casting off any suggestion of sensuality or privilege, when it is precisely my body that allows me to excel at teaching this intimate exam.

"Come with me," I say to this month's medical student. His name is Raymond, a third-year from Yale. When I ask, he tells me that he thinks he wants to be an oncologist, but he's not sure yet. We go down the hall and stand for a moment outside room three, where Maria Lopez waits for us. Raymond tells me he's done several pelvic exams before. Nevertheless, he confesses, he's never quite sure what he's *feeling*. I catch hold of his inadvertent double entendre and think perhaps we're going to have a real conversation, one that addresses the multilevel aspects of the exam we're about to perform: what he's feeling in his doctor's body, both physically and emotionally; what the patient is feeling; and how, as I stand by observing, my body responds, remembering. Then Raymond clarifies. "I can never tell whether the uterus is retroverted or anteverted," he says.

Before we knock on the exam room door, I encourage him.

"Don't worry," I say. "The exam takes practice. It's more important that you listen to Maria and watch her face. Let her give you clues to what *she* is feeling."

Maria Lopez, who has been our patient for years, sits uneasily at the end of the exam table. She has delivered three babies with us and lost one with us, too, a spontaneous abortion that occurred a month ago. Today our job is to make sure everything has returned to normal. We have to palpate her uterus to make sure it's firm and small again after the early miscarriage of her pregnancy. We have to ask her about bleeding, the resumption of intercourse, and birth control. Most essential, we have to inquire about Maria's grief and healing, those extraordinary processes that trail along behind a woman's life like silk scarves.

Raymond, whom I introduce to Maria as *un estudiante*, will conduct the exam. I, in my long flowered skirt and my woman's body, will observe. My own breasts have heft and weight and, when he palpates Maria's breasts, my hands and breasts will respond, and I will know how to direct him, resisting the urge to move his hands aside and show him. When he attempts the pelvic exam, I will become aware of my own vagina, its contractility and its fragility. Surely this happens to Raymond when he examines other men. He recognizes the body's responses and is more careful because at some level the borders between his body and the patient's body meld. I step back and prepare to assist him.

I can never be sure of how Raymond or any student will come to terms with what he's *feeling* when he examines a woman. Like many students on their way to more desired rotations, Raymond might simply breeze through the clinic, unaffected. I might teach him to identify the size of the uterus (a peach, a lemon, a grapefruit), how to twirl the pap spatula deftly around a patient's cervical os, and how to perform a thorough breast exam, but my goal is to teach him what sensations these maneuvers elicit in his female patients. As Raymond begins to examine Maria, I tell him that because I am a woman, I have some idea of what another woman experiences during an exam; even so, I add, no one can ever truly know what someone else is feeling.

But there is another way of knowing. I know how Maria might feel, torn between shame and fear as Raymond steps forward to examine her body, because I have taken care of Maria for a long time: I have learned to anticipate her individual responses and to honor them. I suspect that today she thinks her body has turned against her, expelling her fetus. And yet, like any woman, she cannot escape her body's whims. Tingling breasts and monthly blood flow, hormonal flushes, roller-coaster dizziness, fertile pregnancies, and even lost babies are a part of our lot. If Raymond can understand this—if he watches Maria's face and notes how her legs relax or tense, whether her vaginal introitus contracts in surprise at his touch or loosens around the speculum, whether she moves away from his hands or accepts them—then he too might come to know Maria and help her make peace with her body.

I can also project my own experiences in women's health onto my encounters with other women. Raymond can learn this, too. Like all humans, a woman's parts are private. In order to remain healthy, we must permit trespass, lie on our backs as Maria does now, letting her knees fall open, relaxing her thighs and her buttocks. Surely Raymond too has been exposed and examined, vulnerable and afraid.

He inserts the metal speculum. "Aim down," I tell him. My memory of how this feels is vivid. "Be careful to avoid the urethra."

Maria looks at the ceiling as Raymond peers through the speculum's blades to find her cervix, as he removes the metal device, as he fumbles (now he fumbles, but soon he will perform this gesture as easily and unconsciously as he walks) to reach his lubricated, gloved fingers to the very cul-de-sac of Maria's vagina. She winces slightly, and Raymond begins to sweat. He has hurt her. I see tiny drops spring from the hair follicles on his upper lip.

"This is an uncomfortable exam," I tell him, "and it's important that you're thorough. But remember, she can't see what you're doing. Explain what you're going to do before you do it. Talk to her, and she might be more comfortable." Maria and I exchange glances and roll our eyes. *Eso nos pasa*, I say to her, *por ser mujer.* This is what we women must endure. I keep hold of her hand.

Turning to Raymond, I explain the basic uterine positions: anteverted, retroverted, or midplane. Maria's uterus, I remember from her previous visits, is retroflexed, retroverted to the maximal degree. I tell Raymond that when a woman's uterus is retroflexed, it can cause perpetual distress: pain with intercourse as the penis nudges the cervix and jostles the uterus; difficult exams, as often the retroflexed uterus can be adequately palpated only with an uncomfortable recto-vaginal investigation. I repeat this in Spanish and Maria nods in agreement.

"Identify the thin wall between rectum and vagina. Locate the firm uterine fundus flexed back under the cervix, a bulge that impinges on the rectal canal," I say.

"Wow," Raymond says, beaming, "I think I got it."

He leans into this exam, steadying his right hand, the one that has luckily found the uterus. Maria has turned her face to the wall, but Raymond doesn't notice. Not that he is callous or mechanical. He's preoccupied. First he had to deal with his fear of awkwardness, of hurting his patient. Now he's simply elated that he has succeeded in mastering one more thing in the chain of a thousand things that he must learn. He isn't aware of Maria's embarrassment. No, it's more accurate to say that he doesn't *feel* Maria's embarrassment. Later I will ask him to remember a moment in his life when he was vulnerable and exposed. Then I will ask whether he recalls Maria's turned-away stare, her silent endurance. "Think of how invaded she must have felt," I'll say.

When the exam is over (I have to check as well to be sure that her uterus is normal and her ovaries are free of cysts), Raymond stands back as if he no longer dares to touch her, while I help Maria sit up. Maria's body will take an hour or so to recover. Her uterus will be slightly sore, rattled. Her ovaries will ache. The lubricant will irritate her vagina. Later a gelatinous glob will slip out of her at an inconvenient moment. Her relationship with Raymond will remain a wild contradiction. He is a man and a stranger. He has *seen* her.

I think he too must be lost in a whirl of emotions: pride at his skill; exhilaration at his increasing clinical familiarity with the female body; maybe even an innocent pleasure at the *otherness* of its mystery and velvety passageway, the firmness of the womb, the contrast (unconscious or realized) between this unerotic exam and the lovemaking he shares with his wife. I imagine that he feels ill at ease as well, both indebted to Maria and detached from her—grateful that she has let him practice on her body and yet about to forget her.

After we tell Maria how sorry we are that her pregnancy has miscarried and after she has wept on my shoulder, Raymond and I bid her good-bye. We walk back to the residents' lounge, where he writes the details of this encounter in Maria's chart. As we sit together, Raymond seems to recognize (as if by revelation) that he can't include Maria's version of their transaction but that I, his teacher, am a woman who has been, like Maria, probed and examined. In that instant, he transcends the mechanical and enters the magical. What he writes in Maria's chart is only *his* side of the story. He realizes that he must pay close attention to any hints that he might gather, like Hansel and Gretel's bread crumbs, that will help him expand his vision. If Raymond can recall his most human moments and translate those memories into a shared vulnerability with his patients, he might yet master that metaphoric *knowing*.

"Thanks for your help," he says. "I guess you've been there yourself."

I agree, and he struggles to find a way to ask me, "What's it like for the patient? What was it like for Maria—what is that exam like from a woman's point of view?"

I hesitate, not sure of where to begin or how much I might personally have to reveal, but Raymond leans toward me, interested and fully engaged. I'm touched by his question, heartened by his sensitivity. He puts down his pen, pushes aside his red manual of gynecological facts, for now abandoning his desire to identify uterine orientation or cystic ovaries. He wants to step into his patient's body and know what *she* is feeling. He wants to know how she experiences this exam, and that will help him to understand the subtext of women's health. He's asking me to lead him by memory, by my own body's recollection, as if I might go on ahead, mapping out the tortuous path that he must follow by faith alone. I tell Raymond that he just might become a wonderful doctor.

As we talk, finding language to soar above the level of rote skill, I realize that I'm not simply teaching Raymond and the other male students how to do a proficient pelvic exam. I'm teaching them my body.

Teaching Women's Studies,
E-Mailing Cancer

Carolyn DiPalma

> Experience is [. . .] not the origin of our explanation, but that which
> we want to explain. This kind of approach does not undercut politics
> by denying the existence of subjects, it instead interrogates the
> processes of their creation, and, in so doing, refigures history and the
> role of the [researcher] and opens new ways for thinking about change.
> —Joan W. Scott

Academically trained in feminist theory as a subset of political theory, I
actively employ theory in most of my intellectual enterprises.[1] I say "most"
rather than "all" because there remains a part of me that demands practicality
and applied hands-on ability—to almost the complete exclusion of anything

else. Undoubtedly this is in part a vestigial holdover from my previous professional training in both critical care nursing and international public health. The experiences of supervising a regional trauma center emergency department, working on and helping to organize the first private hospital-based emergency helicopter program in the United States, and teaching health care workers in refugee camps on the Thai-Cambodian border—even during military offensives—have underscored my awareness of the necessity for considering material practices. I have a real "can-do" streak that is all about being organized and getting a task done. Nevertheless, I refuse to participate in the increasingly popular dismissal of theory as an overintellectualized, jargon-filled practice since it is through the insights of theoretical inquiry (through feminist, gender, postcolonial, poststructural, postmodern, and queer theory) that I am often able to explain or understand the world and its daily practices. Encountering the tensions in the ironic pull between theoretical arenas and practical applications often produces the most interesting—and sometimes painful—moments for personal political engagement.

In the fall of 1998 I began my third tenure-track year in a department of women's studies by teaching two theory courses—one an undergraduate course, "Contemporary Feminist Theory," and the other a graduate course, "Body Politics." Weaving various aspects of my own interests into course material meant that in both courses the selected readings moved from high theory to practical examples. For example, in the undergraduate class, we moved from reading Monique Wittig's "One Is Not Born a Woman" and Trinh T. Minh-ha's *Woman, Native, Other* to Elsa Barkley Brown's "What Has Happened Here?" and from Donna Haraway's "Situated Knowledges" to Bernice Johnson Reagan's "Coalition Politics." In the graduate course, we moved from reading Michel Foucault's *Discipline and Punish* and Wendy Brown's "Wounded Attachments" to Emily Martin's *Flexible Bodies* and Kate Bornstein's *Gender Outlaw.* The graduate course, "Body Politics," a new one, was particularly interesting for me. I was using it as a forum for reading widely and gathering material for research into various ways in which sex and race come to be written on the body.

In early October, as I was leaving for a conference, my doctor's office called and asked me to make an appointment for a repeat mammogram. I sent the following E-mail to a friend[2]:

Subject: Thursday

I'm on my way out the door to the airport. The 45 page paper has to be made into a 15 min 3–person combined presentation. This I get to do tonight. I have an appointment at a Kinkos computer for 8:30pm. [. . .] sigh.

The mammogram people called. They compared the films from 3 yrs ago and want another view of the Left Breast (cone compression view) and an ultra sound. I go in next Thurs. [. . .] tick, tick, tick.

So, with these peaceful thoughts as a back drop, I'm off to have fun.

The conference took a fair amount of concentration. However, once our presentation was completed I could think of little else than sundry unfavorable outcomes from the upcoming appointment. It seemed like a very long conference—and teaching seemed miles away—as I explained on my return.

Subject: Monday

> *We left the Kinko's computer at 4:30 am on Friday. Sigh. The conference began at noon on Friday. The keynote speaker's talk was interesting, and she remembered me (which I took to be a good thing). Our paper was the first one on Saturday. After we gave our paper I was wasted.*
>
> *The weather was perfect. It was crisp, a beautiful sunny day—so I played hooky. I walked around the campus, took a trail, sat on a park bench and generally enjoyed the day. I returned in time for the keynote speaker on Saturday and the dinner. Walking around was one of the best things I've done for myself in quite a while.*
>
> *Of course, these various tests for my left breast were much on my mind. I think I was at the stage you mentioned of putting it into a category of not worrying about it until I hear more. I think that stage was finished when the comparison with the old films showed changes in the left breast. Now I'm very sad—and, sometimes, resigned.*
>
> *When left to myself, I'm just sad (and, sometimes, tearful). I want solitude and quiet. I want space. I want time to think and, then, I don't want to think when I have the time.*
>
> *I need to get prepared for my Tuesday classes.*

On Friday, the day after I had the repeat mammogram, I received the radiologist's report from my doctor—and sent the news to a couple of close friends.

Subject: Surgeon

> *According to the radiologist's report, there is "architectural distortion" which appears to be a neoplasm and is "highly suggestive of malignancy." The bottom line is, I need a biopsy of both sites in the left breast. I need to find a good surgeon who specializes in breast surgery, make an appointment and get my old x-ray films. I will, of course, get a second opinion (preferably from another good surgeon).*

I had student papers to grade and classes to prepare for, including reading a book for the graduate class, yet I fell into an emotional black hole for the next day and a half—unable to do anything.[3] When I regained my equilibrium, I was so preoccupied with locating a surgeon and worrying about what the future might hold that I could not think clearly. Concerned I would be perceived as overreacting or as a junior faculty member unable to meet the demands of the position, I was reluctant and embarrassed to reveal to my colleagues my desperation about not being prepared for my courses and not having graded assignments in a timely manner. Sharing the medical information with my peers was not difficult; rather, divulging what I feared would be thought of as lack of attentiveness to my courses or lack of professionalism was difficult. One generous colleague, to whom I will be eternally grateful, unhesitatingly agreed to take my graduate class on very short notice—receiving the book about ten hours before time for class to begin.

After spending years practicing and teaching health care, followed by years practicing and teaching feminist theory, I felt surprisingly removed from professional or intellectual engagement with my body. Of course, I knew many of the possible medical scenarios I might face and was familiar with the politics of women's health care. I also knew much about gendered body image, the signification of the breast and its (problematic) relationship to the social construction of "femaleness" and "femininity."[4] Yet, weaving this knowledge usefully into the experience of calling doctor's offices for appointments, passing the time in waiting rooms, investigating regional cancer centers, surfing the Internet for information, contemplating my future, calling on friends for support, and developing a list of informed questions to discuss with the doctor were difficult. For example, on many occasions I found myself participating in the dominant medical discourse as though it were unproblematic, as though there was an unmediated relationship between words and things, as though I had never done any critical thinking about women's health care or any critique of gender expectations—in short, as though I did not understand that all categories of experience and analysis are contingent and debatable. In retrospect, Heidegger was right, the conversation was having me; I was not having the conversation.[5] Recognizing the existence of medical knowledge as a discourse means recognizing language as a kind of practice and, then, what is not said— the nondiscursive—as a field of other possible practices, other possible knowledge, producing other possible outcomes. My feeling of intellectual distance from my body is actually evidence of my attempt to avoid engaging with the troublesome tension of exploring and understanding both the discursive and material struggles necessary to bring politically informed theory and personal experience together. Positioning myself to address daily practices through theoretical understanding would require recognizing and grappling with the tensions between theory and life—a difficult process.

I have an exquisitely well-developed cynical view of health care. Engaged in both a medical discourse about illness and treatment, and a metadiscourse about authority and embodiment, I expected to have a respectfully aggressive—even adversarial—relationship with my surgeon and, in the case of malignancy, my oncologist. Yet I was amazed to find that the doctors I encountered (with two notable exceptions) were not only informed and competent but also extremely calm, kind, and caring. For example, one doctor spent three hours patiently and collectedly explaining possibilities, discussing options, and answering questions! So, upon reflection, one reason the medical conversation was having me was not merely because orthodoxies of medical discourse are so neatly woven, mutually self-sustaining, and all-of-a-piece, but because I had been unprepared for their appropriate, appealing, and personalized delivery. I had assumed that I would be groping through multiple avenues of medical wisdom in a desperate search to discover connecting threads, relationships, and nuanced implications between disparate insights and practices. Instead, with the tension of health care as an unsettling friendly foe, resisting the seduction of medical wisdom became a far more difficult task. I needed to make my way critically through prevailing knowledge claims, putting pressure on them, while figuratively and literally trying to survive the commonplace and the catastrophic.

It was a struggle to stay focused on my need to seek out and analyze medical advice and at the same time to stay focused on the needs of my students and my courses.

After several weeks of medical appointments, consultations, and tests, on Wednesday, November 4, 1998, two days after my breast biopsy, I received the results of the pathology report from my doctor. The "questionable area" in my left breast was malignant. After telephoning my family and the chair of my department, I sent the following E-mail to friends who were awaiting the news:

Subject: Biopsy

Bad news. I have infiltrating lobular carcinoma. It is fast growing (the tumor is larger than 8 cm!). It is very invasive. It often "mirrors" on the other side. I will need IV chemotherapy for probably about 6 mos (maybe followed by 8 weeks of daily radiation). I need to have a mastectomy within the next 2 weeks. This is not a death sentence, but it will be a long road. At this point I don't have much else to say. I have a lot to do in the next couple of weeks. I'll check my e-mail every couple of days. I probably won't be answering the phone much.

A diagnosis of cancer got—and focused—my attention. The next few days were filled with activities required to turn over my courses and various responsibilities and with reorienting myself to a new set of priorities and processes.

Subject: Preparing

I have turned over my classes and my duties at the university. While I will still participate in some activities, I have rid myself of most anything that might be called an obligation—due in large part to the kind and supportive volunteer offers from friends and colleagues. We have even streamlined my spring schedule to two days a week. If I can work it, fine. If I can't, it is a schedule that can easily be filled by an adjunct professor. And we spent some time getting together the particulars of my sick leave time, figuring out ways to make it work. At this point, it looks like I shouldn't have any difficulties in that area. And we are stopping my tenure clock so I won't be responsible for things like research and publishing during this period.

After being introduced to Reiki Therapy through a thoughtful arrangement made by friends, I have been having treatments. It is a kind of noninvasive, hands-on relaxation and healing ("energy work"). It helps me feel better and is also thought to have some positive effects on the immune system. I had the first session 2 days before the biopsy, have had several since, and I plan to continue this throughout the upcoming events. I figure a couple of hours a week devoted strictly to me working on relaxing and healing has to be time well spent.

I have been tearful from time to time—usually surprising myself by bursting into tears as I go to rinse out a glass, or hang up some clothes, or take out the trash. It is clear to me that this will be a one-day-at-a-time process. It is simply too much to think about otherwise.

I have (perhaps over-) indulged myself in a new-found hunger to have candles all over the house. I went to the store yesterday and went just a bit mad buying candles. Last night it was about 52 degrees. Paul and I had a fire in the fireplace, lit all the candles (an impressive number), turned off the lights, drank some wine, and fell asleep on the floor in front of the fire. The end of a very long week.

The tension of combining the idea of surgery with Reiki and the prospect of chemotherapy with feminist theory meant I was in a constant struggle to make incompatible, or at least unfamiliar, perspectives link together. I was trying to make a kind of coalition, a necessarily self-centric coalition of ideas and practices that may have had little in common except for their intersection in my body and subjectivity. This kind of "coalition-thinking" does not, as Bernice Johnson Reagan has taught us, feel like "home" (358–60).

Although it had been necessary to confide in a couple of students, for all intents and purposes I suddenly disappeared from my classes—leaving it up to my replacements to explain the events leading to my absence. I heard from those who were covering my courses not only about the progress of the classes but also about student reactions to the news of my diagnosis. I was surprised, touched, and, quite frankly, concerned when I heard that some students had burst into tears. I had been busy orchestrating material for the remainder of the courses for my replacements and trying to communicate myriad details about the needs of various students along with course content and directions. Although I had anticipated the reactions of several graduate students with whom I worked closely, in general (and especially with undergraduates) I had not considered the ramifications of students' emotional attachment or the possibility of their genuine concern for my welfare. I realize now—after much time, many cards, calls, and conversations—that what I had thought of as a fairly mechanical (albeit complicated and disruptive) handing over of my courses was in fact an emotionally traumatic experience for many students. This recognition meant, among other things, that I really had to stop and consider my relationship to my students. Many made offers of assistance. A number of graduate students joined a support team of drivers, grocery shoppers, house cleaners, visitors, assistants, cooks, and office helpers that several of my colleagues organized. In the case of my students, I was unsure about what might or might not be appropriate. Would it be an abuse of professorial power to accept a graduate student's offer of volunteering to do my dishes or to drive me to an appointment or to clean my kitchen (or my bathroom)? Would it be insulting or hurtful for me to decline their offers? I needed help. I needed to make taking care of myself a priority. I wanted to challenge my inclination to "do it myself" and to expand in the area of accepting assistance, but I did not want to take advantage of students. This was a major struggle for me. In the end, the best I could do was to maintain a high index of suspicion and a constant awareness of the possibility of inappropriateness, while allowing students to join with friends and colleagues in their offers of assistance. Cancer was proving to be a strange teacher.

With invaluable assistance from supportive friends, family, colleagues, and students, I spent the next two months recovering from the surgery, traveling to Reiki treatments and doctor's appointments, pursuing a variety of medical issues and treatments for complications, awaiting various pathology reports, gearing up for chemotherapy, dealing with assorted side effects from my first chemotherapy treatment, and attempting to celebrate the winter holidays.

Subject: Thinking spring semester

During the spring semester I plan to teach on Tuesday and Thursday afternoons. I'm trying to plan my chemotherapy sessions (each about 7 hours long) for Fridays so that I'll have 3 full days to recover before going back into the classroom. I'm hoping that will help.

I also found out that I can't get a chemotherapy schedule for the length of the semester (I wanted one in order to help plan out my syllabus). Apparently it is a one-treatment-at-a-time schedule, even though they want the treatments to be 21–28 days apart. Apparently the spacing is dictated by the blood work results rather than by the calendar.

There will be several different kinds of chemotherapy. Among other things, the drugs are dictated by the extent of the lymph node involvement, the type of cancer, and the pathology results of certain hormone and other tests. The first four treatments will be one set of medicines and the next four treatments will be another.

The spring semester loomed large in my mind. I was scheduled to teach a course titled "Woman's Body/Woman's Mind"—essentially an undergraduate women's health course. The irony of teaching such a course as a recently diagnosed breast cancer and postmastectomy patient undergoing chemotherapy did not escape me; however, the course was ideal for a number of reasons. First, I was very familiar with the material, the readings were relatively straightforward, and the course could be picked up by an adjunct if I were unable to teach. Second, the course included many speakers from the community (midwives, nutritionists, mental health professionals, AIDS educators, hospice workers, sex therapists, and victim advocates) and a number of videotapes (on birth, disabilities, abortion, cervical self-examination, and violence against women), so it did not depend on my ability to actually stand up and lecture or lead students through a structured discussion of the readings every class period. We would, of course, discuss the readings and apply them to the information provided by the guest speakers or by the videotapes in the style of a seminar discussion. Third, because I structured the course around a number of different topics, the schedule could easily be changed by rearranging designated topics or by inserting different ones. Fourth, the largest percentage of the grade assignment was based on each student's work on a semester-long research project and a class presentation of the project as a work-in-progress. This assignment was accompanied by a detailed timeline requiring topic approval and the submission of a number of references on several different dates. Between the timeline requirements, the presentation, and the final written project, students would independently be able to pursue interests that class materials did not address comprehensively. Any instructor could easily follow any particular student's progress throughout the semester; the entire class would benefit from each student's research via the work-in-progress presentation, and the student presentations would also minimize the needs demanded by a more teacher-centric course.

In addition to course and classroom issues and responsibilities, I had publishing obligations. I was coeditor of a collection of essays on teaching the introductory course in women's studies, and the publisher expected the manuscript in mid-January. Fortunately, the coeditor and I were already in the final stages of manuscript preparation at the time of my diagnosis although we still had to write the introductory chapter. Because we lived several states apart, much of our collaboration had been over the phone, via E-mail, fax, and traditional post. Since the coeditor had other plans that brought her to my area in early January, we were able to sit down together in a very productive meeting, working out many of the remaining details of the manuscript and the introductory chapter. Meanwhile, I also had other concerns:

Subject: Hair loss

> *In the last two or three days my hair has begun to fall out quite dramatically. If I shake my head vigorously hair flies everywhere. If I actually put my hand in my hair and give a small tug I can get a distressingly huge clump of hair. So, today I went to see the wig lady at a local wig store. I must say wigs are not a language in which I hope to become fluent; however, this woman clearly knew what she was doing and in short order had everything all arranged. My wig arrives tomorrow. So, tomorrow I go to the wig lady and get my head completely shaved and get my wig fitted, thinned, cut, and styled. Getting my head shaved seems like a particularly vivid milestone in this process of chemotherapy.*
>
> *The Spring semester begins on Tuesday and I'm looking forward to being back on campus at least two days a week as I teach one course and continue my duties as graduate director.*

I was nervous about starting the semester, about teaching, and about the workload. Would it require more endurance than I had? Would I suddenly burst into tears in the classroom the way I had been doing at home? Somehow, with the ubiquitous assistance of friends, I was able to order my books, finish my syllabus, confirm dates with guest speakers, and reserve videos.

Subject: First day of the semester

> *The last couple of weeks have been very busy. Today the plastic surgeon did a partial closure of the remaining opening. He put the last stitch in at 1:25 pm and (after a frantic cross-town drive and switching cars) I arrived in front of my first class on-time at 2:00 pm. This was a little more drama than I actually needed on my first day back to work, but it turned out fine.*

The students from the support team met me (and the friend who had driven me) at the car and helped carry supplies to my office. A colleague took my list of videos for the semester to the media center, and a graduate student agreed to pick them up and deliver them to my office on the appropriate days. The class was relatively small, about fifteen students, allowing it to be scheduled in the conference room down the hall from my office, so, once I arrived, I never had to leave the building. Even though I suspect most students knew my recent history, I was committed to being open and honest with the class. On the first day I implied we were about to undertake a journey together. I explained the recent events in my life, my desire to teach the course, and the reality that I did not know what the next few months would bring. Therefore, I suggested, they needed to know that although there was a possibility that I might not be able to complete the course with them, I intended to try. I also assured them that I expected them to make use of my office hours, to ask questions, and to apply themselves as they would to any other course. The day went well, and I suspect the students were as hopeful about the positive possibilities for the semester as I was.

Subject: End of week two

> *I am doing well. I am teaching one class (15 students, seminar) and doing graduate advising. I'm getting better at asking for assistance when I need it, and at respecting my body's need to rest and slow down. My old habits for muscling my way through fatigue do not work now. If I muscle my way through I pay for it in dramatic ways (the effects of chemotherapy are quite unforgiving). So, I'm learning to take it easy. I've had a series of friends come to stay. They have taken care of both Paul and me and have cooked until the freezer is simply bulging.*
>
> *My co-editor and I managed through all of this to get the manuscript to the publisher yesterday (one day early)! So we are quite pleased with ourselves. We have one more month to write our introductory chapter.*

I was tired and everything seemed an effort, yet I was establishing a routine, finding a pace, and settling in to the rhythms of the semester. I also discovered useful services, such as people in various offices on campus with access to electric golf carts and willingness to drive me to distant campus locations when the need arose. That is, generally speaking, I had more and more time when I felt that I could carry on with my life and my work without too much difficulty (although it still came in fairly carefully measured doses).

Subject: Pacing myself

I continue to improve. But, with job candidates coming in to be interviewed on top of meeting publication deadlines for several articles and all my other duties, it has been fairly hectic for me. The bad news is these "good" times are somewhat unpredictably truncated by immediate and overwhelming soreness and fatigue. It's as if I'm just cruising along, everything is fine and then—bang: the end of the road. It is always a bit of a shock and usually terribly inconvenient and frustrating. But, I've learned to listen to this, and when I have to stop, I just stop. This is hard to do when I'm facing deadlines of one kind or another, but I just do it anyway. I have little choice. Recovery from these episodes of "hitting the end of the road" is also uneven, but usually longer than I ever think it will be. The effect of all this is that I do less "kicking and screaming" than I used to do and am a little less tearful about having to stop what I'm doing, and have, instead, developed a real respect for listening to my body, respecting its limits, and "letting go" while it re-builds its (albeit limited) reserves for the next bout of activity. I think continuing the Reiki therapy has helped me with this aspect a great deal.

In class we were covering introductory topics, such as the history of women's health care and the politics of professionalism from the healing knowledge of witches to current medical practices; more provocative topics, such as the politics of cervical self-examination and menstrual extraction versus menstrual regulation; and issues of body image and disability. The first two guest speakers came during the third and fourth weeks of class, one a senior health educator of wellness, exercise, and physical activity and the other a nutritionist/dietician—both from the campus health center. The classes were engaging and—in terms of my health, aside from fatigue—uneventful. I had explained my circumstances to the guest speakers prior to their arrival, and they merely went about their business of delivering energetic, interesting, and appropriate presentations. The immediacy of my own health simply was not the focus of our daily classroom activities. Occasionally I would mention fatigue and request assistance with moving the VCR monitor from the side of the room to the front of the room, or while sitting at the seminar table I would illustrate a point on a large piece of paper and hold it up rather than stand up and use the blackboard. From time to time students would ask how I felt or how I was tolerating the chemotherapy. My condition was a known backdrop, which could be discussed, but generally it did not elicit or require active attention from either guest speakers or students. In short, my known and visible health status meant that issues of morbidity and mortality were necessarily the present absence in that classroom—always present, yet absent in most discussion.

One of the effects of feeling better was that I began to consider my situation a bit more theoretically. I began to think about what I was doing, the ramifications of my actions and my motivation. One of the first targets of my musing was my wig. I had never really thought much about the wig. I never wanted a wig. I just got one when my hair began to fall out because, well, because I guess I thought that was what one did, what was expected. I find it curious that I went through the entire wig routine without much attentiveness. Again, I surely know and can readily critique the issues of gender expectations and body image that the use of a wig taps into; however, this was one more occasion where the conversation had me. I was juggling a multitude of issues at the beginning of the semester, and my wig was not even in the top twenty on my list of things to consider. But by the beginning of February my days became more predictable, and when I thought about it, I was not sure why I was wearing the wig.[6]

Here was a clear example of theory and life in tension. I knew I did not need the wig any longer. Perhaps it was a resource that helped to mark a path of normality through a time when surgery put normalness into question. A resource that was valuable at one point but later got in the way. This, too, seems like coalition politics. The terrain of my daily life had shifted enough that the wig-as-normalizing-resource no longer connected to the other vectors of intelligibility that were mobilizing my self-understanding and that were allowing me to get things done. The wig-as-normalizing-resource was pushed out, not because it was bad but because it was no longer in a productive conversation—no longer in coalition—with the other self-producing practices in which I was engaged:

Subject: Wig

> *I announced to my students yesterday that beginning next week I would no longer be wearing my wig, that I'd be teaching bald. I thought I should give them fair warning. It seemed mean spirited to simply show up one day without it. The students were good natured about it. I am just simply D O N E with this wig. I really don't think I could have begun the semester without it. I think I needed to use my energies elsewhere, but I'm clearly done with it now—and school is the only place I wear it. So. A decision has been made.*

When I entered the room at the next class meeting most of the students were huddled in the far corner with their backs to me. I thought it was odd, but there is often much confusion at the start of class as groups of students gather their presentation materials together. Yet, for a fleeting moment I thought they did not want to look at me. I had gone too far, baldness was too much, and this group in the far corner was exercising a form of protest. Out of the corner of my eye I saw a greeting card being passed around. Suddenly it became clear that the students had organized to show their support. The group in the corner turned to face me, surprising me by walking forward together and presenting me with a dish on top of which rested a "bald" cake—an angel food cake without icing—to celebrate and support my decision for baldness. It was a moving and lovely gesture, and again I was quite touched. But it was also more than that. Sharing that cake was a way for all of us to share the complicated and dynamic tensions of that classroom. It was a way for the students to speak out and participate in my experience and for me to join them in their experience. The cake marked a recognition that we were going through an ill-defined and important process together—one at which we were all willing to work. I recognized the moment not as sentimental, but as political, an ironic moment of classroom power in which action, support, awakening, investment, coalition building, and recognition of mortality became political practices of the day. I understood that, for students, too, coming to terms with serious illness meant, in part, facing such a possibility for themselves. Likewise, witnessing and celebrating my recovery also implied the possibility of their own.

From that day on I taught brazenly bald.

As the semester wore on, I continued to struggle with recovery and with the increasingly debilitating side effects of chemotherapy. The new drugs in the last several series of treatments produced bone and nerve pain that interfered with my ability to stand, walk, or use my hands—and caused the loss of all of my body hair (eyelashes included). Sallow and in a constant state of exhaustion, I shuffled slowly forward without bending my ankles instead of walking. Unable to use my fingers, I was often reduced to grasping books and papers as well as the phone and the steering wheel by using the side of my hands or my wrists or forearms. Under these conditions, returning papers to students in class became quite a challenge. Typically, as part of modeling feminist process, at the start of each class I ask whether there are any announcements. These might be the date, place, and time of an upcoming campus or community activity, the reporting of media coverage, or a "real life" encounter about a topic relevant to the course specifically or to women's studies more generally. During these announcements, since the side effects of the chemotherapy were so visible, I often volunteered (limited but appropriate) information about my current health status. Meanwhile, outside of the classroom, publication demands required me to rally my scant energy for the daunting and exhausting task of reviewing page proofs for the coedited collection as well as addressing minor revisions for an essay accepted by a journal.[7] These time-consuming chores and, perhaps most concerning, the effort and strain of cognitive struggle left me feeling run-down and feeble. I was surprised to find that my mind—in addition to my body—was easily tired. At this point I alternated feeling simply weary and debilitated, with pride in my ability to carry on and hope that what I was going through was indeed positive and helpful. I wanted to believe, given the myriad of awful choices, that I had made good ones. Sometimes seemingly mundane events took on new proportions.

Subject: Shock of recognition

> *Yesterday when I was walking with my slow and careful steps through the grocery store (where most of the mini-dramas in my life happen), a woman wearing a large "floppy" cotton hat pushed her cart past mine as I was getting something off the shelf. She smiled looking at my awkward stance and my bald head and said, "You have the same hair-do that I have. You're not having any fun either, are you?" I smiled back, and said, with a small chuckle, "No. I'm not. I have to keep telling people this isn't a fashion statement." She moved on, smiling, and so did I. It felt like 2 aliens acknowledging each other as we passed through life on planet earth. Later, when I reached the produce section, she showed up again. As we were cart-to-cart (so to speak) I asked her (careful to construct my phrase with caution), "Have you been at this very long?" She said "they" thought her cancer was gone but it reappeared in her brain. (I don't know whether it was originally in her brain and reappeared there, or whether is was metastasis—it wasn't exactly clear.) She asked how long I'd been "at it." We talked a few minutes. You could tell by the groceries in her cart that she was buying food for a family that included young children. I wished her luck and said that I hoped she had a good support group. She smiled—sort of dreamily—and said she *really* did. And off we went on our separate ways. A shared moment between strangers. In one way it was fairly ordinary—expats meeting on a train, women meeting in an all-male space—but there was something powerful about it. I thought about it all night. This anonymous encounter. It was like another step in self-recognition. A little lesson in grace, power, and inevitability. There was something about that encounter that made me want to be able to describe myself with the spare clarity of poetry. (Something for which I have absolutely no talent.) An interest I've never had, but I suddenly had a real and deep yearning for it [. . .]. I'm not sure any of this makes much sense [. . .] but it seemed a kind of marker, an ordinary moment that was, instead, extraordinary. An anonymous honesty in the produce section. I wanted to share it with you. (I'm crying as I write and think about this again.)*

Echoing my students' recognition and possible acceptance of their own vulnerability and mortality, I realized this woman was dying. The woman I shared that moment with may well be dead now, her children, family, and friends grieving. Again, theory and life—quite literally—appeared in tension with each other. My connection with the immediacy of mortality was not governed primarily by fear but rather by compassion, understanding, and even identification. This, too, was a teaching, a kind of feminist relationship, a knowledge enabled by the tension of coalition.

The students and I worked our way through a productive course to the end of the semester. Anonymous student comments from the course evaluations make it clear that the students had a positive and personally meaningful semester:

- "I learned so much from this course about myself. [. . .] You really got me thinking about why things are handled the way they are. [. . .] Thank you for being so open with us as a class."

- "One of the most rewarding classes I have ever taken. [. . .] Every topic we covered related to my life in some way. [. . .] I think every woman on campus should take this course!"

- "The speakers were excellent and I liked the broad range of topics. [. . .] By far, the biggest asset to the course was you. Never in my academic career has a professor made students so comfortable. [. . .] And, thanks for being willing to talk about your cancer and leaving your door open for our questions."

- "I felt 'included' in the space in ways I don't in other classes. Actually, I thought the abundance of speakers and videos were *[sic]* more helpful to grasping concepts and relating new knowledge to the outside world. I could incorporate what I learned into life-situations through these aids."

- "This class was an eye-opening experience. [. . .] I enjoyed seeing what I was learning about 'come to life.' [. . .] Also, the fact that you could speak from experience was very motivational."

- "I believe that the most important thing that I have learned in this class is the emphasis on multicultural perspectives of women in health care."

- "I honestly feel truly affected by this course and the materials covered, as well as by you as a professor. My voice was heard and for the first time, I felt like it was truly important."

I continued teaching in the summer while having daily radiation.[8] But that day in early February—that day of the cake—was perhaps the most memorable day of the semester. On that day feminist theory tangibly merged with celebratory feminist practice. I had gotten cancer, but cancer had not gotten me. My body was never separate from my teaching of feminism; it was always implicated. But through the incompatibilities and the immediacy of illness I was able to come to a better understanding of myself and to make a profound connection with my students by enacting a particular—albeit a tense—brand of politics in the classroom. Cancer was a teacher, an adversary, but not necessarily a master.

NOTES

1. Many thanks to Laura Ellingson, Kathy Ferguson, and Paul Larned for their thoughtful comments on an earlier draft of this chapter.

2. The excerpted E-mails included in this essay are taken from my own archives. I saved all E-mail communications (over one thousand) having to do with my cancer experience over the course of approximately one year. Initially I E-mailed only close friends. This particular excerpt is from an E-mail to a longtime friend, also a college

professor, who lives and works in a distant state. Eventually, as the number of interested people with whom I wanted/needed to communicate grew, and in addition to the E-mails directed to specific friends, I began to write a general monthly update—sending it to a large list of friends, colleagues, and supporters. All E-mails are verbatim with the exception of small changes to enhance clarity.

3. My partner of more than twenty years, Paul Larned (a sculptor, who also has a background in medicine), was wonderfully supportive and, of course, terribly concerned. This experience of cancer and its associated events—though not symmetrically—happened to both of us.

4. Examples of writing that address signification of the breast include Bartky, "Foucault, Femininity, and the Modernization of Patriarchal Power"; Blum, *At the Breast;* Chapkis, *Beauty Secrets;* Lorde, "Breast Cancer: Power vs Prosthesis"; Miles, "The Virgin's One Bare Breast"; Sedgwick, "Breast Cancer: An Adventure in Applied Deconstruction"; Weiss, "Splitting the Subject"; and Young, "Breasted Experience."

5. Although there are many examples of this concept in Heidegger's work, here are three. First, from *On the Way to Language,* "Language itself has woven us into this speaking" (112). The second and third examples both come from "Letter in Humanism," found in *Basic Writings.* Second, "In its essence language is not the utterance of an organism; nor is it the expression of a living thing. Nor can it ever be thought in an essentially correct way in terms of its symbolic character, perhaps not even in terms of the character of signification. Language is the lightning-concealing advent of Being itself" (206). And, third, "Thinking gathers language into simple saying. In this way language is the language of Being, as clouds are the clouds of the sky. With its saying, thinking lays inconspicuous furrows in language" (242).

6. See also Hooper, "Beauty Tips for the Dead."

7. See Winkler and DiPalma, *Teaching Introduction to Women's Studies,* and DiPalma, "Reading Donna Haraway."

8. The events in this chapter took place during the fall 1998–spring 1999 academic year. For those interested in the medical particulars, I offer the following brief synopsis. After a biopsy in early November 1998, I was diagnosed with infiltrating lobular carcinoma of the left breast. I had a modified radical left mastectomy with immediate latisimus flap reconstruction. The pathology report indicated an 8–10 cm. tumor (estrogen and progesterone positive, HER 2–Neu negative) and the involvement of one lymph node—thus my cancer was Stage III. The first four chemotherapy treatments (December–March) were Adriamycin, 5–FU/Fluorouracil, and Cytoxan. The last four chemotherapy treatments (March–May) were Taxol. However, due to the cumulative negative side effects (neuropathy) I never received the final scheduled treatment. I began Tamoxifen (20 mg/day) in June 1999, completed daily radiation in mid-August 1999, and had the final stage of reconstructive surgery in December 1999. Improved, but weak and enduring continued "brain fog," I returned to full duties in the fall 1999 semester. Throughout 2000 and into 2001 the confounding weakness and brain fog retreated at a glacial pace. Due to disconcerting side effects I changed from Tamoxifen to Fareston (60 mg/day) in July 2001 and, again, from Fareston to Femara (2.5 mg/day) in January 2002. In August 2001 I had a liver biopsy and in October 2001

I had another breast biopsy—both benign. Although the cloud of recurrence is ever present, generally, with a few ups and downs, my health, attitude, and energy have steadily improved.

WORKS CITED

Bartky, Sandra Lee. "Foucault, Femininity, and the Modernization of Patriarchal Power." *The Politics of Women's Bodies: Sexuality, Appearance, and Behavior.* Ed. Rose Weitz. New York: Oxford UP, 1998. 25–45.

Blum, Linda M. *At the Breast: Ideologies of Breastfeeding and Motherhood in the Contemporary United States.* Boston: Beacon, 1999.

Bornstein, Kate. *Gender Outlaw: On Men, Women, and the Rest of Us.* New York: Vintage, 1995.

Brown, Elsa Barkley. "What Has Happened Here?: The Politics of Difference in Women's History and Feminist Politics." *The Second Wave: A Reader in Feminist Theory.* Ed. Linda Nicholson. New York: Routledge, 1997. 272–87.

Brown, Wendy. "Wounded Attachments." *States of Injury: Power and Freedom in Late Modernity.* Princeton: Princeton UP, 1995. 52–76.

Chapkis, Wendy. *Beauty Secrets: Women and the Politics of Appearance.* Boston: South End, 1986.

DiPalma, Carolyn. "Reading Donna Haraway: A Feminist Theoretical and Methodological Perspective." *Asian Journal of Women's Studies* 5.1 (1999): 50–83.

Foucault, Michel. *Discipline and Punish: The Birth of the Prison.* New York: Vintage, 1979.

Haraway, Donna. "Situated Knowledges: The Science Question in Feminism and the Privilege of Partial Perspective." *Feminist Studies* 14.3 (1988): 575–99.

Heidegger, Martin. *On the Way to Language.* New York: Harper and Row, 1971.

———. "Letter in Humanism." *Basic Writings.* Ed. David Farell Krell. New York: Harper, 1977.

Hooper, Judith. "Beauty Tips for the Dead." *Minding the Body: Women Writers on Body and Soul.* Ed. Patricia Foster. New York: Doubleday, 1994. 107–37.

Lorde, Audre. "Breast Cancer: Power vs Prosthesis." *The Cancer Journals.* San Francisco: Aunt Lute, 1980. 55–77.

Martin, Emily. *Flexible Bodies: Tracking Immunity in American Culture from the Days of Polio to the Age of AIDS.* Boston: Beacon, 1994.

Miles, Margaret R. "The Virgin's One Bare Breast: Female Nudity and Religious Meaning in Tuscan Early Renaissance Culture." *The Female Body in Western Culture.* Ed. Susan Rubin Suleiman. Cambridge: Harvard UP, 1985. 193–208.

Minh-ha, Trinh T. *Woman, Native, Other: Writing Postcoloniality and Feminism.* Bloomington: Indiana UP, 1989.

Reagan, Bernice Johnson. "Coalition Politics: Turning the Century." *Home Girls: A Black Feminist Anthology*. Ed. Barbara Smith. New York: Kitchen Table: Women of Color, 1983. 356–68.

Scott, Joan W. "Experience." *Feminists Theorize the Political*. Ed. Judith Butler and Joan W. Scott. New York: Routledge, 1992. 22–40.

Sedgwick, Eve Kosofsky. "Breast Cancer: An Adventure in Applied Deconstruction." *Feminist Theory and the Body*. Ed. Jane Price and Margrit Shildrick. New York: Routledge, 1999. 153–56.

Weiss, Gail. "Splitting the Subject: The Interval between Immanence and Transcendence." *Body Images: Embodiment as Intercorporeality*. New York: Routledge, 1999. 39–63.

Winkler, Barbara Scott, and Carolyn DiPalma, eds. *Teaching Introduction to Women's Studies: Expectations and Strategies*. Westport, Conn.: Bergin and Garvey, 1999.

Wittig, Monique. "One Is Not Born a Woman." *The Second Wave*. Ed. Linda Nicholson. New York: Routledge, 1997. 265–71.

Young, Iris Marion. "Breasted Experience." *Throwing Like a Girl and Other Essays in Feminist Philosophy and Social Theory*. Bloomington: Indiana UP, 1990. 189–209.

Johnny Mnemonic Meets
the Bimbo: Feminist Pedagogy
and Postmodern Performance

Diane Price Herndl

Like any good bimbo narrative, this one begins in the closet, in front of a rack of clothes. Having just finished the reading for my graduate theory class, I have thirty minutes to prepare for class, dress, make the twelve-minute drive to campus, hope for a parking spot, and walk into the room. It is a typical day. I hate all of my clothes. Like many American women, I see my closet as a reproach, an object lesson in everything wrong with me—I should work less, eat less, exercise more, and then my clothes will be friendlier, and I will be happier. Or maybe I just need to make more money and buy a lot more clothes. Unlike most American women, though, I have an internal voice warning me against this and spend several minutes reminding myself that I have, after all, read Susan Bordo and Frankfurt School criticism and know better than to blame myself or my body or to hope for salvation from the mall.

Having chosen something to wear that doesn't need ironing and will fit no matter what day of the month it is or what I've eaten for the last three days, I stand in front of the mirror to dry my hair while I plan the coming class on Meaghan Morris's essay, "Banality in Cultural Studies." Instead, I think about its relation to my situation and to the banality of my daily routine of clothes hating and Marxist feminist self-lecturing and wonder what the relation is between my personal closet-crises and my professional classroom persona.

As I'm driving into town, past the gravel pit and the place where they're going to build the new museum, I'm suddenly struck by a connection between *Johnny Mnemonic,* the bad movie I watched last night because I was too tired to work, the Morris essay, and my life: Morris writes that (male) cultural studies tend to describe the (usually female) consumer of mass culture as "distracted, absent-minded, insouciant, vague, flighty, skimming from image to image" (651). She argues that this "rush of associations runs irresistibly toward a figure of mass culture not as a woman but, more specifically, as a bimbo" (651). I wonder whether the old image of the absent-minded professor hasn't given way, at least for feminist teachers like me, to that of the bimbo professor. As I think through my day and week, I wish that, like Johnny Mnemonic (a pop culture fantasy of an impossible, enhanced body), I had a computer chip in my brain into which I could download information and out of which I could just upload that information in class. I wouldn't be a bimbo then. I might be falling into Paulo Freire's "banking model" of teaching, rife with what he calls the "narration sickness" of the lecture/memorize/regurgitate model of teaching. But at least I wouldn't come to class spaced out, unable to concentrate, and looking like a ditz.

But when our daily routines include, for instance, running from outcomes assessment meetings to producing annual reports and confronting plagiarism and hostile senior colleagues within the hour, only to walk into a classroom the next hour to teach *Last of the Mohicans* followed by another class on Frankfurt School theories and feminism, to, perhaps, listening to a student in office hours explain that her paper will be late because she has been the victim of domestic violence, I wonder: Are our theories of resistant teaching not at odds with our everyday practices and our material conditions? I'm not raising these questions to complain or despair (much of the time I even *like* my job), but I want to use the congruence or conflict between our personal and professional lives to raise the question about the gap between theory and practice in feminist pedagogy and to offer, perhaps, a moment of meditation about the meaning of the ordinary academic daily rush.

I want to raise questions about feminist pedagogy and the feminist pedagogue herself: Distracted, absent-minded, vague, flighty, skipping from meeting to class to meeting . . . the rush of associations runs irresistibly toward a figure of the contemporary academic as a bimbo. Is this a problem for the feminist teacher? Can a bimbo be a feminist? The contemporary construction of academic disciplines and academic administration—in which professors no longer just teach and do research but are also expected to run the university, raise funds, and serve as counselors to an increasingly nontraditional student body—are at odds not only with the traditional image of the professor as an ivory-tower deep thinker (the original absent-minded professor) but also with contemporary feminist ideas of pedagogy as engaged political action. Can we get engaged in fifteen-minute increments?

On the other hand, such distraction, flightiness, and multiplicity may be the condition of the postmodern academic subject. Can we use that fragmented subjectivity to resist a model of (the) discipline that would picture the academic as Johnny Mnemonic, with a head so full of information and cultural capital that this person will die unless she or he can upload it? Feminist pedagogy has long represented students as more than receptacles for the teacher's information, but can resistance to that model figure the feminist teacher as a bimbo who doesn't know her stuff?

Meanwhile, back in my car, planning class, wishing I'd done my work last night instead of watching a video, I remember the episode we had with AT&T last night. In the middle of *Johnny Mnemonic,* we got *another* call from AT&T asking us to switch our long-distance service or to get their credit card, I'm not sure which. Now I should interrupt myself here to note that we'd been fighting with AT&T for six months over these calls; we'd been getting at least two a week and had been getting increasingly hostile to the callers—we had started asking for supervisors, telling them never to call us again, and the like. Well, this caller wouldn't let my husband talk to a supervisor, wouldn't give us his name, wouldn't divulge the home telephone number of AT&T's CEO (this was our new tactic) so we could call him (we felt sure it was a *him*). My husband, usually polite, lost it on the phone, literally shrieked, threatened, and cursed. It was *so intense!*

That little episode over, we went back to our postapocalyptic, technophobic technophilic movie depicting a world where evil corporations rule, where technology has caused a deadly disease that only more technology can cure, and suddenly I began to notice all the AT&T product inserts in the movie: they were everywhere. Johnny used AT&T equipment all the time—fax machines, telephone call-boxes, Internet connections. The bad guys used AT&T, too. I began to feel surrounded, but I also recognized the banality and the ubiquity of the very things I'm teaching about. Morris's essay examines the problem of cultural studies' approaches to mass culture; in the course of her critique of de Certeau's *The Practices of Everyday Life,* Morris describes the dilemma of how to depict the mass culture consumer, arguing that cultural studies is torn between on the one hand representing the consumer as helpless against mass culture's influence and on the other hand representing the consumer as entirely subversive. That is, it offers a sense that either we are always subverted by the corporate mentality that produces mass culture (she calls this paradigm "they always fuck us over") or we always manage to subvert that corporate mentality by using mass culture to our own, not to the corporation's, ends. She argues that for feminists to participate in cultural studies, we have to work not to fall into a critique guided by a sense of consumer as Other, which always sets up a binary that separates mass culture from consumer, and critic from consumer. Morris suggests that the origin of this kind of thinking may be in our imagining the consumers, producers, and critics of mass culture as really separate and different from each other. She argues for a more complex idea of mass culture that doesn't easily distinguish the three but recognizes the banality and ubiquity of mass culture as something that we all jointly produce. To return to *Johnny Mnemonic* and AT&T, for instance, her critique suggests that I'm neither being fucked over by AT&T's product inserts and phone calls (what they clearly hope for) nor am I, on the other hand, doing what I hope I'm doing, in heroically resisting them by (in my class and in this chapter) exposing their little plot. Just as Johnny can neither escape nor control technology but also isn't entirely done in by technology (he is, after all, saved by a technologically enhanced dolphin—you have to see this to believe it), so can I neither entirely escape nor control AT&T, but they don't control me either. My critique of the film and corporation does not mean that I'm not also a consumer who is, at some level, affected by the representation. We need what Morris argues for: a more complicated sense of subjects and agents.

So you're probably asking yourself about now, "What's wrong with this bimbo? Why can't she stay on task? What's this got to do with feminist pedagogy?" So let me return to the subject.

For many years feminist education theorists have been arguing for an idea of the feminist classroom that is decentered, where the teacher is not always the expert, where learning is more active, where the personal and the professional coincide, and where hierarchies of professor and student are subverted. Many of us have actively put those principles into effect with more or less success and with more or less commitment to actually changing the hierarchy. I'm hardly the first to note that one of the ironies of this kind of pedagogy is that one has to assume a certain amount of power to control the classroom in order to first make it an open classroom and that as long as one assigns grades or even decides how those grades will be decided, there is and will be a hierarchy. What I want to challenge is an idea not exactly of hierarchy but of the persona of the feminist pedagogue, the form of subjectivity that is put on display in the feminist classroom.

In an essay called "Hyper-Feminisms: Poststructuralist Theories, Popular Culture, and Pedagogy," Lisa Starks describes teaching a women's studies course in which she challenges the "anti-fashion" discourse of many feminists, urging her students to see how "classical feminism," which eschews interest in fashion as "silly and unintelligent," actually "aligns itself . . . with the conservative right . . . [because it] employs the same model of the 'self' as does misogynist ideology" (118–19); that is, a model of the self as unique, stable, identical, and substantial. She urges her students to adopt a poststructural model of the self (using Michel Foucault and Judith Butler) to see how we "perform" gender and selfhood. She very consciously argues that she's not urging her students to become "fashion freaks" but to see fashion and style as "an art form and symbolic system," not as something that can be "morally correct" (120). She suggests using Madonna videos as a way of discussing the staging of identity and the performing of gender. Although I like this idea, I would point out that what remains in Starks's example is the feminist pedagogue herself as an apparently unified subject bringing to students' attention the shifting of another's identity—specifically, the shifting identity of a mass culture female icon. As in Morris's critique of cultural studies' separation of mass culture from consumer and from critic, here we see an analogous segregation: Mass culture icon is separate from student, who is separate from professor.

What I am suggesting is not just exposing the instability of subjectivity or analyzing the problematics of agency but of staging and performing the postmodern, poststructural multiplicity of identity in the classroom. But such a performance, I warn you, may come at a price, carries significant risk, and may ultimately be no more antihierarchical than traditional feminist pedagogy.

Let's return to that day in my life as a bimbo professor, then. Having parked my car, dropped off my bag in my office, and walked down the hall to the seminar room, I outline for my class the dynamics of my day and week. I talk about the demands on my time that week, about how scattered I feel, and about the dangers of being so busy. But I also stage for them the pleasures of it to problematize the notion that shifting from idea to idea quickly means that one doesn't think things through. I begin to draw connections, however fragmented, between the closet(ed) practices of my daily life, *Johnny Mnemonic,* the ubiquity of AT&T, Morris's concept of mass culture consumers as bimbos, and my own flighty movement through the day's theory assignment. The class is somewhere between a hysteric's free association and a carefully organized lecture. It goes against the grain of the feminist classroom I'd set up at that point because I do all the talking. But it also goes against the grain of a lecture because I dramatize "lecturer" as anything but a unified, in-control individual; it reveals the identity of the critic and the consumer of mass culture. It is the lecture of a fragmented subject; it is the lecture of a bimbo.

Let me say at this point that I'm acutely aware of the problems with this suggestion from two different points of view. For one thing, this performance occurred in a graduate seminar, late in the semester after I'd already carefully demonstrated to the class that I knew theory and that I could occupy the critic's position without (apparent) contradiction. I had already proven myself in this classroom and had already done what Jane Tompkins argues, in "Pedagogy of the Distressed," that we always *really* want to do in teaching our classes: I had been able, as Tompkins puts it, "a) to show the students how smart I was, b) to show them how knowledgeable I was, and c) to show them how well-prepared I was for class" (654). In other words, I had up to this point maintained that image of the unified individual who was competent. Furthermore, as I said before, it was a *graduate* class. They were able to follow the game and to recognize subjectivity as fair game. Second, though I am no Jane Tompkins, I am tenured, fairly secure in my position in the department and college, and have very little to lose. Michael Carroll, in a response to Tompkins's essay, points out that her pedagogic suggestions are "really aimed at those who are already securely established" (600). So, too, are mine. Imagine performing the bimbo professor in the first week of a first-year composition class or in a class full of hostile, antiwoman (much less antifeminist) students! I'm not so naïve as to think that would work. On the other hand, I think there are problems of teaching postmodern and poststructural ideas of the "self" when *performing* a unified self.

I want to stop here in the middle of my argument to point out my difficulty, finally, with even making an argument. As soon as I advance one idea, counterarguments rush in; I deconstruct my own position; and I challenge and take issue with myself. And beneath it all is the hope that what I'm doing, even here in this essay, is proving how much I know, how smart I am, and how well prepared this essay really is: I can not only make the argument but can dispute it, too. This is, of course, the ultimate problem with staging the multiplicity of identity: it becomes a matter of showing that I'm not just the split subject, but I am also the subject in control of that split, aware of the split, "securely established" enough to display my division. What begins as an attempt to subvert is itself subverted, and I'm back at Morris's dilemma, seeing subversion of one kind or another everywhere I look.

So Johnny Mnemonic needs to meet the bimbo; this is precisely *where* Johnny Mnemonic meets the bimbo: Knowing it all and having all the information packed away in my brain makes me Johnny. But moving from idea to idea, unconvinced by any one argument, makes me the bimbo. And maybe *that's* the complicated position of the feminist pedagogue and of the postmodern subject of teaching.

POSTSCRIPT: THE BIMBO ON CHEMO

Performing the Embodied Subject

So what does all this stuff about bimbo subjectivity have to do with the professor's body? Isn't this just more of that professorial insistence on the mind? Even when the bimbo professor starts off an essay about clothes, doesn't she end up like every other academic and shift over to subjectivity?

So let me start over and try again to return to the body. Two days before I was to deliver at a conference a version of what you've just read, I was diagnosed with breast cancer. In between that diagnosis and surgery, I went to the conference, gave my paper as if nothing were going on, and spent the rest of the conference shopping as if it were to be my last shopping trip ever, which in fact I thought it might be. Nine months later, I was back in the classroom, trying to do the "Johnny Mnemonic Meets the Bimbo" lecture again. This time, though, the bimbo performance was quite different. For one thing, this time when I went into the closet to decide about clothes, I had to decide what to do with my bald head—wear a scarf? a hat? a wig?—and I had so little energy that there was no way I could get dressed, drive in, plan a class, park, and make it to the seminar room in thirty minutes. Think something more like an hour and a half. And this time, even my brain is different; instead of getting a little silicon chip installed in my brain as I'd fantasized, I have a little plastic fitting under the skin of my arm, with a tube running up the vein into my heart, so that they can efficiently administer the drugs that we hope will kill the cancer but that we know will also give me "chemo brain" or "chemo fog," a side effect of chemotherapy that is, at least for the bimbo professor, worse than even the nausea. Nausea can be treated; nausea goes away. Chemo fog lasts and lasts; I have little short-term memory—I go down to the kitchen to get out ice cream to make a milkshake, forget what I'm doing, and go back upstairs to bed. Several hours later my husband finds a puddle of melted ice cream; this happens many, many times. My encounter with technology has hardly made me a repository of easily uploadable information; my encounter with technology has truly given me a bimbo subjectivity.

But my (now former) university doesn't have a sick-leave policy for faculty, so I am teaching that graduate theory class again, but this time the bimbo professor is on drugs (Adriamycin, Cytoxan, methotrexate, fluorouracil, Zofran, Ativan, and Trazadone, plus some steroids), is bald, has gained sixteen pounds, and still has very little short-term memory. The state of my body has really altered the performance of the bimbo; I *look* much less like a bimbo than I could ever manage before, but my *mind* is much more the bimbo's than ever. The state of my body has also altered my performance as professor.

One standard model for the performing professor has traditionally been a separation of the public and private selves of the teacher. Part of that has involved a presentation of the professor's self as all but disembodied; we are to be all mind in the classroom. (This is the same sort of fantasy that underlies the figure of Johnny Mnemonic: The enhanced brain occludes the very body on which it depends.) When I was in college, two of my professors lost their wives to cancer; though I knew this, it was never really made a part of the class. Most of the students in the classes—who were not as connected with the department as I was—had no idea. When I was in graduate school, one of my professors went through breast cancer treatment; I heard about it through back channels, but it was never an explicit conversation between us, despite the fact that I was writing about illness. When I had to go back into the classroom during chemo, I thought about trying to pass as able bodied. I had a wig and, except for the weight gain, really didn't look all that sick (in fact, I was sometimes irritated that I *didn't* look sicker because people assumed that I therefore didn't *feel* all that bad). Would my students be able to get past the distraction of my illness? Would I be playing unnecessarily on their sympathies by presenting myself as a cancer patient as well as their professor? Would I feel that too much of me (whatever that is) was at stake in letting them that far into my life? But when it came to it, I realized that there were good pedagogical as well as political reasons for making this supposedly private reality a part of my public persona.

The political reasons were easy for me. Our culture is so accustomed to thinking of cancer as a death sentence and of chemotherapy as unendurable that I thought it might do students good to see someone living a life that looked a lot like normal. I wanted to make it more difficult for them to see the cancer patient as other; I wanted to trouble their ideas of what it is to be sick. These reasons are, of course, as pedagogical as they are political. But I also wanted to emphasize for them the distinct embodiment of subjectivity and to stage the splits of embodied subjectivity for them in a visible way.

One component of this embodied split subjectivity was cyclical. I had treatments every three weeks throughout the semester. As people who've been through chemo or been through it with others know, what that means is a three-week cycle of different ways of inhabiting your body: For a week you feel horrible; for a week you feel weak and tired but not really bad; and for a week you feel fine. Then you start over. I put this schedule on the syllabus; I planned classes to accommodate my energy levels. We talked in class about the relationship between my embodiment and the pedagogy in the class; we talked about accommodation. And regardless of whether it was part of the plan, I performed differences of subjectivity for them every three weeks: They would see me struggling to maintain a thought some weeks and functioning normally others. When we got to issues of mind/body connections that semester, we made my condition part of the discussion. Who could deny the effect of the body on the mind under those circumstances?

A particularly useful text to teach under these circumstances is Naomi Scheman's "Though This Be Method, Yet There Is Madness in It," an analysis of Descartes's mind/body split as a manifestation of a paranoiac relation to the world. Scheman argues that oppression is often a matter of those with the power of mind using and exploiting the bodies of others—stealing their labor and then representing that labor as disenfranchising, making them just bodies and incapable of using proper judgment. She argues that other oppressed groups—specifically gay men, lesbians, and the people with disabilities—are oppressed less by the theft of their labor than by a representation of them as unable to control their own bodies: "The privileged are precisely those who are defined not by the meanings and uses of their bodies for others but by their ability either to control their bodies for their own ends or to seem to exist virtually bodilessly" (351). Further, she argues, those who are privileged are able to make even very different performances of self cohere, so that we can "think there is a natural unmediated connection between intention, will, and action, because if we are privileged, the world collaborates with us, making it all work, apparently seamlessly, and giving us the credit" (358). My performance of the bimbo professor on chemo made it impossible for the students to avoid seeing the seams, not only in my life but in others' lives as well. The gaps between intention, will, and action were just too visible. It challenged an idea of any performance of professor (or student for that matter) as precisely a performance. It challenged the way that we see ourselves coming to school as disembodied minds attending to only scholarly things.

Now, two years later, I carry that sense of embodied subjectivity into all my classrooms, even though it is less necessary. As someone in remission, I pass perfectly well for able bodied and am in many ways actually able bodied again. To perform illness now might well be seen as just a ploy to get sympathy. But to perform the privilege of the able body is also to lose the lesson of that embodied subjectivity, a loss I would feel profoundly in my classes and in my life. I suppose the real irony is that the bimbo did meet Johnny Mnemonic, but it didn't happen at all as I had planned. But then things never do, and that is part of the myth of subjectivity, too. By performing the embodied professor, by performing the professor who is not just mind in the classroom, we can help our students see the multiplicity that is, after all, the subject.

WORKS CITED

Bordo, Susan. *Unbearable Weight: Feminism, Western Culture, and the Body.* Berkeley: U of California P, 1993.

Carroll, Michael. "A Comment on 'Pedagogy of the Distressed.'" *College English* 53.5 (1991): 599–601.

Freire, Paolo. *Pedagogy of the Oppressed.* Trans. Myra Bergman Ramos. New York: Continuum, 1993.

Johnny Mnemonic. Dir. Robert Longo. Tri-Star, 1995.

Morris, Meaghan. "Banality in Cultural Studies." *Logics of Television: Essays in Cultural Criticism.* Ed. Patricia Mellencamp. Madison: U of Wisconsin P, 1990. Rpt. in *Contemporary Literary Criticism: Literary and Cultural Studies.* Ed. Robert Con Davis and Ronald Schliefer. 3rd ed. New York: Longman, 1994. 642–66.

Scheman, Naomi. "Though This Be Method, Yet There Is Madness in It: Paranoia and Liberal Epistemology." *Feminist Social Thought: A Reader.* Ed. Diana Tietjens Meyers. New York and London: Routledge, 1997. 341–67.

Starks, Lisa S. "Hyper-Feminisms: Poststructuralist Theories, Popular Culture, and Pedagogy." *Gender and Académe: Feminist Pedagogy and Politics.* Ed. Sara Munson Deats and Lagretta Tallent Lenker. Lanham, Md.: Rowman & Littlefield, 1994. 111–22.

Tompkins, Jane. "Pedagogy of the Distressed." *College English* 52.6 (1990): 653–60.

"I've Got a Blind Prof":
The Place of Blindness
in the Academy

Rod Michalko

"Look! Look!"
"A dog, a dog!"
"It's a seeing eye dog!"
"He's blind!"
Then silence, a very loud silence. "Forward, Smokie, right, find the chair." My guide dog Smokie competently guides me to the chair situated at the large desk located at the front of N17—a large lecture hall in the university where I teach sociology.

An earlier version of this chapter appeared as "Blindness Enters the Classroom" in *Disability and Society* 15:3 (2001): 349–59. On June 4, 2001, Smokie died of liver cancer. I dedicate this chapter to him.

"Good boy, Smoke," I say as I remove his harness, place it carefully on the chair, and give him a well-deserved treat. I wait the few seconds that it takes Smokie to settle himself comfortably under the large desk, and then I turn my body and face toward the still silent mass of more than eighty students. The class list I received two days earlier showed an enrollment of eighty-three students for this new term in Introductory Sociology. As I stand there facing the class, I sense the mass that fills the room, and I hear the students as well—not their voices, they aren't speaking clearly now—but movement in the seats, bags being put on the floor, papers shuffling, throats clearing. This lecture hall holds seventy-five people, and as I cast my gaze over the rows of seats inclining from where I stand toward the back, I wonder where the extra eight students are sitting or if they are even present.

I run my hands through my hair and smile at the class. There is no need to call for silence, and so I begin my first lecture of the new term. "This is Introductory Sociology 100.12," I tell the mass, "so if you want biology, chemistry, or psych, or something, you're in the wrong room." There are a few murmurs of laughter, but I don't sense anyone leaving. I continue: "For those of you who didn't notice, there's a dog under this desk." More murmurs of laughter. "His name is Smokie and he's my guide dog," I say. "Guide dogs guide blind people," I continue. "So," I draw this word out, "I guess that means I'm. . . ." The laughter now goes well beyond the murmur.

"My name is Rod Michalko," I tell them, "and it's my privilege to be your professor for the year." I then turn and walk to the chalk board. I run my hand along its ledge and locate a piece of chalk. Raising it to the chalk board, I say that I'm going to write my name on the board. As I am about to write my name, I stop and face the class. "Anything written on here?" I ask. A few "no's" come from the mass. "Come on, you guys, louder, let me know, I don't want to write on someone else's junk." Loud laughter now and a resounding "No!" springs from the mass. I print my name on the chalk board and turn to face the class. "Can you read that?" I raise my hands as I ask this question, beckoning another loud response. I hear a resounding "Yes!"

"Not bad for a blind guy, huh?" I say. The laughter is now bouncing around the room, and the mass begins to speak loudly. The students have now come to life. As I hold my hand up and speak over the din, the class settles. I now begin Introductory Sociology 100.12.

But I begin something else as well—something much weightier than introducing more than eighty first-year university students to the discipline of sociology. I'm beginning to introduce them to blindness. For most, if not for all of the students, blindness has entered *their* classroom for the first time. Blindness has come into their classroom *with* me and *in* me (Michalko, *Mystery* 23–34; Michalko, *Two in One* 174–83). There is much with and about me that is not so unusual for them—I am, after all, a white, male professor, a social identity with whom students are more than familiar. But these interpretive categories are shoved aside as blindness radically makes its way to the foreground of the students' interpretive processes. They sit there in surprise; some are confused, and others sit at their desks in disbelief. "I couldn't believe it when you walked in with Smokie at the beginning of the class," one student told me about halfway through the term. "I phoned my mom right after class." He continued, "I told her, 'I got a blind prof!' I just couldn't believe it."

Yet, this disbelief goes much farther than merely the expression of surprise. For example, a former student dropped in to visit me about a year after he had graduated. During our visit he, Stuart, was reminiscing about the first class he took from me. He said that about a month into the class, Brian (the student who sat next to him) became suspicious of my blindness. Stuart said that Brian pointed out that "He looks right at me," as he put it, and asked Stuart whether he thought I was really blind. We both laughed. "It's true," said Stuart, "Brian really thought you could see, and he thought the class was, you know, one of those experiments. He even had me looking for one-way mirrors on the wall."

Many students have told me similar stories over the years. What can (should?) we make of such stories? There is, of course, the obvious quantitative explanation: Students rarely, if ever, experience a blind professor, and, when they do, they are surprised and "can't believe it." As Tom Shakespeare says, "Because of the widespread segregation of disabled people, many non-disabled people may not have come into contact with disabled people" (49). As explanations go, this one is certainly plausible. But to leave it at that is to ignore the particular social context in which blindness makes an appearance and within which surprise and disbelief are framed. It ignores the *scene* in which blindness is a frame. To understand people's surprise and disbelief when blindness unexpectedly "shows up in a picture," let's conduct a "scenography," to borrow from Butler (28), and thus interrogate the ways in which a scene is put together, staged, and socially constructed (Shildrick and Price) in such a way that blindness becomes a surprising and even unbelievable feature.

To conduct such a scenography I first examine the social organization of a university classroom into which blindness enters. What makes the entry of blindness here so surprising and unbelievable? Has blindness been in the classroom before—before the blind professor entered? Is disability just one more contingency, just one more human feature? Or does a disabled body harbor a particular and valuable pedagogy? Are professors merely "talking heads," or do our bodies speak as well, and, if so, what do they say in the classroom, and how are they heard?

THE PROF'S BLIND, HE CAN'T SEE!

I'm in N17 facing my Intro class for the first time. It's a new academic year and I'm quite excited. I'm very familiar with this classroom because I've taught here before. More than this, I've been in classrooms most of my life, and this one is really no different from any other.

The students' desks are only a few feet from where I stand and are arranged in theater fashion, rising on an incline to the back of the room. My desk is, of course, at the front of the room and is very large—a big table really. It has the usual stuff on it—a lectern and a slide projector, both of which I place on the floor next to Smokie. There is a smaller, podium-like table next to the large desk. It, too, has its usual stuff; it houses a VCR as well as a computer with PowerPoint. I notice, despite my blindness, the overhead fluorescent lighting, which floods the classroom with an almost unbearable brightness. And, of course, lurking behind me is that ever-present and proud symbol of university life—the chalk board.

I am just as equipped as my classroom. In my shoulder bag are about eighty copies of the course outline, printed up very nicely. I also have copies of the two books we will be reading in Introductory Sociology this year. A paper clip is attached to one end of the cover of each book so I will know which way is up when I hold the books up for the students to see.

Everything is set; the students embody a quiet anticipation; I sense more than eighty pairs of eyes now on me, now on Smokie. Smiling, I return the look. I focus my gaze first toward the rows of students nearest me, then I raise my gaze, moving slowly left to right, across the middle and to the back of the room. I then reach down, give Smokie one more quick rub behind his ears (an act designed more to reassure me than him), straighten up, and walk around to the front of the large table. Introductory Sociology 100.12 is about to begin.

My course, along with every other course in this and every other university, is about to begin in the midst of the ubiquitous, taken-for-granted sense of sight. Like the air we breathe, sight is everywhere in my classroom, and, like the air, it is not noticed and not even seen. The classroom—its equipment and social organization—bears the mark of sight; students see and assume this of one another, and they assume that they all see the same things and in the same way. There is no blindness visible anywhere in the classroom . . . till now.

Until Smokie and I entered the classroom, blindness was on no one's mind, and, just as important, neither was sight. But now what? This is a university classroom, after all. There are textbooks for the students to read, overhead slides to see, words to copy from the chalk board, exams and term papers for me to write and grade, students to watch for signs of cheating—this site is full of sight. Now what that blindness has entered this site of sights? Now what that the professor is blind? I have a lot of explaining to do.

I begin the course by doing just that. There are lessons in my explanations—lessons regarding the assumptions and practices of our society. For example, I ask the students how they get the prof's attention during a class and how they communicate their desire to speak. The students now have an opportunity to notice for the first time in a critical way the universal classroom symbol of the raising of the hand. This is our first sociological lesson of the year—the interpretive transformation of a visual event (the raising of a hand) into a communication event bathed in meaning—"I want to say something." This leads to our second sociological lesson—the construction of new symbols from the building blocks of culture. Students always suggest the interactional practice of interrupting as a way to symbolize their desire to speak, now that they have a blind professor. "Excuse me" or "Rod" are now established as the oral events that are transformed into the communication event of "I want to say something."

The next sociological lesson has to do with the phenomenon of reading. Reading, and doing so *with the eyes,* is an assumption as universal to the classroom as is the raising of the hand. I ask for a volunteer and a student comes to the front of the class. I ask her to close her eyes; then I hand her a copy of the course outline, and ask her to figure out how to read it without opening her eyes. The class comes alive, laughing and talking. Within a few seconds, the class begins shouting suggestions to the student standing beside me tentatively holding the outline. Sooner or later, either from the student herself or shouted from the class, comes the suggestion "Get someone else to read it to you." "Good," I say as I take the outline from the student's hands. "That's what I'll do when it comes to grading your term papers." Sociological lesson number two: Print is a cultural phenomenon and not something that stands by itself outside of the context of contemporary society. There are many ways to read, and even though visually is the dominant way, it is not the only way. Another sociological lesson: The implicit connection between vision and print is an ideology that dominates in our society, leading to the hegemonic privileging of sight (Barton 56).

There are other such sociological lessons during this first class, but I mention only one more, namely, recognizing one another. Sight is also privileged in this regard. We see one another, and we recognize one another. Does this mean that those of us who don't see, don't recognize anyone? How will the prof who can't see come to recognize his students? How will he know who's asking a question? What of those students who skip class—will he know? Does he even know that there are students in the classroom? Are there other sociological lessons (Barnes) to be gleaned regarding the phenomenon of recognizing one another when addressing it within the particularity of having a blind prof? This time I leave such addressing and gleaning to the imagination of the reader of this chapter. Surely there is a lesson in this, too. However, let me provide a clue to these other lessons. Do nondisabled university teachers bring their bodies into their classrooms as well? Or is this bringing restricted to those of us whose bodies are noticeable? Is there anything to notice about the nondisabled body? What does the body say when the nondisabled teacher enters the classroom?

So far I have addressed some of the ways in which sight is implicitly embedded in our classrooms. Sight is not merely a physiological function. Instead, it represents a symbolic order and is used to privilege that order as both the dominant ideological and the normal way of being-in-the-world (Corker, *Deaf and Disabled;* Oliver, *Understanding Disability*). I used the occasion of blindness in the classroom as a way to critically interrogate this order as it manifests itself here.

I SEE, THEREFORE I KNOW

As for every sociologist, the fundamental topic of my research and my teaching is society, and, like every sociologist, I try to get my students to look at their society. But, unlike every sociologist, I problematize this looking as well as the understanding that society is seeable. Looking at society is somewhat paradoxical especially when considered from the point of view that students have been living in society from their birth. Still, if we (sociologists) are asking our students to look at their society, where would they look? Where is society, after all? What sort of sight can see society?

My students can see many things, and I ask them to point to some of them—to their desks, to my desk, to me, to each other, to themselves—and they have no difficulty whatsoever doing so. I then ask them to point to society, and this is where the trouble starts. When I ask the students to point to my desk, not only do they know where to point, *they also know where to look.* The latter presupposes the former. But when it comes to pointing to society, knowing where to look loses its presuppositional and taken-for-granted character. Students are never sure of where to look, let alone where to point. This is not the case when I ask students to point at my desk—they know where to look and thus where to point, and this knowledge is steeped in an implicit understanding of the sense of sight as a necessary condition for knowing—"I see, therefore I know" (Michalko, *Mystery* 78).

But, like the rest of us, students also know that they live in a society; they know that society exists. Yet, their sense of sight with its subsequent ability to look fails them when I ask them to point at their society. Their bewilderment at this inability may be understood as a temporary and pseudoblindness. The students cannot point at society; they cannot even look at it; they have gone blind!

The sense of sight that the students so implicitly and so naturally relied upon as the conjoining of seeing and knowing has failed them. This temporary and pseudoblindness, however, penetrates our classroom *as a teacher.* The students and I begin to re-view what they know without seeing—we discuss knowing ideas, thoughts, and emotions, and we ask what it means to know a friend, a family, each other, and ourselves. We begin to interrogate the role of sight in this knowledge. The discussion then moves from the role of sight to sight as a role.

Somehow the students know that not only do they see, but that others also do. The question now becomes, how? How do we know (see) that, like us, others see and, like us, others see that we see? From this form of questioning flows the first and most important of all class assignments: "When you leave here today, I want you to spend the rest of the day, this evening and tomorrow looking and thinking about how you know that people around you can see and how you know that they can tell that you can also see. You have to do this without asking anyone whether they can see and without telling anyone that you can see."

Students come to the next class with all sorts of responses to this assignment. Here are some examples: "He waved to me and I waved back, right across the parking lot." "I smiled at her and she smiled back." "I got all ready, I looked at myself in the mirror and made sure I looked okay before I left my room." "You know what she said? I heard this before about a million times, but I couldn't believe it when I heard it this time. She said, 'I just gave him a dirty look and kept walking.'" "My psych prof just put up a slide, a slide of the brain." "'See you later,' I just said 'see you later.'"

Students were beginning to experience what Berger calls the "first wisdom" of sociology—"things are not what they seem" (23). Although not in these terms (yet?), students experience the first trope in understanding the social character of their world. They do so by problematizing the common-sense understanding of sight as a strictly physical fact. Like everything else, sight needs to be achieved, and this can be done only through social action, interaction, and language (Corker, *Deaf Studies*). Seeing and knowing this requires something more than the sense of sight. These students learned that in order to see and know their society, they must refocus their gaze by positioning themselves within a standpoint that offers them a view of society. They also learned what philosophers from Plato to Heidegger have learned over the centuries, namely, that sight cannot see itself. They learned this when blindness (the teacher) entered the classroom; they learned this from both my blindness and theirs. Despite the blind teacher and blindness as teacher entering the classroom, the story doesn't end there; in fact it doesn't even begin there. Blindness entered the classroom long before Smokie guided me into N17 that day.

THE ECHO OF BLINDNESS

Contemporary conversations about knowledge and the institution often focus on the way that academic discourse legitimates itself by disavowing the historical, cultural, and corporeal specificity of its speaking. By exposing the way that objective and neutral methodologies repress the precise locations from which the speaker comes, academic discourses have begun to interrogate themselves from within, calling scholars to account, so to speak, for their own inescapable epistemic contingencies. (Roof and Wiegman ix)

Disavowal as a form of self-legitimization engaged in by academic discourses has traditionally been a preferred method for resolving the problem of subjectivity in the academy. This problem as well as its solution is an articulation of modernity, and we owe this legacy primarily to the Age of Enlightenment. The precise location from which the speaker comes has been traditionally understood and positioned as a barrier to objective knowledge, and this positioning has generated the solution of objective and neutral methodologies. Method—framed within a positivistic understanding of the world—is modernity's way of removing (repressing) the particular situation of the speaker/inquirer. This methodological repositioning of the speaker/inquirer relies upon an imagined location possessed of the power (Foucault, *Order of Things, Archaeology of Knowledge*) to neutralize the influence of subjectivity. The problem of subjectivity is taken care of by dehistoricizing, deculturing, and debodying the subject with the subsequent production of knowledge.

The Western tradition has continuously made use of visual metaphor with its concomitant spatial metaphor to express the problem of subjectivity and its solution (Jay). Thus, particular locations blind us to a clear and objective view of reality. We (particular subjects) must get out of the way in order for reality to come into view. Particularity blinds us to the objective view of reality, and any knowledge production from particular locations is knowledge blinded by subjectivity. Even though Roof and Wiegman point out that academic speakers are beginning to interrogate themselves from within and are called to account for their own inescapable epistemic contingencies, the problem of subjectivity conceived of as blinding knowledge production remains a dominant ideology within the academy to this day (Smith, *Writing* 73–95).

It is this version of blindness that precedes Smokie and me as we enter the classroom. The students sitting in front of us have had more than a decade of formal education; they have had several years of seeing the point, of not being blind to the facts, of looking at things objectively, and of trying to see what the teacher is getting at. They have had many years of educational practice of seeing that seeing is enlightenment and blindness is ignorance. They have had years of encouragement to step out of the darkness and into the light. (See what I mean?)

And now the very contingency that the students have been taught to avoid—the contingency that represents the quintessential barrier to knowledge—walks into their classroom and positions himself as their professor.

Blindness as the contingent representation of ignorance begins to resonate and echo around the classroom. The sounds of blindness reverberate in the exclamations: "He's got a seeing eye dog! He's blind!" And in the questions: "How will he mark my exams? How will he know who I am?" These remarks are expressions and representations of the more fundamental question "How can he know, if he doesn't see?"

My blindness is, to borrow from Roof and Wiegman once again, my "inescapable epistemic contingency." Exposed as I am in front of more than eighty students, flexing my fingers gently around Smokie's harness, I find at least some means of escape. Recall that I tell students how I will mark their exams and papers and I demonstrate how I read. By showing students that I do the ordinary things that other ordinary professors do, I escape, albeit to a small degree, the extraordinariness of my contingency. I make use of the common-sense version of blindness (which not so coincidentally includes the medical sense) as a condition (contingency) in order to demonstrate that I can minimize the "negative effects" of blindness on my teaching (Zola; Oliver, *The Politics of Disablement* 46–53). But this also serves to emphasize the version of blindness that greets me as I enter the classroom. My blindness echoes the sound that is already resonating there.

I need to do more than account for my inescapable epistemic contingency. I need to escape the conception of my blindness *as contingency* in the first place. If not, my presence *as professor* is, as Roof and Wiegman say, decultured and, more fundamentally, disembodied. After all, the students, unlike me, are without contingency in relation to sight—they don't see their eyesight as such. They are simply people, not people with eyesight. They don't happen to see, they simply see. I, on the other hand, am not simply a person, I am a person with blindness, with a disability. My blindness is a contingency, a condition I happen to have, I am a person who happens to be blind, at least in their eyes. My students do not see their sight as a contingency that they must escape. They see and thus potentially know. I can't see and thus can't know. I will be teaching ideas that must be looked at (examined) and ultimately seen (understood). I will be teaching "seeing people" to see sociologically. In the words of DiBernard, I would be involved in "teaching what you're not in the presence of those who are" (132).

I enter a university classroom in which blindness is already present, a presence couched within the understanding of it as the binary opposite of sight. Because our culture metaphorically (and often concretely) connects seeing with knowing, my presence in the classroom represents an initial echo of blindness as an obstacle to knowing. Seeing blindness as merely an inescapable epistemic contingency doesn't necessarily position it in a location of knowing. After all, inescapable contingency resonates with the sense that if blindness *could* be escaped, it should be. Blindness is not typically treated as a location of epistemic advantage or standpoint (Harding 146–60; Smith, *The Everyday*

181–207) in the way that "woman," for example, is. Womanness, as a site of inquiry and as an epistemological standpoint, does not formulate woman as contingency. Instead, there is something essential to be experienced and learned from the standpoint of womanness. Yet, blindness and other disabilities are usually framed within the non-disability ideology of conditionality and contingency (Titchkosky, *Disability, Self, and Society* 121).

Such an ideology is exemplified in DiBernard's work. A nondisabled university professor, she introduced a course in disabled women's poetry. Whatever complacency she harbored with respect to her new course being merely another university course was, in her words, "quickly shattered the first night when a woman in a wheelchair wheeled into the room." "I knew then," DiBernard continues, "that I have a lot of work to do in coming to terms with my own relationship with and feelings about disability and my identity as an able-bodied person" (132).

In the face of disability, DiBernard not only faces the epistemic challenge of coming to terms with disability, she also recognizes herself (her identity) as located within able-bodiedness. "I feel my identity now not as a woman who 'happens to be' able-bodied, but as a woman whose able-bodiedness is a location for which I need to take responsibility." DiBernard says that she needs to acknowledge her able-bodiedness "as the place from which I experience the world and from which I do my work." DiBernard's experience and work flow from her able-bodiedness, and, as a teacher, she has retrieved her embodiment. He body is no longer "happenstance" or contingency; it is now the place (location) from which she experiences the world, from which she works, and from which she teaches (132).

But DiBernard's able-bodiedness did not come to her from her experience or her work until she taught a course on disabled women's poetry and, more significantly, until the woman wheeled into her classroom that night. Disability gave her her able-bodiedness. DiBernard's able-bodiedness now comes to her as identity and not merely as contingency.

But does DiBernard's able-bodiedness return the favor to disability? Does she see the disabled body in the same way she sees her own body? Does the disabled body now occupy the space of epistemic location, or does it remain mere contingency? Like those with abled bodies, do we (those of us with disabled bodies) also experience the world and do our work from the location of our bodies? DiBernard hopes that her students (the able-bodied ones) will come to understand their bodies in this way, but, as she writes, "it's a long journey to make in fifteen weeks if people with disabilities have not even been visible before" (132).

We can glimpse an answer to these questions from DiBernard's hope. Despite her new found epistemic location, DiBernard still refers to disabled people as "people with disabilities." She still understands the "problem of disability" as the "problem of essentializing," of seeing only the disability when looking at someone who is disabled. DiBernard has not yet grasped disability as essential to the experience and work of a disabled person and thus as essential to the weaving of a social identity. Although her own (able) body is now commingled with identity, the disabled body remains contingent and conditional. We are not so much disabled people as we are people with disabilities. DiBernard's newfound epistemic location permits her to see herself not as someone who happens to be able-bodied but as someone who is able-bodied. Yet, the location of able-bodiedness does not permit the same for the disabled body.

In a similar fashion, my students learn a great deal about their able-bodiedness (eyesight) when Smokie and I (blindness) enter the classroom. They learn, for example, about cultural practices such as making eye contact, giving dirty looks, looking wide awake in class, and so on. They learn that eye contact and looks are not merely a natural function of eyesight but are instead cultural productions. Some of the students begin to turn their gaze toward their own eyesight, and some of them even begin to take responsibility for their seeing. It is at this intersection between the body (eyesight) and identity that I must take responsibility for my blindness and join my students. This responsibility marks the beginning of the development of a social positioning so necessary for the inclusion of identity into the practices of teaching and learning. Identity is not merely a subjectivity that must be removed in order to know, as the Age of Enlightenment would have it. The task of the speaker/inquirer is to engage in the risky business of maneuvering identity, including the body, into the social position of speaker/inquirer. This maneuvering risks and therefore must resist the understanding that identity and the body represent knowledge itself; instead, identity and the body represent the "critical space for critical inquiry" (Titchkosky 2003). Speakers/inquirers must maneuver in the space of their identities and bodies and not obliterate this space as a remedy to modernity's problem of knowing.

This conjoining of the body and identity in the classroom with my students is a daunting task indeed. Like DiBernard, I, too, am tempted to let my blindness (my body) reveal the connection between able-bodiedness and identity. I am tempted to reveal the epistemic location of able-bodiedness, and I join DiBernard in the hope that my students will see both their identity and epistemological standpoint in their bodies (eyes). This hope, however, will remain just that, a hope, unless I (blindness in the classroom) continue the attempt to depict my blindness as mine—as my identity—and as a location from which I experience the world, from which I work, from which I teach, from which a reality (one as legitimate as those of my students) comes to me, and especially as a location *in which I live*. This is to depict blindness and all disability as a social identity—an identity that embodies living and learning and not one that is contingent and from which we must escape.

WORKS CITED

Barnes, Colin. "The Social Model of Disability: A Sociological Phenomenon Ignored by Sociologists?" *The Disability Reader: Social Science Perspectives*. Ed. Tom Shakespeare. London: Cassell, 1998. 65–78.

Barton, Len. "Sociology, Disability Studies and Education: Some Observations." *The Disability Reader: Social Science Perspectives*. Ed. Tom Shakespeare. London: Cassell, 1998. 53–64.

Berger, Peter. *Invitation to Sociology: A Humanistic Perspective*. New York: Anchor, 1963.

Butler, Judith. *Bodies That Matter: On the Discursive Limits of "Sex."* London: Routledge, 1993.

Corker, Mairian. *Deaf and Disabled, or Deafness Disabled?* Buckingham: Open UP, 1998.

——— . "Deaf Studies and Disability Studies: An Epistemic Conundrum." *Disability Studies Quarterly* 20.1 (2000): 2–10.

DiBernard, Barbara. "Teaching What I'm Not: An Able-Bodied Woman Teaches Literature by Women with Disabilities." *Teaching What You're Not: Identity Politics in Higher Education*. Ed. Katherine J. Mayberry. New York: New York UP, 1996. 131–53.

Foucault, Michel. *The Archaeology of Knowledge*. London: Tavistock, 1972.

——— . *The Order of Things: An Archaeology of the Human Sciences*. London: Tavistock, 1970.

Harding, Sandra. "Standpoint Epistemology (a Feminist Version): How Social Disadvantage Creates Epistemic Advantage." *Social Theory and Sociology: The Classics and Beyond*. Ed. Stephen Turner. Boston: Blackwell, 1996. 146–60.

Jay, Martin. *Downcast Eyes: The Denigration of Vision in Twentieth-Century French Thought*. Berkeley: U of California P, 1994.

Mairs, Nancy. *Waist-High in the World: A Life among the Nondisabled*. Boston: Beacon, 1996.

Michalko, Rod. *The Difference That Disability Makes*. Philadelphia: Temple UP, 2002.

——— . *The Mystery of the Eye and the Shadow of Blindness*. Toronto: U of Toronto P, 1998.

——— . *The Two in One: Walking with Smokie, Walking with Blindness*. Philadelphia: Temple UP, 1999.

Oliver, Michael. *The Politics of Disablement*. Bassingstoke: MacMillan, 1990.

——— . *Understanding Disability: From Theory to Practice*. New York: St. Martin's, 1996.

Roof, Judith, and Robyn Wiegman. *Who Can Speak? Authority and Critical Identity*. Chicago: U of Illinois P, 1995.

Shakespeare, Tom. "Joking a Part." *Body and Society* 5.4 (1999): 47–52.

Shildrick, Margret, and Janet Price. "Breaking the Boundaries of the Broken Body." *Body and Society* 2.4 (1996): 93–113.

Smith, Dorothy. *The Everyday World as Problematic: A Feminist Sociology*. Toronto: U of Toronto P, 1987.

———. *Writing the Social*. Toronto: U of Toronto P, 1999.

Titchkosky, Tanya. *Disability, Self and Society*. Toronto: U of Toronto P, 2003.

———. "Disability Studies: The Old and the New." *Canadian Journal of Sociology* 25.5 (2000): 197–224.

Zola, Irving. "Healthism and Disabling Medicalization." *Disabling Professions*. Ed. Ivan Illich. London: Marion Boyars, 1977.

My Body, Myself:
A Quadriplegic's Perception of
and Approach to Teaching

Richard Radtke
with
James Skouge

Several months ago, just before Christmas, my wife and I, along with our daughter, Ocean, were returning home from a working vacation in the Philippines. I am a fisheries oceanographer, raised in Indiana, but long-settled in Hawaii as a professor at a university. I travel widely in my work, often to remote areas. My wife, Judith, is from the Philippines, and we decided last fall to embark on a homecoming to her native village. Ocean, now seven years old, had never visited Judith's family. It was time for a visit. There was also a program for people with disabilities that I wished to establish, and I wanted the opportunity to study the marine life that was not too distant from Judith's home. The two-week trip was wonderful. Everyone's wishes were fulfilled. We arrived at the Manila airport for departure on a Sunday evening with mixed emotions about flying home. "Could we stay a little longer, Daddy?" Ocean pleaded.

As we waited in the ticket line, my wife was approached by an airport official who spoke with her in hushed terms in their native Tagalog language. I knew they were talking about me, just by observing his furtive glances in my direction. I interrupted. "What is it that you want?" I demanded.

"He wants you to have a physical examination by an airport physician before they will issue our boarding passes," said Judith. "He says that you are an invalid and that it is airline policy that all invalids pass a physical examination before being allowed to fly."

I looked at two old people, a man and woman, just ahead of us in line. "Are they invalids?" I asked. "No," he said, speaking directly to me for the first time. "They are old. They are not invalids."

"Let me see the airline manager," I commanded. And so, after some minutes, a manager appeared.

This is and always will be the story of my life, a struggle against prejudice and fear, ignorance, and perhaps even envy. I am paralyzed from the neck down from multiple sclerosis.

PERSONAL HISTORY

I am a physical person stuck in a paralyzed body. In this chapter I would like to share with you a few of the lessons I have learned about making life work.

I love being out of doors and involved in great adventure. I always have. In fact, that is why I chose my profession. I love fish and I choose to follow them all over this world. But maybe that's jumping ahead.

I played college football. Grew up on a farm. My physical structure is six feet four inches, and in college I weighed up to 240 pounds. My sense of self was largely defined by my size and strength. I'm not sure I realized that until my multiple sclerosis hit me like a thunderstorm, forcing me into a wheelchair within two years. That was in the early 1980s, after I had already secured my Ph.D. I was married at the time and soon thereafter had a son. That marriage broke up. My wife and child moved away. Many things inside me died. Thereafter, I couldn't even bring myself to watch a football game. Years later, I have changed. Sports are once again very much a part of my life. But it has taken time and growth to make that reconnection.

In order to make the leap from football player to quadriplegic I had to make a personal evaluation of my life. That meant accepting that the more physical part of my life was dead in some way. I needed to accept myself without my physical abilities, which is how I now live. The passages have been many, including hills of frustration, anger, and disgust, and valleys of depression and diminished self-esteem. Becoming a quadriplegic meant the end of privacy and the near total dependence on others. Strange and frightening. The things of sleepless nights. With my wife and child gone, my health in disarray, and my career in question, I confronted a choice. I could lie back and await death, or I could choose to construct a life. I chose the latter. This choice has become a lifelong learning process for others and me.

Typically, when I meet new people on the university campus, they ask me what classes I'm taking, assuming that anyone in my situation would be a student. Well, maybe I am—a professor but a student of life.

As far back as I can remember, I dreamed of adventuring in Antarctica. We didn't have much literary material on the farm, but we did have encyclopedias, mostly out of date. I devoured the images of penguins and icebergs. After facing my MS, I resurrected my Antarctic dreams by writing a scientific proposal to the National Science Foundation, together with a colleague, proposing an expedition. We never mentioned my disability, of course. After external review, we were notified that the proposal had been accepted on its merit. We were overjoyed.

Due to Antarctica's remote location, I was notified that any researcher going there was required to pass a physical examination (similar to a military physical). As you may surmise, I did not pass. I had my overall health in my favor, however. I was and still am a vegetarian with a daily regimen of physical therapy. The examiners found no medical problems or risks. I just presented the anomaly of being unable to move. This was the dilemma the National Science Foundation faced: healthy man, cannot move. I requested an exemption. It was denied. In case of fire, they said, I would pose a significant safety hazard. This denial became my invitation for resistance.

I began a letter-writing campaign, requesting support from anyone with any influence, mainly people I had never met but perhaps had voted for, including representatives, senators, and even the president. Senator Inouye from Hawaii, who had lost an arm in service to his country, came to my assistance. I was granted permission to make the expedition.

The trip was arduous, unforgettable, and eye opening. I knew that nothing would ever stop me again. I was able to touch (I still have the feeling) the fish of my dreams. I held a penguin and assisted fellow scientists. I became part of the Antarctic drama. This was to be a major defining juncture in my life. The year was 1987—six years after the onset of the MS.

Many years later I faced a much more formidable test of resolve. I wanted to follow migratory fish into the high Arctic, specifically into the upper northwest corner of Greenland. I've always been passionate about extreme coldwater species and here was my chance. The NSF accepted my proposal. The funding was in place. But money isn't everything, of course.

The difficulty arose in getting to the research site because it was necessary to land at the U.S. airbase in Thule, Greenland. The U.S. Air Force has its own standards of fitness and conduct. There was to be no compromise. I received an official letter at my lab, stating that it was "too dangerous" for me, a quadriplegic, to travel and camp in the extreme cold of the Arctic. It was a nonnegotiable denial of access to the U. S. Air Force Base. My letter-writing campaign, this time, was of no avail. Even retired generals tried to help and failed. I was crushed. Then fate smiled. My despair transformed into astonishment when I received an E-mail from a bed and breakfast accommodation in a remote Eskimo village right in the heart of my required research area. The hoteliers explained that occasionally a Canadian pilot in a twin Otter landed on a gravel patch near their village, bypassing the Thule airbase. I was on the phone immediately, confirming the truth of this unexpected turn of events. We would fly in from Canada, free from military oversight. The trip was successful. I returned some weeks later to Hawaii with volumes of data and stories.

As I write this, I'm thinking of the German philosopher Goethe, who described "the hesitancy concerning all steps of initiation and creation" before truly committing. Goethe recognized a fundamental truth: The moment that one definitely commits, Providence moves. The next year I filed the first lawsuit of my life. It was against the United States Air Force. We settled. In that year I was allowed to land on the base, reside there, and use the facilities leading to an out-camp on the tundra near a glacier-fed lake. Perhaps roadblocks are passages. Does that seem like a contradiction in terms?

To be a field biologist in a wheelchair is to see and hear rejection every day, sometimes clearly voiced but most often masked and implied. "You can't do that." "That's not possible." And of course the great legalistic cry, "We worry about liability—the danger you pose to yourself and others." Perhaps these hundreds of rejections bring me closer to my goals. As a quadriplegic, I have now scuba dived with giant clams in the tropical Pacific, thanks to the National Geographic Society; studied giant catfish in Thailand; coelacanths in Indonesia; sturgeon in China; salmonids in Alaska, Canada, and Norway; mahi mahi in Spain and the Philippines; and local species at home in Hawaii.

It is tough to travel. Nature isn't accessible by any standards of the Americans with Disabilities Act. A favorite phrase of mine, especially when I have just returned from a trip, is "give me two weeks and it will be better then." Things do get better as you distance yourself a bit. Pain and problems dissipate. Accomplishments invigorate.

I flew to Thailand to research giant catfish in the Mekong River, traveling with an attendant, John. As our base of operation we stayed at a medium-star hotel in Bangkok. Medium star or no, the bathroom was inaccessible. My wheelchair would not roll through the door. Consequently, each time I needed a shower or the toilet, I had to be carried, all two hundred pounds of me. On the first day of our adventure, as I was slung over my attendant's shoulder, I heard a loud crack, felt sharp pain, and saw stars. My head had hit the frame of the bathroom door, with the edge of the frame slitting my forehead above my right eye. Warm blood streamed across my eye, down my face, and into my lap. John propped me on the toilet, shoulder against one wall, and taped a wet washcloth to my forehead. I remember thinking that as long as there was no permanent damage, it was worth being cut to be in Thailand.

The next day, bandaged but unbowed, we mounted an elephant to get to the river. A crowd of people worked as one to get me situated and comfortable on the pachyderm. One can learn a big lesson from working in underdeveloped countries. Physical access in this world resides first and foremost in the heart and attitude of people. Physical barriers become inconsequential. In Thailand there were no curb cuts or ramps, yet any time we came to a curb or faced a flight of stairs, people materialized seemingly from nowhere. I had no problems getting around in Thailand—but using the bathroom, yes! I still have a scar above my eye, a badge that reminds me of the giant catfish.

Perhaps more than any other country, Norway has opened my eyes to the concepts of universal design and access. For whatever reasons (perhaps related to socialized medicine), my disability has never seemed to be a limiting factor in Norway. Restaurants never require me to go through the kitchen. Taxis with wheelchair lifts are available in every major city. Hotel bathrooms are accessible. People with a myriad of disabilities move about the streets. Passersby actually smile at me on the sidewalk, making me feel a part of humanity. Who are these Norwegians? We visited a fish laboratory some thirty miles outside of Tromsø, far above the Arctic. It was a long trip down a rough gravel road. I expected to come upon the worst-case scenario at the end of the road. Instead we arrived at a well-kept building that was totally accessible—on the edge of a fjord. Even the stairs leading to the water level of the fjord were made accessible by an open elevator attached to a track. Such accommodations are unheard of in U.S. labs.

I requested to go on a field camp. Rather than receiving a denial of access, I was asked how I could best be assisted. On a typical day the journey would require ninety minutes. This was not a typical day.

Facing headwinds of twenty-five miles an hour whipping eight-to-ten-foot waves, I took five and a half grueling, pounding hours to reach the destination. Although wedged into my wheelchair with every conceivable cushion and towel, I fell to one side and then the other with each pounding surge. I didn't know how long I could endure the ordeal. As I was jostled to my right, I would see the wall clock ticking in some state of suspended animation. As I'd jolt to my left, I would see the great waves through the portholes, often well above my head, crashing over the bridge and surging across the decks above.

Suddenly, through the porthole, just inches from my face, appeared a puffin in summer plumage flying just at my shoulder height. I was struck by its beauty, a magnificent, wild creature so close at hand. It seemed to fly with me forever. I reached outside my body and flew with the puffin. I forgot the pain. Although I was being beaten badly by the waves, the world that I treasured was close enough for me to touch. I knew what I wanted. I could see my future.

Safety was always a consideration, but not an excuse. Ropes dangling from a giant crane were tied to the frame of my wheelchair and, with me in, I was ever so gently raised some fifty feet up a cliff face from a small boat to disembark for the island of Spitzbergen.

My adventures have their share of juxtapositions. In Japan I had the rare opportunity of traveling first-class and with every amenity. I represent an enigma, however, to the Japanese. On the one hand, I am a university professor. Professors are highly esteemed in Japan, far more than here. On the other hand, I am in a wheelchair and "disabled," which suggests to the Japanese that I should really be at home, out of sight, cared for in the arms of my family. This conflict became apparent when I was invited to present a paper at a prestigious international symposium in Tokyo. The conference organizers knew that I was a professor, but they didn't know the rest.

My attendant John and I arrived at the registration center. We were welcomed. Our hosts hid their shock and dismay and went into a huddle, coming up now and again for a quizzical glance. Their spokesman approached and in the warmest of Japanese hospitality directed us to a nearby five-star hotel, with the assurance that it would surely meet our needs with all its amenities.

Everything was first class, everything that is except for the undersized doorway to the toilet and the tub. John, although large and strong, could not possibly carry me into the bathroom. So he dropped me to the floor, removed my clothes, and dragged me naked across the five-star wall-to-wall carpeting. ("Highly esteemed American professor dragged naked into bathroom.")

John propped me up on the toilet, leaning my shoulder against one wall, and gathered his strength. We waited for Mother Nature to do her calling, with ample time to laugh and observe the inviting Japanese bathtub, blue tiled, chrome plated, and sumptuously sunken, not five feet away across the bathroom tiles. "Come to me. Forget your troubles. Soak and relax," the great five-star tub beckoned. "Bath time!"

John drew the warm water. Nature called. And with renewed strength, he transferred me from toilet to tub. I slipped into the warm waters and relaxed. In fact, relaxation is part of the problem with multiple sclerosis. Jell-O is perhaps the food item that best illustrates the transformed state of my body. I can't be grasped. I can't be held. I can't be caught. "I've got to get out of this tub," I told John. "I can't get any more relaxed than this." But try as he would, John couldn't catch me. He drained the water. And there I lay. A great white form, relaxed to exaggeration.

"Call the front desk for help," I whispered. "Tell them to send a couple of five-star bellboys." Sure enough, in moments two uniformed gentlemen were at the door. "Take your hats off, gentlemen, we've got a job to do." It was a bit of a Marx brothers situation. Three men engaged in a catch-and-release activity they had never imagined. Hesitant at first, the bellboys grabbed my arms and legs and anything else that seemed to be a protuberance, shouting in what

I imagined to be the most colorful Japanese. Suddenly, with a great heave-ho, my gelatinous body slithered from the tub, crossed the tiles, passed through the orifice called a door, and lay white and dripping on the five-star sheets of the sumo-sized bed. We thanked the bellboys profusely. They wouldn't take a tip. They left. We laughed.

It costs a great deal to stay in such a hotel in Japan. And although we certainly got our money's worth, I awoke the next morning with no inclination to pay for another night. We bypassed taking a bath. I wasn't even that eager to use the toilet (much to John's relief). We dressed and headed to the symposium, where we explained to our hosts that a change in venue was in order. They were accommodating.

It seems that the Japanese social system provides special inns for the elderly, including persons with disabilities. It is an internal system, not usually open to outsiders or visitors. With just one phone call our hosts made the arrangements. John and I moved into an inn located some miles away from the city center in a suburban zone. It was totally accessible. Even the Japanese bath was accessible by a lift. The inn had no restaurants, just a cafeteria. Again, totally accessible, with marvelous local food. John was a linguistics major who spoke fluent Japanese. He was also six feet three inches tall. So I guess the two of us stood out. Our hosts assigned graduate students to transport us in the mornings and evenings, providing a wonderful opportunity for us to build relationships with people whom we would otherwise never get to know. One evening we even attended a graduate student party, meeting young people with whom I have subsequently worked both in Hawaii and elsewhere.

So what is the lesson in this? Maybe it is that when you are on the margin of life, surprises happen. Unique, unexpected, and wonderful social opportunities emerge. My "disability" forced me to move to other housing and interact with a different echelon of people, helping me to learn the lessons of self-reliance and serendipity. In the meantime, those bellboys got a lesson they'll never forget.

Not long ago I went to China, traveling there with my attendant Zac, who was also a student studying to become a high school teacher. When I arrived in Beijing one startling fact immediately became clear. Nothing was accessible. Forget worrying about a bathtub in Tokyo. We couldn't even get off the plane. It had come to a halt a quarter mile or more from the terminal, greeted by motorized steps parked at the plane. The steps would have been challenging enough, but getting to them was nearly impossible because there was no aisle chair to transfer me from the seat to the stairs. Zac did not have the physical strength to throw me over his shoulders, carry me down the aisle like a gunnysack of corn, and then negotiate the narrow steps to the tarmac.

Ground crews arrived. Many people talking, gesturing, watching, then pulling and tugging and dragging and grunting. Bruised and shaken, I was extracted from the plane. "Deplaning" is a good word for it—forty-five minutes of it, to be exact. It was good to hit that tarmac. We boarded a bus with just one step to scale and made our way to the terminal. Our suitcases were waiting. The best we could find for ground transportation was a tiny cab. We flagged it down. I was squeezed into the front seat, with luggage piled so high on my lap that I couldn't see out. My wheelchair was folded and crammed into the back seat alongside more luggage and Zac. Sometime later we arrived at the hotel.

I learned at the hotel that persons in wheelchairs are perceived as non-persons because they are under someone else's direction. Consequently, it was nearly impossible to get anyone to address me directly. People would look past me to my attendant. (This is not unique to China, by the way, perhaps just more extreme). By the second day in Beijing, I knew that my exploits were going to be enlightening to me and anyone with whom I would come into contact.

All my life I had dreamed of scaling the Great Wall of China. After a two-hour cab ride, again squeezed into the front seat with knees pressed between chest and dashboard, I found the Great Wall with its impending majesty spread before us. My attendant did not speak Chinese, so we had hired a translator at the hotel. Thank goodness. I was extracted from the cab, reinstated in the wheelchair, and pushed to a viewing area to see the great serpentine wall rest across the crests and valleys of miles of Chinese hillsides. "There are many steps to surmount," announced our interpreter. "It will be impossible to get beyond this point."

"Impossible?" I asked. "Getting here was impossible." I had to know for myself. The steps weren't visible from our vantage point, so I asked Zac to check them out. He disappeared for a few minutes and returned shaking his head. "It's impossible," he reported. "There are forty-five steps. There is no way."

What Zac was actually saying was not what I was hearing. What, in fact, I heard from Zac was that we would have to try a different way, something yet uninvented. I realize now that I do that as a matter of habit—reframe obstacles as challenges. So I assessed our surroundings to see what, if anything, could help us achieve the objective. In this case I was looking at hundreds if not thousands of Chinese soldiers. They were everywhere. Young, uniformed, and bored. "Oppressive," I had felt. "Bored soldiers . . . hmmm."

I instructed the translator to please ask the soldiers if they would help to lift me onto the wall. She was reluctant. "Those are soldiers," she said. "They are on duty. It is better not to talk to them."

"They are bored," I said. "Please ask." Shyly she approached one of the uniformed youths who was standing just six or eight feet away. She spoke so quietly that I couldn't hear her voice. He listened; she gestured in my direction; he turned and stared at me, trying to visualize the request. Then with a smile, he turned and walked to a cluster of men some distance away. They huddled, looking at me over their shoulders. I sat smiling, watching. More men than could be counted suddenly surrounded us—a great Red army.

At my insistence Zac showed them the safe points on the wheelchair for lifting and carrying, and then like a flood wave I was swept aloft, sitting in a throne, above the heads of this sea of uniforms. Up we climbed, first in silence. Then with expressions of great joy and laughter. The sky was so blue. I was back in Norway reaching out to touch the puffin. Then down I came, landing perfectly atop the Great Wall of China. Almost on cue, the soldiers backed off to give us breathing room and a view. I was filled with emotion. Great pride in accomplishment. Great appreciation for human kindness. I signaled the soldiers over, buying a Chinese army cap, complete with red star. The soldier perched it on my head, amid great laughter. Then, once again, I was swept to the sky for the descent.

Later that night back in the hotel I lay in bed thinking that although I cannot move, there are many ways I can teach using my body.

I am the director of the Ocean of Potentiality Project at the University of Hawaii, which is codirected by Dr. James Skouge (an able-bodied colleague). Together we orchestrate all kinds of camps and field activities to support young people with disabilities to consider careers in math, science, engineering, and technology. We use my body as one of our teaching tools. At this point in this chapter, that probably isn't sounding too strange.

We take young people to some of the most beautiful and remote areas in Hawaii to conduct field experiments and to build the kinds of relationships that camping and outdoor adventures permit. Many of our group have significant disabilities, including mobility, communication, and emotional challenges as well as deafness and blindness. Many have been overprotected and underchallenged. And most have never met the likes of me.

As camp director, I fully participate in all activities. The campers are encouraged to assist me (as well as themselves and others) in every aspect of the outdoor life. They join me in paddling inflatable canoes, netting fish, hiking in cloud forests (I have an all-terrain wheelchair), pitching tents, cooking over campfires, exploring coral reefs, and so forth. One young blind woman, who most adamantly did not want to go into the stream in an inflatable boat, changed her mind after assisting in the ordeal of transferring and launching me. "I'd better go, too," she said. "He may need help out there."

Our camps are typically four days and three nights, including a very long first day that sometimes includes predawn flights to neighboring islands, complex ground transportation, and most recently, an arduous hike for the able bodied and a helicopter ferry for those of us in wheelchairs. So, by the time we arrive, set up camp, and get dinner prepared, it has been a long day. Due to limitations of my energy levels, I typically do not greet people during this arrival phase. I do not perspire, so as the day gets hotter, so do I. I also speak softly, and it is difficult for me to move my head very much in either direction. Consequently, I stay mostly in the background throughout the hustle and bustle of the first day. People who don't know me may wonder who I am. They have heard the name, but they are befuddled.

Usually after our supper we gather for an initial meeting. A microphone and amplifier are attached to my headsets. The group of thirty or more people are gathered in a circle around me. I introduce myself and welcome them all. I explain that I am paralyzed from the neck down and ask the newcomers to suggest what they think my capabilities might be. Many suggest that I can watch TV and work on a computer. They don't yet know that I am a scientist. Then we show slides, and I share with them in pictures and words some of the great adventures of my life. Thus begins our relationship of the next several days, as they begin to experience the life of a scientist.

I encourage campers to interact physically with others and me. We orchestrate a process by which young people introduce themselves by touching each other's hands, including mine, which lie motionless in my lap. We ask group members to assist in feeding me, pushing me, and adjusting my many pieces of equipment, including my computer headsets. Through touch and proximity, fear diminishes. (Wheelchairs can be very intimidating, they make for distance. We try to think of ways to break through.) At a recent camp, five people assisted in wheeling me into a stream, where they bathed me with buckets of cold water. It was as cold a bath as I've ever endured, something neither the youths nor I will forget. Great laughter and bonding.

I am not the only adult with a disability at our camps. We invite many role models with disabilities to join us. Mr. Makia Malo always attends. He is a big Hawaiian man who is blind and a great storyteller. In the wilderness his cane is not enough. He puts his hand on a youngster's shoulders and makes his way from the tents to the campfires to the boat launch, always talking to the participants, drawing them out, touching them as they lead him along. "Watch your step, Makia, rock ahead."

There seems to be power in helping. Perhaps this is especially true for young people with disabilities who are normally not in the helper position. I remember that the greatest dread of my life when I was initially taken by MS was the realization that for the rest of my life I would have to be helped. If that sounds strange, please slow down and think about it. We are raised to become independent. We are raised to help others. So what happens when those core values become unreachable? Self-esteem plummets. A mosquito lands on your cheek. You hear it buzzing. You feel it crawling. You know it's rubbing its legs in eager anticipation of sucking your blood. Do you ask the stranger beside you to help? At what cost to self-esteem?

We try to share with our kids that it is all okay to be helped. Being helped is a universal part of the human condition. It is also essential, however, that each of us become helpers in return. No one stays out of the loop. No matter how profound the disability we are all responsible to one another and to our natural environment. All of our camp activities include community service, whether it is washing the service dogs or cleaning up a beach. All of our camps also expect random acts of kindness, no matter how small. An ambulatory person gathers water in a bucket. A wheelchair user pumps the water from the bucket, through a filter, and into the drinking containers.

I would like to reflect on the universal issues of fear and prejudice. I learned early on in my "disability" that my life as a "normal" person was over. If I were to survive and thrive in this world as a quadriplegic, it would be under an entirely different set of circumstances. I would have to overcome my shyness. I would have to sacrifice my privacy. I would have to be willing to give my body to strangers. I would have to break through walls of prejudice that are reinforced and rebuilt every day that I live.

So every day I learn new lessons. I share my stories. I try to include humor. I present myself as a whole person. I give lots of talks. Even when it is a scientific presentation, I try to share my family and my love for high adventure. I want people to see me, not the wheelchair, not the paralysis, not my invisibility when they turn away, and not the fear when they sneak a glance thinking I'm not watching.

I realize that I am at a disadvantage at public forums, so I always schedule a talk. I want people to see me directly and hear my voice. I want to become for whatever brief moment the center of their attention. I want people to see and perhaps face their fear.

I show pictures, sometimes funny things. One slide depicts me sitting in my wheelchair underwater on a reef in Samoa. I'm wearing a mask and tank. A speargun is tied to one of my gloves. The picture was entirely staged. We threw a rusting wheelchair off the boat, arranged it just right some thirty feet under water, and then posed me for the photo. It is funny, though; it catches people off guard. I tell them things aren't very accessible on the reef and that perhaps the Americans with Disabilities Act needs to be revisited. People laugh. Then I tell them how much I love water and to be weightless, how I wish I didn't have to have two guides, one on each arm, steering me where they think I might want to go. For a quadriplegic, water is freedom. My dive partners know how much I value it. They pull me to the right, but I want to go left and linger above some giant clam. They see my eyes through the goggles. I communicate. "Stink eye," they call it in Hawaii. We turn to the left.

I show them slides of my wife and daughter. They see me in dogsleds in Alaska or perched in the bucket of a front loader in Antarctica, smiling through my fur-lined hood, a penguin in my arms. They see that I am an adventurer, wholly embracing my passage through this life. I tell them about my service dog, showing them a video of her skills in pushing buttons and retrieving fallen objects. And when I'm finished with my talk, people approach me. They want to acknowledge me. They want to touch my hand or most certainly my service dog—this beautiful golden retriever who more than anything is the icebreaker of my life. No one fears my dog.

THE PUFFIN'S RETURN

Not long ago a life insurance agent knocked at our door. I was sitting in the living room. Judith invited him in, offered him a chair, and slipped away—leaving him to make his sales pitch to me. He talked with great enthusiasm about his company and the protections they guarantee, comparing and contrasting, citing statistics and figures with great enthusiasm. "Would you be interested?" he finally asked.

"Perhaps I would," I respond. "I am quadriplegic, however, from multiple sclerosis. Would that impact at all on my eligibility?"

"You are what?" the young man stammers. Then he looks. He really looks, realizing that I don't move. "I'm sorry, sir," he said. "You will not qualify."

"It's not a problem," I say, "just a challenge." The salesman reaches out a hand, as if expecting a handshake. Thinks better of it and puts his hand in his pocket. Displaying an uncomfortable smile, he says good-bye. The door closes just as Judith appears from the kitchen with a tray of refreshments. "He left already?" she asks. "Yes, but we can still drink the juice."

Judith holds the glass to my lips. I suck through the straw. Through the porthole I see the puffin in spring plumage soaring just beyond the glass.

Assistive Technology

There is a world that I enter every day of my life in which I am free, powerful, capable, and without limits. I am talking about the world of computers and digital technologies. Computers are high on my list of best friends. In my lab I am wired up with as many as three headsets controlling computers, phone, and voice dictation. My service dog curls up at my feet and I become cyber-connected. The phone rings, and I whistle to activate a switch. "Hello, this is Rich Radtke," I say. I am there. I am powerful. Prejudice cannot touch me.

My students scan any and all print materials, including the mail. Video is dumped onto our hard drives. Our slides are digital, even our microscopes. We employ a wireless LAN (Macintosh "airport" technology), so anything we write or view is shared among the workstations. Both at home and at work I spend hours on the Internet—reading newspapers and journals, listening to music, and communicating with colleagues. I publish widely. My techniques for writing and publication are various. Sometimes I dictate my initial draft, recording my voice digitally, using SimpleSound on the Macintosh. I then E-mail this sound file to a secretary who wordprocesses it and E-mails it back. I am then in a position to revise and edit the text version, using an on-screen keyboard, word prediction, a head-controlled mouse, and a sip-and-puff switch in my mouth. On other occasions I dictate my initial drafts using voice—recognition software. Both of these strategies allow me to produce written text without having to touch a keyboard. In fact, there is no keyboard that is visible on my computer. People visiting my office for the first time are puzzled. By moving my head, sipping, puffing, and speaking, I control and access the world. These technologies are extensions of my body. Perhaps a few more details are in order.

I value my privacy and I have to struggle to maintain it. My extreme physical disabilities leave me vulnerable to losing it. The telephone provides a good example. I want the freedom to dial and speak with whomever I choose. I do not want to ask others to dial for me, nor do I want them answering my phone and transferring my calls. For these reasons I want to dial and answer my own phone, and I most certainly do not want to use a speakerphone. So I dial through my modem using a phone directory on my computer. If the number is unlisted, I dial for operator assistance. I maintain two modems on my computer: one for the phone and the other to download data. This way I can talk and work. I push technology to its limits and I challenge you to do the same. I use the same headset and microphone that switchboard operators use. I answer and hang up my phone with a whistle. I have now given up recreational whistling. Once when my son (an avid whistler) was enjoying computer games with me, he whistled in response to a deft play and set off my phone.

When I am wired to my computer, I am transformed. I have relied on the HeadMaster by Prentke Romich and a Screendoors program, which is a screen-typing program by Madenta Communications. The HeadMaster is an infrared device that has three emitters situated on my head with a receiver on the top of a computer. The receiver is plugged into the mouse port. The three emitters that sit on my head allow me to move the cursor on the screen by moving my head. By using a connected sip-and-puff switch I make selections. I am partial to Macintosh computers, but I have used the HeadMaster with PC machines using Windows and WIVIK. The ScreenDoors program is an on-screen typer and word-prediction program that allows me to type efficiently. Under the best circumstances, with a computer with lightning speed such as a Macintosh at the level of a G4, I can type twenty words per minute. Not bad for a neck guy. I don't worry about spelling errors. Thank goodness for spellcheckers. I often sit for seven to eight hours in front of my computer. I have no problems staring into screens, but after looking at a screen all day, I typically choose not to watch television at home. My work is silent without key clicks. Often I forget that I cannot move.

My voice is soft. And because I do not have a great range of motion in my neck, it is often difficult for me to get others' attention. In extreme cases, such as when my lab assistants are wearing their Walkmen, I activate an alarm, purchased through Radio Shack, attached to an X-10 module, which activates the computer.

As anyone with multiple sclerosis will attest, we are often overwhelmingly fatigued at the end of a day. When I am giving a lecture or presenting a seminar, it is not always easy to take a nap or a break at the right time. When lecturing, I project my computer graphics and videos while speaking through a portable speaker system called SpeechMaker (Forward Motion). I have used it in lectures around the world. Even though my voice is just a whisper it is magnified enough for all to hear.

I illustrate my lectures with multimedia, using PowerPoint slideshows (Microsoft Corporation) with my own photos that we store on Kodak CD ROMs as well as Quicktime movies that we produce from our edited videos. I rearrange my "slides" for different classes, accomplishing everything with my HeadMaster (have lectures, will travel).

When I am away from my laboratory and in need of large data sets, I download my data onto portable hard drives or CD ROMs. In this way I am virtually unlimited in the amount of information I can take with me on my journeys. This arrangement lets my cursor do the walking. Because I am not able to turn pages manually, we digitize all text, using an AppleScanner with OmniPage Pro as an optical character reader. Usually I open numerous manuscripts simultaneously and use the search features of Microsoft Word to locate, sort, cut, and paste my articles and lecture notes.

Microscope work and image analyses pose vexing problems for a person without arm or leg movement. I am not able to easily view microscope preparations. As part of a solution, we view our samples using a high-definition video camera attached to the microscope's eyepiece, displaying them on a high-resolution television screen. These images are then digitized and stored. Pictorial images consume a large amount of disk space, but it is still possible to place almost fifty images on a CD, and DVDs greatly expand this capacity. This arrangement allows me to manipulate and manage the large amount of data necessary for the research I conduct.

This year we have created a "field-based" computer lab for teaching. Using the wireless "airport" technology, we are networking ten Macintosh iBooks, utilizing screen-to-screen software that allows me to view and interact with all the computers on the network. We work with young people with and without disabilities in our Ocean of Potentiality Project in Hawaii and our Dreamcatchers program in Alaska. Under field conditions, a dozen or more of us can learn from one another. This represents a tremendous teaching advantage in that once I am hooked up to the computer I can interact with my students without having to physically move my body to each of their computer desktops. We look forward soon to having wireless connectivity to the Internet from our field stations.

Service Dogs and Attendant Care

My beautiful golden retriever stays with me twenty-four hours a day, often finding her place underneath my desk next to my feet. We have designed my computer workstation so that she can restart the computer should it crash or freeze, which has come in handy on a few occasions when I've been working alone. She also turns on and off lights, hits elevator buttons, and turns on the television. Perhaps most important, however, is her companionship and presence. People approach me now in ways that they did not before I acquired the dog. People will talk to her and reach out to pet her. They will ask me about her, and soon we are engaged in conversations. These are the same people who are fearful of establishing eye contact with me under less-inviting circumstances. Many owners of service dogs have reported similar phenomena.

I am a research professor. Most of my teaching occurs informally with my graduate and undergraduate students in the lab. Running a full-time research laboratory requires a bevy of undergraduate students. I try to surround myself with young people who are passionately interested in science while open to learning about the culture of disability and being responsive to my physical needs. Over the years I have recruited numerous students to act as my personal-care attendant. For the most part this has worked out well. The student attends classes during the day when I need the least assistance, does his homework in the lab, and then lives in our home with my family. Usually my attendants are young men, physically strong, with a passion for learning marine biology. I value the contact and interaction that I have with young people. They keep my spirit young. I know everything from "Macking" to the latest rock groups. We laugh together. In recent years I have been successful in obtaining facilitation awards from the National Science Foundation to cover attendant costs on field trips, but this has come with its baggage of paperwork. Many of the costs associated with attendant care I pay for out of pocket. Many people believe out of ignorance that my medical costs are covered by social programs. But I fall outside of the social "net." What I get I pay for. "Publish or perish," you might say.

It would not be fair to end this chapter without confronting the honest truth that prejudice against persons with disabilities abounds in our world. I struggle daily to succeed. I live a life that is on a tightrope, swaying, with no safety nets and no end in sight. I work with people who are field scientists, working under difficult conditions and proud of it. For many, "macho" is an accurate word of description. I do not, of course, fit their image of a professional in our field. Recently in my presence a colleague challenged my right to work. "He can't go in the field. It is much too dangerous for a person in his condition. Only the fittest can accomplish this type of research." He said it within my earshot, as though I were deaf. My blood boils. On a typical day at the university, colleagues scurry past my open laboratory door without so much as a greeting. To greet me, of course, they might have to enter my lab, approach me, and perhaps even touch my hand. These same people complain that I am unfriendly and aloof because I do not attend their TGIF functions, never appreciating how inappropriate such functions are for me. They are held outdoors with noisy conviviality. I would overheat. My voice would be lost in the conversation.

Some colleagues have gone so far as to suggest that I be assigned a smaller lab and office space, suggesting that my mobility impairment reduces my need for physical space. How small and mean! Others complain that my accommodations are too expensive and perhaps even unfair. Why should I merit assistive technologies? Why should department funds be utilized to make the bathroom accessible? Often I am a lone voice, arguing for my professional needs. It is not a comfortable position to be in. I become branded a troublemaker and complainer.

The issues surrounding accommodations are particularly galling. Some faculty have complained that I am receiving special privileges when I ask for materials in electronic format. This sets me up to lose. If I am granted an accommodation, my work is held in suspicion, as though I were granted special favors.

How I am treated varies. If I go into a restaurant the waiter or waitress invariably asks the person with me what I will have for dinner. I have instructed my attendant or those who travel me that if such questions arise they are to refer the questions to me. In more than one instance as I was waiting to be put on a plane, I have heard flight attendants talking about me in plain sight as if I don't exist. In most cases I quickly try to bring about the idea of my existence.

Body language can mean a lot, especially when I am not able to move that much. Those who know me can tell you that I say much with the tone of my voice and the use of my eyes. Those with whom I have scuba dived will tell you that I swear by my eyes. I think it is just the look, as we would say in Hawaii, the "stink eye." I change the inflection of my voice when I'm impatient or tired, or I host other types of personalities without changing the words that I use.

My body teaches so much.

**The Day the Foreign Devil
Came to Class:
My Teaching Body in China**

Pam Whitfield

The first day I walked into my American Literature classroom, students chatting in the hall opened a wide swath for me. My own students already stood rigidly at attention behind their flimsy wooden desks; as I placed my bag on an equally flimsy wooden podium, they spontaneously applauded me. Then the class sat down en masse, their open, expectant faces like vessels waiting to be filled. Nervous and sweating from the hike up six flights of stairs in a subtropical August, I removed a paper-and-bamboo fan (courtesy of China Airlines) from my bag, spread its blades with both hands, and began to fan myself vigorously. The room erupted again, this time into uncontrollable laughter. Thinking that they found an Asian implement humorous in the hands of an Anglo, I simply smiled and said, "Let's begin class." Two years later I visited a female graduate at a vocational college where she taught English. Ai Chun watched me adroitly open another paper fan, this time single-handedly, and swish it slowly and femininely under my chin. "I'm glad that you have learned how to use a Chinese fan," she teased.

I taught English education majors at Zhangzhou Teachers College for four adventurous years; I became proficient in Chinese, adopted the social norms and mannerisms, and eventually married a local man. But when I first arrived in southern China, my head swelled with pedagogy and enthusiasm, it never occurred to me that my body would have to assimilate, too. Everyone from the department dean to the freshmen insisted on calling me "Miss Pam." I told them they were being *tai keqi,* too polite. Only four years later, back in the United States, did I realize that they were also trying to feminize me.

My residence permit described my vocation as *zhuan jia,* "foreign expert." The first day I met with my superiors in the English department, they handed me a stack of textbooks and a class schedule. When I asked about syllabi, they shrugged. "Oh, you're the native speaker. You know what is best to teach and what the students should learn. Anything you do will be good, we are sure." So I was already in, perhaps in deeper than I realized. The challenge was to seize the opportunity—and the autonomy the school authorities surprisingly granted me. I knew a thing or two about Chinese education from studying in Beijing; I understood its teacher-centered approach, the students' passivity, the emphasis on rote memorization, and the use of writing models. And I saw these qualities not as operating in a vacuum but as connected to traditional cultural values. But I still had my goal: to teach my students to think critically, speak out, and become actively involved in making meaning. Oh, I had noble ideals. But my body kept getting in the way.

I could be picked out in a crowd by the color of my hair or the way I moved. Local folk pointed, giggled, and formed staring squads. They followed me through the market as I shopped, commenting on my clothes, brushing the hair on my forearms with curious fingertips, listening to my bookish Chinese. The woman I bought noodles from offered to take my cut-off shorts home and hem them. "The American teacher shouldn't wear rags," I heard her whisper to her daughter.

I liked being called teacher. More often I was a foreigner, a *lao wai,* a white devil, or a western friend, depending on who was doing the labeling. I was a white capitalist imperialist from the country that ordinary Chinese discuss the most. I was the only non-Asian woman in this oversized crossroads town. And I was not feminine. I wore plaid lumberjack shirts, I laughed loudly, I walked twice as fast as everyone else and climbed stairs two at a time when I was late for class, which was often. I rode my bike too fast, darting in and out of traffic, elbows and knees jutting out. I preferred pants, didn't cross my legs when I sat, and my pale blue eyes were spooky up close. In retrospect,

I can't imagine what my students and colleagues found we had in common. Maybe a taste for difference.

After only a few days of teaching, I realized that my classes were swelling with new faces, which was unprecedented, since I taught literature to the entire junior class of my department and writing to the sophomore class in two sections. Students from other departments had heard about me, evidently. At the time I surmised that they wanted to hear standard English spoken; in retrospect, they probably sneaked in to enjoy the spectacle. In this college the typical professor stood squarely behind the podium, read from the text of a prepared lecture, used the blackboard for making illustrations or clarifications, and seldom addressed questions to the students. Younger teachers had begun to use some direct eye contact and discussion, but the latter was formal and stilted. I moved around on the narrow dais and occasionally fell off it. I waved my textbook for emphasis, made facial expressions to facilitate students' comprehension (so I hoped), and stored pens behind my ears to their infinite amusement. I looked my students hard in the eye, willing them to analyze as they absorbed. I got them to talk back to me and soon to talk back to each other. Once I playfully threw a piece of chalk at the senior class smart aleck who sat in the front row, shocking everyone, including myself. I filled my blackboard with scrawled notes after only fifteen minutes of class; I pointed and gesticulated and walked up and down the narrow aisles between desks, banging my big American hips on the sharp corners. My body constantly belied my sex; I made big, jerky moves, I read with flourishes, spoken and otherwise, and it took me a year to learn to use my fan correctly.

Although I felt compelled to demonstrate what Chinese colleagues termed "an active teaching style" and to make learning more student-centered through dialogue, journals, collaboration, and debate, I also desperately wanted to fit in. I admired the homogenous Chinese, their compact, fit bodies and the graceful way they had of spooning soup or turning a page. They never seemed to hurry, yet got everything done. They rode their bikes slowly, spoke evenly, used their eyes modestly, and turned hospitality into a fine art. Women wrapped arms around other women's waists as they strolled the side alleys after dinner, and grown men walked hand in hand. Everyone was comfortable in her body but me. And everyone got touched, from the toddler cradled by his grandfather's hands to the elderly neighbor whose niece brushed her hair each morning.

After a month of teaching in Zhangzhou, I accepted an invitation to visit six rambunctious, giggling junior women in their dorm room. After the customary round of tea and fruit, I heard one girl urging another in Chinese, "go ahead, ask her . . . can you touch . . ." I realized that they wanted to touch my hair. "Of course, please," I answered in English, and six sets of fingers reached out to stroke and comb my brown locks, reddened by the subtropical sun. Suddenly, we began to laugh—and share on a physical level.

The Chinese don't worry about personal space; they sit thigh to thigh in crowded trains and at dinner tables, and they lean across each other's laps during conversation. In the students' dorm that night, I realized how my body had yet to acculturate and how much I missed being touched. I'd been in Zhangzhou for one month, and no one had hugged me. No one had even touched my arm, except in crowded streets, to warn me of a trash heap or an upcoming bike. When I stood to leave, the women pushed Li Qun, their bravest roommate, forward and into my path. She shyly asked, "Can I embrace you?" I grinned and suddenly was surrounded by six short, warm bodies, all clinging to my waist. I felt like I was melting or blooming—maybe both.

When I recall my teaching stint in China, what I remember is how hard I tried to give my students some power and how they deferentially kept trying to give it back to me. Even when they grew comfortable with my westernized pedagogy, they worried that by removing myself from the ideological center of the classroom, I might lose face or feel less integral to the process of learning. My ultimate purpose was to make myself obsolete, but they kept repositioning me on that foreign expert pedestal. I learned to see myself as a white bird, flying between the grimness of their everyday lives and the Disney World of an Americanized classroom. So I looked for things a white face and an assertive body could fix. When the college president invited me to his office for a PR visit, I sat through three cups of tea and the requisite chitchat, being careful to keep my legs crossed and not show my teeth when I smiled. When he signaled the end of the interview with an offhand "if there's anything I can do for you," I told him that my female students had to carry buckets of water for bathing and clothes washing up three flights of stairs in the dormitory because the pump hadn't worked properly for a year. I offered to let the women use my washing machine and shower, startling the smile right off his face. Two days later a female student stopped me on the sidewalk to inform me that her dorm floor now had running water. Smiling slyly, she said, "We know it was you."

The longer I remained in China, the easier it became to forget my ethnicity. The local folk became accustomed to me sitting in noodle stalls, buying detergent, or bargaining for tomatoes. The staring lessened, the faces grew familiar, and Zhangzhou began to feel like my town. I became so used to being the only Anglo that I often suffered from the illusion of fitting in. Chinese mirrors are often undersized and grimy, so I could go for days without acknowledging that I was fatter, taller, paler, bigger-nosed, or simply less graceful than those around me. Then I would glance at a plate-glass window as I pedaled by it or visit a major city and see other foreigners and be rudely reminded that I, too, stood out like a sore thumb. I stayed in China so long that I began to stare at other Anglos, perhaps out of a subconscious desire to make them aware of their embodied difference, too. I seldom befriended foreign tourists; they reminded me too much of myself. I had gotten good at negotiating China in spite of my whiteness, and it became painful for me to watch other westerners stumble through this crazy, welcoming, abhorrent land.

I came to China thinking I could create change, but China was subtly transforming me. I found a tailor to make me a half dozen long skirts because I found that they were cooler and easier to bike in. I imitated the modest Chinese women by mounting my bike from the left-side pedal—it reminded me of riding my horse back home. I bought shirts with flowery patterns and thin strappy sandals. I assimilated into the Chinese diet and began to shed pounds as if my body wanted to fit into those tiny bus and train seats. I learned to drink tea daintily, allow my hosts to speak first, and refuse gifts three times before accepting them. I let a student give me dancing lessons because the campus ballroom provided the only weekend entertainment besides card playing in the dorms. Twirling around the concrete floor in a waltz, with multicolored Christmas tree lights twinkling on the walls, I imagined I was homogenous, compact, gentle.

Strangely, I began to reserve my ethnic identity and assertiveness for my classroom. Meanwhile, the Chinese language became an outlet for my aggressions. As my spoken skills improved, I spoke more, enjoying the boisterous, harsh tones and the higher volume of Mandarin. I felt I was being rowdy, but others heard normal language use. "You're more Chinese than the Chinese," Shao Min, my best friend, told me. She meant it as a compliment.

The threshold of my classroom became a border I crossed every day. When I entered the room, smiling to see the students scramble for a bench, my mind clicked into English, and my body did, too. The students needed my white face and so-called authentic English to inspire them. They had indentured themselves to the public school system so the central government would pay for their college education. Most of them knew they were going back to their villages and mountain towns to teach English grammar and pronunciation to middle-school children who planned to be farmers like their parents, but my students all harbored dreams of international travel, a translation job, or even graduate school.

My classroom energy became a promise—English was exciting, English made things happen. At Thanksgiving I stripped off my L.L. Bean jacket and tied up the sleeves so I could demonstrate how to stuff a turkey. I stood by the window and recited Ezra Pound from memory, pantomimed an American family at dinner, or marched military-style across the wooden dais to explain poetic meter. I got their bodies involved, too—in skits and role playing. I'd hand one student a placard reading "mean shop owner" and another a shoe with a broken heel, telling her she had just worn it out of the store and now wanted her money back. Our spoken English classes got so loud, so dialogue-dominated, that the department assigned me to the soundproof listening lab, citing a (fictitious) classroom shortage. We shut the door, pushed the desks against the walls, and held mock cocktail parties where everyone practiced conversational English with a pretend drink in hand, and I circulated through the knots of guests, playing hostess and making introductions.

But when the bell rang and my students filed out, I walked down the stairs behind them, listening to their banter and thinking in Chinese. I had to go buy a fish, put air in my bicycle tires, and visit a colleague who'd just had surgery. Returning from the hospital, I paused to buy a half dozen sticky rice balls for my husband. The peasant woman who bagged them barely looked up at me when I asked the price, *duo shao qian*. She only saw my cotton skirt and sandals and heard locally accented Chinese. But a stooped-over woman standing behind her tottered over and asked me, *Ni shi bu shi bendi ren?* "Are you one of us?" Dropping the pastry into my bike basket, I replied, "Only half, but I'm working on it," cracking her up along with another gold-toothed granny who'd stopped for an earful. She was probably losing her eyesight, but as I gathered my skirt and daintily mounted my bike, I said "thank you" just the same.

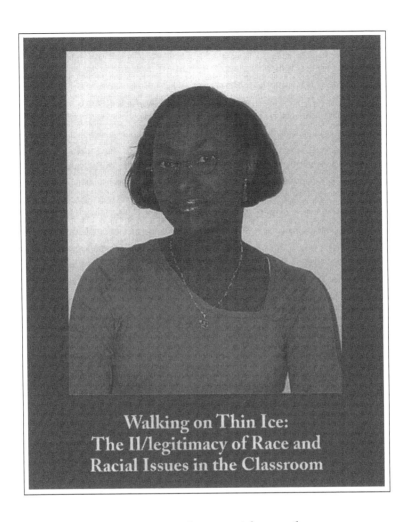

Walking on Thin Ice:
The Il/legitimacy of Race and
Racial Issues in the Classroom

Simone A. James Alexander

"Why are there so many women's texts on this syllabus?" questioned "Tom," a student of my "Third World Novel" course. This was my first attempt at addressing the contradiction that Margaret Andersen addresses. She writes, "At the same time that educators say this is a multicultural world, they teach a deep sense of otherness and ask students to think as if we were all alike. Thus, while we acknowledge that there are different groups in society and different cultures in the world, at the same time, we deny it by maintaining a reference point on human culture and society that is centered on the experiences of a few" (6). In my teaching I therefore aim to de-center the center, an "all-white, womanless curriculum." I informed Tom that I was attempting to promote curriculum continuum and to connect unconnected spaces by illustrating connections among my students, their learning, society, and me. My goal is to heighten awareness of and tolerance for difference and to promote inclusion rather than exclusion. Tom's questioning of my rationale for choosing more texts by women than by men resulted from his literary training and background. He had been trained to read and accept (white) men's texts unconditionally; to witness this "drastic transformation" of the curriculum was unusual and unexpected. I had inundated the curriculum with works not only by women but also by women of color, third-world, immigrant women, who are branded by otherness and deemed peripheral by mainstream discourses.

Alternatively, my privileging texts by women of color could have been too personal for Tom; he viewed this act as my pushing my own agenda. I am a black, Caribbean-born, and female professor who teaches predominantly white, middle-class American students. By choosing texts that speak to and about myself, I made Tom feel as though the woman of color was forced on him in both body and text. Arguably, Tom foregrounded my gender, my body, and color and was reacting to what he felt was overkill, that is, a black woman teacher talking about black women. Tom's questions and others like them provide an entrée to this discussion.

The Third World Novels course is one of three rotating electives I teach. It meets once a week for two hours. In addition to the electives, I teach two sections of Freshman English, which are required of all faculty. Each section meets twice a week for one hour and fifteen minutes and consists of sixteen students, all freshmen. One section of the course had one black female student; the rest of the students were white. The elective was a little more diverse. In a class of thirteen students, three were Asians (all male), four African Americans (three females, one male), and six Caucasians (four females, two males). In another elective, Survey of African American Cultures, there were five African American students (three females, two males), eleven Asian students (all female), and four Caucasian students (two males, two females).

By probing the effectiveness or noneffectiveness of debating race and racial issues in the classroom, in this chapter I examine how race, gender, and class to some extent determine classroom dynamics. I address the expectations and responsibility that both students and the institution expect the teacher to shoulder and how these expectations change when the teacher is of color. I argue that though the classroom is seen as a liberatory forum where issues of race are openly addressed, it also functions as a repressed space. Though the head of her class, the teacher, ironically, not only suffers from bodily restriction in the enclosed classroom but also tailors her discourse to suit the needs of her students and the institution. Similarly discomfited are the students, as they, too, are repressed by classroom restrictions and governed by race- and gender-restricted discourses. Although the teacher's racial identity can affect her students' responses to race and racial discussions, it also affects her authoritative presence in the classroom. The subject of classroom debates can become the object of her students' gaze. This gaze takes on mythic proportions when the teacher is othered, an exotic, alien being. Apart from being a black, Caribbean-born (Guyanese), middle-class woman, I have traveled extensively and lived on four continents. Although I have not recently lived in the Caribbean I have maintained a distinct Caribbean accent.[1] But my discernible difference is not simply a matter of skin color and linguistic difference. I also speak and have taught the Russian language.[2] I am not merely a black Caribbean-born professor but a black Caribbean-born professor who speaks Russian fluently.

To my students and some colleagues, my privileged status as a multilingual professor is itself an anomaly, one that was underscored in a recent job interview when the chair of the English department and the hiring committee questioned what I intended to do with my unusual background and qualifications. I countered that I viewed my unusualness as an asset and my backgrounds not limiting but complementary. I should add that he had quickly corrected himself, replacing the word "unusual" with "exceptional." Although I was told that my educational background would be an asset to the department and the institution, I did not get the job.[3] Although the chair did not voice this openly, I can safely assume that the unusualness in my qualifications lies not in the fact that I speak Russian but that I am a black woman who speaks Russian. I can't but think the university was not yet prepared to deal with such an oddity.

The teacher of color occupies an ambiguous position, powerful and powerless, both subject and object. As an agent of knowledge, she also becomes the object of her students' gaze and occasionally their derision. Not only is the teacher's discourse tailored to meet the needs of both her students and the academic institution to which she has obligatory ties, but her body is constrained as well. I feel as if I am walking on thin ice. Yet there are still many uncharted and unbroken silences on race that, despite dangers, should be brought to classroom discussions. As a generous contributor to the unspoken silences in the classroom (I, too, have added to the silence by remaining silent), I try here to confront (albeit in writing) the source/force of my discomfort. Thus, I reclaim myself, my body. In this self-legitimizing process, I would like actively to engage colleagues and especially my students and offer possible solutions that we all can use in classroom discussions as means of countering racism.

ENGLISH 101

I received my initiation in identity and body politics in my second year in a tenure-track position at a private liberal arts college in New York, where I taught English 101 to incoming freshmen. Despite its location in a largely

multicultural community, the college was and is a predominantly white institution. After coming to grips with my students' initial expressions of shock
and surprise upon realizing that I am othered, triply so, black, female, and
Caribbean, I began to feel a sense of belonging in the classroom, which pur-
portedly provided me with the acceptance and acknowledgement that I
sought at the institutional level. This sense of home, however, was short-lived,
shattered by "Ryan." In response to an assignment on cultural differences,
Ryan blatantly exhibited his intolerance to my race. The assignment, based on
Doris Lessing's short story "The Mother of the Child in Question," asked students to illuminate and comment on societal and individual prejudices and
cultural differences. In this story an immigrant mother is repeatedly questioned and coerced by the district's social workers to send her youngest child
to a school for the "mentally disabled." The mother remains steadfast, refusing to surrender her child to the local authorities and insisting that her daughter attend the same school her four siblings attended. I posed questions: Why
was the story titled as it was when the overriding issue appeared to be the
child's condition and devising ways and means to help her? Was the title an
allusion (insinuation) that the mother's decision not to send her child to this
mandated school was itself questionable? Ryan responded that the mother did
"a wrong thing and her decision, not to comply with the authorities, was fool-
ish because as an immigrant she would not have been entitled to such 'luxu-
ries' [as a special school] in her homeland." He also observed that the mother
didn't speak and/or understand English well and was ignorant of American
culture. After questioning further the mother's decision not to send her child
to a school for the "intellectually challenged," Ryan concluded, oddly, that
"Whites are afraid to take blood from Blacks because they suffer from sickle
cell anemia." Ryan's (written) outburst was not only an attack on my race but
also an attack on my body as he read it. African American scholar Carla Peterson correctly points out that the "body is never simply matter, for it is never
divorced from perception and interpretation . . . and it is subject to examination and speculation" (ix). Indeed it is true that the (black) body "is subject to
examination and speculation." At the same time, however, it is also perceived
(at least in Ryan's view) as "simply matter," sometimes, as here, "diseased" matter. My body is always already a "highly contested site of meaning" (xv), evidenced by Ryan's mis/reading of it. He attempted to make the black body
invisible and/or ridden with dis-ease. My "diseased" body equates with having
no body at all. Thus, the body becomes, to echo Peterson, both "invisible and
hypervisible" (xi). In spite of my attempts to keep it out of sight and "out of
speech," in part by my dressing it professionally in suits, it was exposed to the
white male gaze and derided. Vanessa Dickerson argues, "all too often when
the black female body is looked upon or made the object of the gaze, the body
is still perceived as unworthy, if not worthless" (197). Ryan unveiled and
announced the worthlessness of the body. Moreover, viewed as a collective

(black) representative, I was held accountable for the dis-ease that plagues the entire black race.

Ryan's attack on my racial identity on one level effaced my gender as well as desexualized my body. Because my body was seen as collective, my gender was also erased. In Ryan's eyes, the black body is homogeneous, yet in another way my body is gendered, visibly female. However, although I was quite aware that Ryan's comment was racially motivated, prejudiced, inappropriate, insulting, and ignorant, unquestionably provoked by my race, I remained silent. My silence temporarily stifled my own dis-ease with his unsolicited response. Later I quietly "voiced" my dis-ease by humbly writing at the bottom of his paper: "What is the relevance of this statement? And how does it enhance your essay?"

Obviously, by making my body the object of the gaze, Ryan overlooked my intellectual abilities and reduced me to racialized, sexualized body. Henceforth, Ryan viewed my teaching, an activity usually deemed intellectual, as an act of impersonation, an out-of-body experience. My apparent physical defect, in his eyes, is closely linked to an intellectual defect. Ryan's prejudice was reinforced by the stereotypes that have circulated about black bodies. Tragically, these stereotypes are still in circulation. This was confirmed by a former professor, who, upon hearing that I had landed a tenure-track job just out of graduate school, commented that this was "affirmative action at its best." My qualifications and the fact that I had completed a master's and a Ph.D. with no financial support from my department were totally overlooked and thereafter dismissed. Instead, my professor preferred the myth that black women (African Americans) are the primary beneficiaries of affirmative action. His comments speak directly to Carla Peterson's sardonic observation that "African Americans need affirmative action because, as pure bodies, they are incapable of intellectual thought and cannot compete fairly as workers in the marketplace" (xvi). My intellectual abilities were discredited and affirmative action indicted, with my hiring seen as simply a matter of race and, ironically, privilege. My professor's uninformed critique and false presumptions of minority hiring engaged what Carrie Tirado Bramen calls "inferential racism" (118).

In the instance just mentioned, my racial identity was attacked; in other instances, my ethnicity is subjected to ridicule. One such incident occurred in a class in which I introduced various novels by Caribbean authors. As I entered the classroom one morning, one of my male students, "Robert," started to chant "Kinky Reggae," the song made popular by Jamaican-born Bob Marley. Taking a break from his melodious pastime, Robert asked whether I was a Rastafarian and practiced "Rastafarianism." I learned later that he wanted to know whether I was familiar with reefer. Though the Rastafarians (in the Caribbean) are noted for their dreadlocks (along with their symbiotic relationship with nature, among other things), Robert thought he noticed a striking resemblance between us. At that time, I wore, and still do, my hair straight. Had Robert taken the time to look at me he would have noticed that I did not fit the physical stereotype he intended with the word "Rastafarian." But by focusing on my ethnicity, he negated my body, which functioned conveniently as a site for manipulation. His queries were rebutted with silence.

FROM BODY POLITICS TO CLASSROOM POLITICS

In my ongoing effort to separate the body from brains/intellect, I attempt to keep the body out of sight and out of classroom debates by employing a strategy of "decorporealization." Peterson claims that "one sentimental strategy" that black women employed "in coming to voice . . . was that of decorporealizing the eccentric black body, rendering it invisible and privileging the soul or mind instead" (xii). My attempt to decorporealize the black female body means not that I subscribe to the popular mainstream discourse that views the black body as unseen/obscene but that I wish to lessen the presumption of incompetence that plagues it. I hope to give agency to the teacher's intellect by deflecting the gaze from her body. Though race is pivotal in determining this presumed incompetence, Pamela J. Smith argues that often gender damning takes precedence over race as she wisely determines that "even being of the 'right' race does not diminish . . . this presumption of incompetence" visibly linked with women (31). I embodied this linkage.

The dynamics of the elective I taught last spring, "Survey of African American Cultures," were noticeably different from others. First, the class mainly consisted of students of color. Second, the African American students dominated the classroom discussions, and third, the Asian students were mostly silent. In this classroom of color, I consciously worked to undermine my own authority to be noticeably impartial, allowing students to express themselves freely as they saw fit. The black students took full advantage of this transferral of power by "stepping up to the podium" and openly speaking about racial encounters, paralleling the injustices that various characters in specific texts experienced with those they themselves had experienced. Some of the issues raised included police brutality in the black community, racial profiling, and the presumption of guilt based on race. James Baldwin's "If Beale Street Could Talk" provided a perfect stimulus for discussion. Arguably, my presence boosted the black students' assertiveness, for here stood one of their own. In this instance the classroom provided a forum, an outlet for students who otherwise may not have had or seized an opportunity to speak and be heard. During these discussions the white students were also noticeably silent. I wondered whether they didn't understand the texts or were dissatisfied with the discussions.[4] The situation was soon elucidated by one of the two white female students. "Amanda" E-mailed me to detail her dissatisfaction with the class, her discomfort in openly discussing the issues at hand, and her fear of being disregarded by the others. She added that another reason for her not participating much was that she did not find the class challenging and structured enough. This structural imbalance, she said, was a result of my allowing personal experiences in "nonpersonal" discussions. Amanda suggested I employ the Socratic method for our discussions because, in her experience, this method had been most effective for establishing the needed structure and authority.[5] Undoubtedly Amanda is one of those students, who, in Sheila Minn Hwang's words, "assume[s] that authority comes in specific packages and that a particular kind of authority is necessary for effective teaching" (159). I employ Pamela Smith's proposal for a possible solution—I "swallow the rage that results from experiencing discrimination." Smith writes: "[S]ince black women are presumed to be unintelligent and not sufficiently credentialed," we should "write scholarship about race and gender that is both experiential and analytical" to assess the effects of discrimination and racial prejudice (32). Thus, I combine analysis and lived, bodily experiences—despite Amanda's objection—in the classroom—and here.

Amanda's fear of speaking candidly about race and racial issues may have been justifiable. She was ill at ease in a "colored" classroom, on the one hand, and on the other, her privileged life sheltered her from the injustices and discrimination that inner-city students face daily and that appeared in our texts.[6] Cheryl Johnson writes, "one manifestation of students' dis-ease with the black female professor is their hesitancy, sometimes downright fear, of engaging in dialogue with her about African American literature and culture" (132). Amanda's refusal ultimately served to undermine my power and authority in the classroom, an authority, which in Indira Karamcheti's words, "has already been problematized by the fact of visible difference" (138). Amanda viewed the undermining of my authority as self-inflicted and irresponsible, an indication of incompetence. Her disapproval of the intermeshing of the personal (autobiographical) with the fictional/analytical is key because it suppresses the "relation [between] pedagogy and 'the personal.'" The suppression of this relation is viewed by Roger Simon as "the result of a strategic embrace of notions of objectivity borrowed from traditional disciplinary studies and seen as necessary for achieving academic legitimacy" (91–92). By suggesting that I adopt a Socratic approach in my teaching, Amanda both embraced and posited traditional canonical discourses as the standard for all other discourses. Traditional discourses unconditionally embrace objectivity, which results in depersonalization. To Amanda, not only did the content of my African American course fall short of achieving academic legitimacy, but I did, too.

Amanda was totally against the conflation of the teaching body and my self. In her view the two should be distinct. But how does one study/teach African American literature/culture separate from the black self, the black body? Amanda's request to treat as distinct and separate the black body and the black discourse on slavery, for instance, was in my mind an impracticable demand, especially given the needs and desires of my other students to relate their lived, bodily experiences with the textual ones about which we read and wrote. Black literature has been one of recovery, recovering what was lost or deliberately excluded and rendered insignificant by mainstream (popular) discourse. The emerging literature, which focuses on self-representation, attempts to recover not only the self but specifically the black body. Saturating contemporary works, this self-recovery process is evident and unavoidable. It is almost impossible to remain disembodied in the process of teaching works by African American authors about African American peoples. As a woman of color I find that these textual issues of race, racial prejudices, and body politics speak to me directly. My teaching is inevitably a "situated, embodied act," to reemphasize Simon. Simon concludes: "'to teach as a Jew' [his] Jewish body will have to be seen more clearly, more concretely," meaning, "refusing to leave [his] difference at the door" (100). Like Simon, I refuse to leave my difference at the door. I therefore personalize the readings as an act of legitimizing them. As a further counter to alienation, I incorporate and integrate issues on diversity and alterity not only in my electives but also in both sections of my English 101 class. I visibly assert myself as black and female through text choices. One such text is Ralph Ellison's *Invisible Man,* though it may seem ironic that I would choose to teach a book that chronicles a man's invisibility to assert my presence and my visibility. Unlike the invisible man who claims that when people "approach [him] they see only [his] surroundings, themselves, or a figment of their imagination—indeed, everything and anything except me" (3), I feel my visibility/invisibility is accentuated by my race and my gender, which are critical to my teaching (body). In a sense, my identity is betrayed, given away by my body. Indira Karamcheti illuminates this exposure/intrusion in concluding that "indeed, the minority teacher is already known, *in personal terms:* ethnicity, race, is, among other things, an already familiar genre of personality" (Karamcheti's italics, 138). Karamcheti correctly notes that our notable ethnic and racial differences make us "walking exemplars of ethnicity and of race" (138). But again within this visibility we also embody our invisibility. Offering a case study of students in a women's studies course, Lisa Bowleg writes that the invisibility of race does not apply to the woman of color but to white people, who have the privilege of seeing "themselves as generics (that is, as 'just people')" (116). Although I lack this privilege, I enjoy the privilege of incorporating texts in my syllabi that embrace and celebrate difference and otherness. Engaged in the act of transgressing the supposed divide between the personal and the pedagogical, I am "engage[d] in the practice of self-inclusion, the politics of the personal" (Karamcheti 138). The pedagogical and the personal should not be seen as opposite. They are complementary. By including specific texts and asserting my self in discussions I transform the curriculum.

Speaking about the limitations that women of color face, Sheila Minn Hwang corroborates my experience that "students tend to make assumptions about correlations between one's ethnic background and one's area of expertise" (159). Though Hwang is Asian and teaches British Literature and I am black and teach African American literature and literatures of the Diaspora, we share a similar fate. Like Hwang, who, "because of [her] Asian face, must constantly defend [her] right to talk knowledgeably about British literature" (159), I, too, in spite of my black face, am forced to defend my position as an African Americanist/Afro-Caribbeanist. My blackness and the fact that I teach African American and "minority" literatures do not spare me the label of incompetence, as Amanda's questions and suggestions of my academic legitimacy evidence along with departmental questioning of my teaching approach and techniques.[7] I am living proof that one's visible, embodied ethnicity does not always permit one to lay claim to the literature that speaks to and of that ethnic group.

Although in the preceding example my ethnicity is a detraction and disclaimer, in other cases, it provides a visible link with textual references for my students. Establishing a link between the text and myself seemingly provides some identifiable comfort, a therapeutic remedy as practiced by "Martha." Too bashful to address openly issues of race and discrimination in the classroom, Martha did so without inhibition in a written assignment on James Baldwin's "Notes of a Native Son." In class Martha, normally enthusiastic about our debates, was unusually silent. However, she informed me subsequently by E-mail how much she enjoyed the discussion and was appalled by the discrimination that Baldwin experienced in spite of his education. She writes that she was "simply shocked that someone with Baldwin's education was subjected to so much hate and discrimination. It is even more appalling when you considered that he attended an Ivy League university." Martha was troubled by the injustices Baldwin faced and the mistrust of white people that he later developed as a result of these injustices. Evidently she thought that his education would shield him from the injustices that she linked exclusively to the experiences of uneducated (poor) blacks. Martha saw a link between Baldwin and me and realized, maybe for the first time, how insignificant one's education could become amidst racism and racist perceptions. On one hand, the personal narrative in which she acknowledged the injustices was probably her way of ensuring that the rage of racism that embodied Baldwin did not infect me, and on the other hand, it may have been her attempt to build my trust in her. Martha cautiously did not voice her opinion in the classroom with her fellow students, who interpreted Baldwin's essay simply as a personal (autobiographical) narrative that had nothing to do with reality. Yet her refusal to address such issues except in a paper intended for my eyes put me on the defensive, tempting me to see the written response as an "act of pleasing." In this situation the classroom functioned as an inhibiting, suffocating space. And it reveals that Martha, though white, was subjected to what I had experienced as a black woman: She was trapped, physically and linguistically, in this predominantly white classroom.

EVALUATIONS: A MARKER OF COMPETENCE?

Whereas students use written evaluations (a privilege) as a forum to voice their disapproval and discomfort with both the class and the teacher, the teacher has no such institutional forum, no real outlet. Because evaluations represent a subjective practice, I ask whether it is fair to place a preponderance of weight on students' evaluations when judging a teacher's competence—or incompetence. Addressing the danger of relying heavily on students' evaluations and the occasional self-imposed blindness or lack of vision of colleagues, Smith cites the Association of American Law Schools: "Nonminority colleagues often do not recognize the hostility and questioning of ability that colleagues and students can direct at a minority professor. The failure to acknowledge these factors can cause some faculty members and administrators to give undue weight to [student] complaints and to respond inappropriately" (31).[8] The dominance and frequency of in-classroom questionings have distracted attention from the sometimes more profound out-of-classroom questionings by the institution. Because of the atmosphere of fear and prejudice, the teacher often does not feel safe discussing the possible racist motivations for bad evaluations with other faculty members. I experienced my own bouts of skepticism at the end of a fall semester. After giving my students a written assignment to construct a counternarrative to Judy Syfers's essay "I Want a Wife," I was dumbfounded by "Sara's" response. In her essay she wrote a sister-narrative titled "I Want a Girlfriend." Sara graphically, with sadomasochistic detail, described the kind of girlfriend she (as male speaker) desired and the violent, abusive, sexual relationship that should define this relationship. Assuming a male identity, Sara wrote that she wanted to be complimented on the size and satisfaction that would be derived from her male anatomy. In an after-classroom session with Sara, I voiced my concerns about and discontent with the content of her sexually wired essay. She did not see eye-to-eye with me and saw nothing abnormal or unusual about her written response. She apparently thought that by her assuming a male identity it was acceptable to stereotype the male body since it was an "out of body" experience.

A few days after I was debased and labeled by Sara along with her classroom supporters as closed-minded because I objected to her sexual descriptions and innuendoes, my dean asked whether I thought that the term-end bad evaluations were racially motivated.[9] Although I knew that her questioning *in this case* was well intentioned, I refrained from offering a verdict for I fear being accused of masking my "incompetence" or "playing the race card," playing for sympathy. And although at this point my fears of talking openly about the evaluations with the dean were unfounded, they were later confirmed.

BRIDGING THE DIVIDE: CLASSROOM VERSUS INSTITUTION

One possible solution to student and administrative challenges to teacherly authority and teacherly selfhood, as well as to the multiethnic syllabus, is to acknowledge that race and gender matter and directly address them, exposing prejudices. However, one should note that the classroom is a place where students are groping for identity and power and where the teacher, at the same time, is attempting to assert hers, the reason difference is made to matter so greatly. Even though the classroom provides a forum for dialogue among the races, this forum is effective only if it is defined by sustained dialogues. At the same time, classroom debates should not be posited as the cure-all of prejudices and dis-eases.

The institution also plays a pivotal role in bridging the divide between teacher and students, between in- and out-of-classroom debates. Although one possible way to transform the curriculum is to add diversity to it, the institution also has an obligation to diversify the faculty to reflect the changing needs. The need for more diversity in the mainstream curricula, evidenced in my English classes in which race discussions spill over, should be addressed and implemented. Even though diversity should be a component of mainstream courses, electives should not be regarded as adjuncts to mainstream curricula but as part of the whole. To foster collegiality and to create a productive environment, institutions need to undergo changes; rather than adopt the notion that the "student is always right," they should instead take into consideration that a student's questioning of a teacher may be the result of personal differences and prejudices. Evaluations should not be the sole marker of competence, and the teacher should not be graded on this single assignment; her overall performance should be taken into account. Institutions should also cater to the needs of the changing profession(al) or individual. They should be aware of new scholarship on and by women of color, familiarizing themselves, either in planned faculty forums or personal discussions, to better understand the professor and to better assess students' complaints. This interaction would help the administration and students to become more accepting and tolerant of difference and individuality, permitting personal growth, which eventually leads to institutional growth. Administrators should be willing to listen to suggestions that may not support theirs but yet are not necessarily outlandish. The challenge, moreover, is not solely to pursue the course of integration and diversity in the curricula but to extend it beyond classroom debates and remain committed not only to students but also to women professors of color. To this end it would be helpful if minority faculty are given a forum to voice their discomfort and experiences, whether good or bad. Whether the views of the woman of color are in agreement or to the contrary, she should not be penalized or marginalized for expressing them. When the woman of color becomes legitimized, bodily and/or textually, thin ice will not beckon and threaten.

NOTES

1. Although Guyana is geographically located on the South American continent and is the only English-speaking country in the region, it is considered part of the Caribbean community because of the cultural and linguistic similarities and governing policies it shares with other Caribbean nations. It is also a member of the Caribbean Commonwealth Community. Similar to other English-speaking Caribbean countries, Guyana was colonized by the British, hence its former name, British Guiana.

2. I lived in Moscow for six years, where I obtained a first and a second degree in Russian language and literature. While completing my dissertation, I taught Russian language to undergraduates at Rutgers University, New Brunswick. More than half of my students were first-generation Russian immigrants.

3. I found out later that another West Indian friend was offered the job, which she turned down because of unsuitable conditions.

4. While I noted the white students' discomfort, mine was tempered. I responded to comments as portrayed herein, sometimes refraining from offering an opinion so as not to be accused of being prejudiced one way or the other or of inciting racism. Though being uncomfortable with addressing race and related issues should not be a source of contention in seminars that have race incorporated in the titles, one can never take things for granted. I have had students who were sincerely stunned that race and racism and the vestiges of slavery were so prevalent in a class that spoke to and of the black experience. Students complained that they were expecting to be introduced to the cultural aspects of the black experience and not be engaged in empty rhetoric, trespassing on the racial aspect of the black experience and unnecessarily digging up the past.

5. I feel that authoritative distancing on the professor's part is necessary to foster students' expressing themselves freely in an atmosphere that promotes the exchange of ideas and various interpretations. It is rather ironic that Amanda called for my authoritative presence in the classroom and, in the same breath, accused me of being too opinionated and too visibly present.

6. In conversation with Amanda, I learned that she was a transfer student and had lived in Boston all her life. Both her parents are medical doctors.

7. In a meeting with Amanda, I proposed arriving at a less rigid pace of learning so her concerns could be duly addressed and represented and all her needs could, I hoped, be met. In spite of our meeting and unknown to me, Amanda took the matter to the dean, who later, in a brief conversation, requested that we meet to discuss in detail strategies for countering issues such as students' expectations and teachers' oblig-

ations. Though this meeting did not take place, a few days after Amanda filed her grievance, I was contacted and informed by a senior faculty member that she had been asked to conduct a classroom observation, specifically in this literature class, on my teaching praxis and practices. I assume that the reason this meeting did not take place was that the classroom observation took place without event and I was given a flattering and laudatory report. Apparently there was no need for further investigation.

8. Pamela Smith herself is an assistant professor of law at Boston College Law School and has faced discrimination by both students and the institution.

9. Evaluations are normally given to students at "New College" about three weeks before the end of the semester. Customarily, we professors are instructed to give them to students to fill out, at the end of the session, in our absence. I followed this instruction, but before I was able to leave the classroom a few of Sara's friends stood in front of the class, using the blackboard as a cushion for the evaluation sheets, and drew straight lines through the number one on all ten questions. One is the lowest score, ranging on a scale from one to five.

WORKS CITED

Andersen, Margaret L. *Denying Difference: The Continuing Basis for Exclusion in the Classroom.* Memphis: Memphis State UP, 1987.

Andersen, Margaret L, and Patricia Hill Collins. *Race, Class, and Gender: An Anthology.* New York: Wadsworth, 1995.

Baldwin, James. "Notes of a Native Son." *The Art of the Personal Essay: An Anthology from the Classical Era to the Present.* Ed. Phillip Lopate. New York: Anchor/ Doubleday, 1994. 587–604.

Bowleg, Lisa. "'When I Look at You, I Don't See Race' and Other Diverse Tales from the Introduction of Women's Studies Classroom." *Teaching Introduction to Women's Studies: Expectations and Strategies.* Ed. Barbara Scott Winkler and Carolyn DiPalma. Westport, Conn.: Bergin & Garvey, 1999. 111–22.

Bramen, Carrie Tirado. "Minority Hiring in the Age of Downsizing." *Power, Race, and Gender in Académe: Strangers in the Tower?* Ed. Shirley Geok-Lin Lim and Maria Herrera-Sobek. New York: MLA, 2000. 112–31.

Collins, Patricia Hill. *Fighting Words: Black Women and the Search for Justice.* Minneapolis: Minnesota UP, 1998.

Culley, Margo, and Catherine Portuges, eds. *Gendered Subjects: The Dynamics of Feminist Teaching.* Boston: Routledge, 1985.

Dickerson, Vanessa, and Michael Bennett, eds. *Recovering the Black Female Body: Self-Representations by African American Women.* New Brunswick: Rutgers UP, 2001.

Ellison, Ralph. *The Invisible Man.* New York: Vintage, 1995.

Gaine, Chris, and Rosalyn George. *Gender, "Race," and Class in Schooling: A New Introduction.* Philadelphia: Falmer, 1999.

Gunning, Sandra. "Now That They Have Us, What's the Point?: The Challenge of Hiring to Create Diversity." *Power, Race, and Gender in Académe: Strangers in the Tower?* Ed. Shirley Geok-Lin and Maria Herrera-Sobek. New York: MLA, 2000. 171–82.

Hill, Douglas. "What Students Can Teach Professors: Reading between the Lines of Evaluations." *Chronicle of Higher Education* (16 March 2001): B5.

Hwang, Sheila Minn. "At the Limits of My Feminism: Race, Gender, Class and the Execution of a Feminist Pedagogy." *Power, Race, and Gender in Académe.* Ed. Shirley Geok-Lin and Maria Herrera-Sobek. New York: MLA, 2000. 154–70.

Jay, Gregory. "Taking Multiculturalism Personally: Ethnos and Ethos in the Classroom." *Pedagogy: The Question of Impersonation.* Ed. Jane Gallop. Indianapolis: Indiana UP, 1995. 117–28.

Johnson, Cheryl. "Disinfecting Dialogues." *Pedagogy: The Question of Impersonation.* Ed. Jane Gallop. Indianapolis: Indiana UP, 1995. 129–37.

Karamcheti, Indira. "Caliban in the Classroom." *Pedagogy: The Question of Impersonation.* Ed. Jane Gallop. Indianapolis: Indiana UP, 1995. 138–46.

Lim, Shirley Geok-Lin, and Maria Herrera-Sobek, eds. *Power, Race, and Gender in Académe: Strangers in the Tower?* New York: MLA, 2000.

Peterson, Carla. "Foreword: Eccentric Bodies." *Recovering the Black Female Body: Self-Representations by African American Women.* Eds. Vanessa Dickerson and Michael Bennett. New Brunswick: Rutgers UP, 2001. ix–xvi.

Simon, Roger I. "Face to Face with Alterity: Postmodern Jewish Identity and the Eros of Pedagogy." *Pedagogy: The Question of Impersonation.* Ed. Jane Gallop. Indianapolis: Indiana UP, 1995. 90–105.

Smith, Pamela J. "A Message to Sapphire and Her Sisters in Academia." *Women in Higher Education* (February 2000): 31–34.

Winkler, Barbara Scott, and Carolyn DiPalma, eds. *Teaching Introduction to Women's Studies: Expectations and Strategies.* Westport, Conn.: Bergin & Garvey, 1999.

Wyatt, Elizabeth Gail. *Stolen Women: Reclaiming Our Sexuality, Taking Back Our Lives.* New York: Wiley, 1997.

Moving Bodies

Petra Kuppers

Dance has a dominant aesthetic that talks about ideal bodies, complex movement, lightness, and skill. But dance also has many different faces, embracing
different ideas of beauty and playing with different bodies. Our postmodern
stages, well used to achieve ever more different flights away from traditions,
occasionally present dance companies with disabled performers, big dancers,
and older movement artists. But the reality in our dance classrooms and teaching studios is often a different story.

In this chapter I present moments from my teaching experiences as a disabled dance leader—moments accumulated during my teaching at Manchester Metropolitan University, Swansea University Adult Education Department, Bryant College, and various university workshops and community
groups in the United Kingdom and the United States.

MELTING

To touch the steely wheel of a chair and to feel its smoothness, running lightly, a student puts her foot on the rim of my wheelchair's wheel, just as she would place her palm on my shoulder to lift herself upward in a complicated move. Her foot explores and glides and touches my hand, which in turn glides over her foot and provides me with leverage to move off the chair and onto the floor. She sits in the chair, exploring its potential for movement.

CONTACT

Contact improvisation is a recognized movement form or dance technique. It relies on balance and weight transference rather than fixed body patterns or clearly articulated lines. It doesn't call for an ideal body in the way that other codified dance forms do, and many disabled dancers have embraced Contact as their form of choice. The core skills you develop as you work your way further into Contact are listening to your body, listening to the other's body, finding points of contact, ways of moving with the other, and letting your weight swirl you into movement. Things change as you work with contact; touching starts to signify differently. When you are in a jam session and participants are flowing together, touching becomes movement and movement potential instead of a metaphor for interpersonal communication. Your body fragments in a positive, living way because your attention is not held in only one center but instead multiplies into different sensations and different loci of connection and flow.

BLOCKING

It is the beginning of a new academic year. My new students stand in the dance studio at Manchester Metropolitan University in Britain, anxiously looking at me. I have wheeled into the space and introduced myself as their teacher. Every time, I see doubt and questions in the eyes of the young people in front of me. Not one among them uses a chair or a crutch—dance departments are still seldom set up both physically or conceptually for the same categories of difference among bodies. As long as techniques such as ballet dominate in the curricula, very few disabled people will graduate because ballet demands a very specific set of skills and body shapes. So what am I doing in the dance studio? How does this soft, big, supported body fit in? What is the tragic story behind my painful limbs? These are the questions I see formulated before me.

FLOWING

Dance is about human movement, space, bodies, and energy. It allows forms of communication and knowledge that we cannot express verbally. Thus we move. I give the students instructions, let their bodies loose in the dance studio's space, and move among them as I direct their attention. As we all swarm and fill the spaces between the walls, changing our walk or locomotion according to the energy instructions I give them, I ask them to become aware of the people around them and to pay attention to the kinesphere of their fellow movers. The kinesphere, principally explored by Rudolf von Laban, is somewhat akin to the private space surrounding bodies in social interaction. It holds the extensions of the body, providing a space of possibility around each one, the sum of its potential movement. The kinesphere is small in everyday social action but can be enlarged and worked with in dance or performance, as attention is projected outward. Our kinespheres can become so large that a person standing at one end of the dance studio can touch and communicate with the kinesphere of someone at the other end, transmitting movement impulses and intentions. Kinespheres have different shapes: Some people move more dominantly in their upper regions or prefer wide movements to narrow, high ones. Certain places might be dead spots; many people in Western culture hold dead spots on and around their back and neck muscles, keeping rigid and not paying attention to these areas of their body. As a dance teacher, I pay attention to these shapes and aim to round them, enlarge them, and let them become living entities that allow for new forms of community and communication.

TOUCHING

Back in the dance studio we move, directing attention to our beings in space, our kinespheres touching and bouncing. Warmed up, the students shift their attention away from their social knowledge about disability and begin to move differently around me and see and touch me with new eyes and bodies. The chair moving in space has a different trajectory from that of their bodies. The continuous motion and the glide of the wheels on the floor have a different effect from that of bipedal motion with its ups and downs and its binaries and jolts. The students become familiar with my ways of moving and incorporate that knowledge into the passes we can make, the comings-together and comings-apart. Without focusing on the binary difference between them and me, we all become aware instead of the multiple differences between one and the other.

As the improvisation continues, I might gather all of the dancers together, restricting the space allowed for movement. We might all create a knot in the middle of the room, exploring points of connection, stepping points, and avenues of descent onto the floor and ascent toward the ceiling. Or I might manipulate the energy and flow of the movement, thereby controlling speed, stops, and continuity. We might move together on the edges of exhaustion, task-based instructions disallowing notions of seeing one's body as an aesthetic object. When you are focused on touching someone's foot, or freeze into a line of four, or mirror someone, you cannot "stand outside" and see yourself as an entity moving gracefully, checked against an image of unity fixed in your mind. As the dance takes over, individual bodies blur. Languages change. My teacher's body becomes just that, no longer an uncomfortable body.

SHIFTING

I dance with most of the students in their first session, even if I am scheduled for conceptual rather than practical courses. Learning to see my teacher's body with new eyes and a different sensibility opens up invaluable knowledge to all students: the differences between social and phenomenological stories surrounding body-knowledge and an awareness of the readings of bodies we engage in on a daily basis. My goal in performance and choreography is to make bodies and spaces strange and interesting. We extract differences from the everyday in a pleasurable way, finding beauty and dignity in unsuspected places. By using my body tactically, I allow my students to experience difference viscerally *and* conceptually as a source of interest and fascination—not only difference between nondisabled and disabled but also, beyond that, difference among nondisabled people and the valuable, exquisite nature of their own, different selves.

Dancing Revolution:
A Meditation on
Teaching and Aging

Brenda Daly

Write yourself. The body must be heard.
—Hélène Cixous

"What did you think of the presentation?" I asked the eighteen students in
English 339, "Literary Theory and Criticism," following their attendance at a
talk by Jane Tompkins and Gerald Graff in the spring of 2000. I was expecting these students, all of them undergraduate English majors, to debate the
pedagogical question Tompkins and Graff raised in their title, "Sage on the
Stage or Guide on the Side?" Instead one student blurted out, "They're so
old!" As others nodded in agreement, I countered foolishly, "But they're my

age!" Since I was too surprised to turn this exchange into a teachable moment, I have been haunted ever since by this classroom scene: the moment I became aware of my aging teacher's body. How, I began to wonder, am I to act in this newly "old" body? I recalled with embarrassment having danced a little jig in that same classroom to wake a drowsy student. We all enjoyed the moment—including the sleepy student—but afterward I wondered: Am I too old to dance and too old to teach? If Parker Palmer is right, such fears of aging are widely shared by teachers. As he says in *The Courage to Teach*, "Day after day, year after year, we walk into classrooms and look into younger faces that seem to signal, in crude ways and subtle, 'You're history. Whatever you value, we don't'" (48).

Fall semester 2000 has ended; nevertheless, according to my "Ladies of Rylstone Calendar," whose pages I have not turned since the academic year began, it is still August 2000. Above the caption, "Beautifully preserved," is the photograph of a nude: a middle-aged white woman, her breasts discreetly hidden behind a large cooking pot, stands in her kitchen, ladling preserves into jam jars. August, now long past, was the month I learned, as I was preparing to return to the classroom after a summer of writing, that I had a potentially precancerous condition. When the doctor phoned, explaining the need for a biopsy, which she called "minor surgery," I was typing the syllabus for English 339, "Literary Theory and Criticism." Calmly, with only mild annoyance at the inconvenience, I called to schedule the surgery for late September and then quickly returned to my work. A few days later, as I handed out my syllabus, a student called my attention to at least three typos on the first page! I was embarrassed but intrigued; with my mind elsewhere, my body had been writing itself, recording disturbances. Throughout the month of September, I worried—unnecessarily, as it turned out—that the demise of my body had begun.

Wednesday, December 22, 2000, 11:05 A.M. A Lutheran Brotherhood salesman arrives, earlier than scheduled, to explain my options for long-term care insurance. I am annoyed, mostly because I have allowed him to schedule this appointment at a time that interferes with my writing but also because I don't want to think about aging. I know, however, that long-term care insurance will cost less if I buy it before I turn 59. Nevertheless, I ask, "What if I wait until I'm 65?" With fingers on the keyboard of his laptop, he answers, "I'll turn you into a 65-year-old in just a second here, and we'll figure the cost." He smiles at his joke, but I don't. "What if I limit my coverage to five years?" I ask next, explaining, "I'd rather be dead than linger on if I am unable to take care of myself." He zooms me back to age 59, explaining that for a higher monthly payment, my long-term care coverage can be adjusted for inflation. "The problem with that plan," I reply after he shows me the cost, "is that I'm an English professor who may not be able to afford such a large monthly payment, especially after retirement."

Having had almost no time to write during fall semester, I hoard my morning hours over the holiday break. These hours belong to me, not to students who view me, understandably, primarily in terms of their own needs. And these hours certainly do not belong to an insurance man who sees me as one more sale in the year 2000.

In the year 2000.

In the year 2000 I acknowledge that, despite my ability to exercise an hour a day with Jane Fonda and the eternally young women on her videotapes, I must make changes in my teaching schedule. I no longer have the stamina to teach two eighty-minute classes on Tuesdays and Thursdays so that, ideally, I can write on alternate days of the week. Preparing to make this change, I rationalize: Committee work has already "stolen" most of my writing days; what difference will it make? It's true. Despite a Tuesday-Thursday teaching schedule, my writing time—as is probably true for most faculty members—is usually "stolen" by required service to the university: preparing for classes, answering an increasing number of E-mails, reading and evaluating applications for grants and leaves for a college committee that I currently chair, grading papers, and writing letters of recommendation for students. More and more I find that I am able to write only during the summers. Given these realities, I arrange to switch from a two-day to a five-day teaching schedule for spring semester 2001. After making this change, one of my inner voices says, "It will be good to have a gentler rhythm, a more even tempo, for each work day." Another voice protests, "Does growing old mean slowing down until, finally, I will be forced to give up the things I love the most—writing? teaching? dancing? Death is not the problem (or so I tell myself); what I can't seem to accept is the time between now and then.

I would prefer not to think about aging. The primary reason for my resistance is that, as Elizabeth Spelman reminds me, our culture fears the body, a fear that intensifies as the body ages. "What might be called 'somatophobia' (fear of and disdain for the body) is part of a centuries-long tradition in Western culture" (126), Spelman explains. Men have claimed "transcendence," actively creating culture, according to Simone de Beauvoir, whereas women have been regarded as "immanence," as wombs. According to Spelman, that is why feminists such as de Beauvoir, Betty Friedan, and Shulamith Firestone have argued that "the source of our liberation lies in sundering that connection" (126). Yet Spelman cautions feminists against disassociating ourselves from the body. Instead, she argues, feminists must challenge this attitude toward the body because somatophobia "contributes to white solipsism in feminist thought": (1) It ignores an important element in racist thinking that holds that certain races are more "body-like," that is, "more animal-like and less god-like" (127); (2) it leads to the notion that superior groups—of a certain gender, race, or class—have better things to do than caring for the body, thus predicating one group's liberation on the oppression of the other group;

and (3) it leads, by divorcing the concept of woman from the concept of a woman's body, to "the idea of a woman who is no particular historical woman—she has no color, no accent, no particular characteristics that require having a body" (128).

Such a disembodied feminist—without color, accent, or body—becomes an oppressor of others. Thus I must acknowledge not only that I have a body but also that I inhabit an aging white middle-class (or is it working class?) body. When I enter the classroom, I cannot leave this body behind, although my culture would have me do so. I was reminded of this cultural code in 1963 when, at the age of twenty-two, I was about to begin my first teaching job. Instead, I had to inform the principal at Hopkins High School in suburban Minneapolis that I was married and pregnant. The principal, disapproval in his eyes, immediately released me from the contract. Embarrassed and without questioning his assumption, I knew the unwritten rule: He couldn't have a pregnant woman in the classroom. I felt trapped in my pregnant body, afraid of being eternally condemned to the realm of immanence as my mother had been. Because my mother had had no money of her own, her responsibility for the care of seven children made her completely dependent upon my undependable and abusive father. It also left her no time for a life of the mind. Hoping to escape her fate, despite my pregnancy, I enrolled that fall in a graduate program at the University of Minnesota. Oddly, the more my body swelled, the more invisible I felt on campus. Following the birth of my son on a Saturday evening, one week before winter quarter ended, I attended my last Wednesday-evening seminar. When a male student commanded me to stand up. I stood. For the first time, and only after it was over, my pregnancy had been acknowledged.

I understood that I had violated a taboo simply by appearing in a university—a place of the mind—in a pregnant body. Over the next fifteen years, as a mother and a high school teacher, I became a feminist. Although I did not return to a doctoral program until 1978, one of my first postdegree publications focused on mothering. In *Narrating Mothers,* which I coedited with a younger colleague who was (and is) also a mother, we consciously and persistently resisted the binary opposition, immanence/transcendence, as we examined the maternal perspective in twentieth-century women's narratives. My essay, "Teaching Alice Walker's *Meridian:* Civil Rights according to Mothers," explains how, as a teacher, I came to understand that mothering is not the same for all women. Judith Fetterley had alerted me to the fact that gender makes a difference in how we read, and in 1985, while I was teaching an extension course in a racially mixed neighborhood in northern Minneapolis, my students taught me that African American women and white males interpreted *Meridian* differently from the way I did. Yet, African American women readers did agree with me on one point: that mothering is central in *Meridian.* By contrast, young white men did not even notice mothering in the novel! After this teaching experience, because I had read Adrienne Rich's *Of Woman Born* in 1976, I recognized that I could no longer read—or teach—as a (white) man. Along with many other feminists, I acknowledged that consciousness is embodied.

Now, as I confront the "flesh loathing" that I sometimes feel toward my own aging, white, heterosexual, middle-class teacher's body (with its working-class past), I understand that I must learn to differentiate between cultural attitudes toward aging and my own experience of it just as, earlier, I had learned to differentiate, as Rich recommended, between the institution of motherhood and my actual experience of it. I am not at all certain, however, that such differentiation is possible when it comes to aging. Since the birth of my son thirty-six years ago, I have known—known viscerally—that I cannot escape death. Yet, since my mother's death in 1997, I have also resolved to resist at least some aspects of aging. This resistance, I believe, makes me hungry for dancing. As a girl, I loved to dance, and when I dance now the experience reminds me of the girl I once was. In the fifties and into sixties, that lively girl could rock and roll, jitterbug, and twist and bop with abandon. That may be why, in 1999, as I was leaving my own fifties behind, my partner and I signed up for dance lessons. What a joy to dance again!

At the same time I found myself drawn to the rhythms and images of dance in fiction, and in a wild experiment in "Twentieth-Century Fiction," I invited thirty, mostly white, male and female nonmajors in their late teens and early twenties to dance their responses to fiction. We began by discussing images of dance in David Leavitt's "Family Dancing" and Lorrie Moore's "Dance in America." During the next class period we assembled in a gym where the dance instructor, Linda Sabo, explained that dance is "culture inscribed on the body." Under her guidance, students learned a few basic movements before choosing a character from one of the two short stories to portray in dance. After improvising movements for their character, Sabo asked them to dance with another character. In retrospect I view this experiment as a kind of acting out, a way of avoiding the task of facing my anxieties about aging. Yet, as a result of this experiment, I began to ask new questions. If dance itself is a language—a symbol of the act of creation itself, a pantomime of metamorphosis (Circlot 72–73)—how, I wondered, does the language of dance differ from the language of literature? How does the body speak? What exactly is the language of dance?

Defining dance for inexperienced students, Lorrie Moore's teacher-narrator says: "I tell them dance begins when a moment of hurt combines with a moment of boredom. I tell them it's the body reaching, bringing air to itself. I tell them that it's the heart's triumph, the victory speech of the feet, the refinement of animal lunge and flight, the purest metaphor of tribe and self. It's life flipping death the bird" (47). I agree; that's it exactly: Dance is the purest metaphor of tribe and self. In this sense the body is the text, and the text the body. Critic Arlene Elder also suggests such an intimate relationship when she uses the phrase "dancing the page" to describe the native dance rhythms in M. Scott Momaday's novel, *The Way to Rainy Mountain*. As Elder's phrase implies, dance is a phenomenon shaped by cultural codes and beliefs, a metaphor of tribe and self. If dance is defined as "a pantomime of metamorphosis," its rhythmic movements "speak" of the inevitable transformation of body and culture, self and tribe. According to this formulation, body and mind and individual and culture cannot be separated. Aging, like other transformations of self, occurs to an individual but always within a tribe, a culture. In short, cultural beliefs are shaping my experience of aging.

Physician Christiane Northrup makes this point—that beliefs about aging influence the actual physiological process—in *Women's Bodies, Women's Wisdom* by summarizing the results of an experiment on the Tara Humara Indians in Mexico: As reported by Dr. Deepak Chopra, endocrinologist and internationally recognized authority on how consciousness affects our bodies, certain members of the Tara Humara tribe ran the equivalent of a marathon or more every day and had regular races between groups. The most intriguing aspect of their culture, Northrup emphasizes, was that they believed that the best runners were those in their sixties. Indeed, according to researchers, the best lung capacity, cardiovascular fitness, and endurance were found in the runners in their sixties! Yet, as Chopra emphasizes, "for this belief to translate into physical reality, the entire tribe has to believe it" (Northrup 435). Certainly, this belief—that the body improves with age—is not shared by the American "tribe," of which I am a member. Moreover, as I learned when presenting an earlier version of this chapter, men and women experience aging differently. For example, one man who has been supportive of my feminist scholarship in the past declared bluntly that the topic of aging is "narcissistic"; by contrast, upon hearing my topic, women have commented almost uniformly that men gain status as they age, but women lose it. These gendered responses helped me to identify the primary source of my fear of aging in the classroom: the possible loss of respect from students.

I first encountered my fear of this loss of respect almost thirty years ago while reading Joyce Carol Oates's *Do with Me What You Will*. As Marvin Howe, an aging lawyer, tries to explain to Elena, his much younger wife, why he needs her so desperately, he recounts an experience at a stag party: "The master of ceremonies had been building up to this. He made us all believe that something truly amazing was going to come on stage. . . . And then . . . two bicyclists pedaled out, and they were women, naked, but then it became obvious that there was something wrong with them: they were very old women" (Oates's ellipses 554). Although I was only thirty-two years old when I first read this passage, I identified with the aging women who are figures of ridicule: "They were very skinny, they were riding these bicycles, like circus bicycles, decorated with balloons and paper flowers" (554). At first, Howe says, the audience was surprised, but then they laughed. But when one old woman fell, Howe explains, he was reminded of his aging mother, and at that moment "the bottom had fallen out of the universe" (554). That is why, Howe says, his life depends upon the youthful Elena's staying. He needs her to function as a mirror in which he can see himself as youthful, regardless of his age. By contrast, if an aging woman chooses a younger partner, she is likely to be ridiculed. The reason is obvious: An aging woman *is* her body, is immanence, whereas an aging man is not.

Despite this encounter with the sexism of ageism in the early 1970s, I have been very slow to recognize my own internalized ageist attitudes. For example, although I began studying images of women in the early seventies and although I tried to be inclusive, I had completely ignored grandmothers! Only after becoming a "nana"—which is what my Mexican American grandson calls me—have I found myself reading more and more often from the perspective of an aging woman. Yet I say very little about aging women in the classroom. Little by little, I am attempting to change this behavior. For example, when I inform students that, according to reader-response theorists, we read from different subject positions, I now include age along with the more familiar categories of race, gender, sexual orientation, and class. Last fall (2000), to illustrate this reader-response concept to students, I used my personal experience as a grandmother to describe how I read the chapter called "Three Sisters" in Sandra Cisneros's *The House on Mango Street*. Since becoming a grandparent to two beautiful Mexican American children, as I told students in "Twentieth-Century Fiction," I have become attentive to "three old ladies who smelled like cinnamon" (105). These three sisters are not ordinary women, I explained, but personifications of what Jean Wyatt calls "Mexican social myths of gender [that] crystallize with special force in three icons: '*Guadalupe*, the virgin mother who has not abandoned us, *la Chingada (Malinche)*, the raped mother whom we have abandoned, and *la Llorona*, the mother who seeks her lost children'" (244). What intrigues me, I told my young students, is that Cisneros has transformed these icons into mentors who bless Esperanza, rather than discouraging or delimiting her feminist desires. Students were polite as I expounded on Cisneros's feminist transformations of the mythical identities of these three women, but they were obviously not as engaged as I.

What attracts me is Cisneros's notion of aging women who bless, rather than any notion that discourages or delimits them. This notion of a "mentor who blesses"—similar to what Erik Erikson calls "generativity"—is not always easy to achieve. Generativity, according to Erikson, is the "instinctual power" behind many kinds of caring; more specifically, it refers to "man's *love for his works and ideas as well as for his children*" (131). Erikson explains that it may first arise during parenthood but can be generalized to include many workers and thinkers who need to teach, not only for their own sake but also for that of others. In 1964, when Erikson's words were first published, women's ideas were rarely valued; their work was limited to the care of children. Yet the concept of generativity may be expanded to include a woman's need to generate feminist ideas—that is, the need to continue her own creativity—as well as her need to nurture the young in her care, both inside and outside the classroom. My feminist ideal, then, is to become a creative older woman who blesses the young, rather than fearing, envying, or delimiting them. To learn how to achieve this goal—which can be challenging in a competitive academic culture—I have begun seeking grandmother-mentors. My search has only just begun, but thus far, such generative feminist mentors are not easy to find either in life or in literature.

One reason for the absence of generative aging women is that they are not honored in Euro-American culture. Alan Cheuse makes this point in a short story called "O Body Swayed," which depicts an aging woman who is abused by school children. As Cheuse's title suggests, his story is a fictional updating of Yeats's "Among School Children," with specific reference to the lines "O body swayed to music, O brightening glance,/How can we know the dancer from the dance" (lines 63–64). The aging woman in the story, Jane Harrison, is a former dancer, now confined to a wheel chair, who has recently returned to the United States for hip-replacement surgery. The story opens as Jane, recalling with embarrassment her "little dance" with a flight attendant in the lavatory somewhere over the Atlantic, asks the same attendant for help in leaving the plane. It is fear of this kind of dependency that prompts me and others in my age bracket to pay money for long-term care insurance. In our society aging parents cannot count on help from their adult children; in fact, even if the children are willing to help, parents may prefer the help of someone they pay, as is the case with Jane in "O Body Swayed." Jane is not at all gracious about accepting help from her son; in fact, in an effort to escape him and his wife, she finally agrees, though reluctantly, to be interviewed by a young reporter. "Just come the hell over," she tells Amy Kunstler, "I'm in a bloody wheel chair, and you can push me to the park" (25).

As they talk, joggers, skateboarders, and bikers go whizzing by, and Harrison repeatedly asks Kunstler to slow down. The issue of generativity surfaces when the reporter asks, "So you're not making anything new?" Harrison lies: "I am, actually. . . . A very new piece. Quite embryonic right now, though. But definitely in the works" (28–29). Following this exchange Harrison becomes even more cantankerous, undoubtedly because she feels defensive about lying and angry that she is not in fact working on a new piece. She cautions Kunstler not to get her hopes up about doing a story about her: "I'm a bit more difficult in person than my pieces might make me out to be." Kunstler responds, "I don't write psychological criticisms of movement, Miss Harrison. Unless I'm trying to find some connection between a piece and the American psyche" (29). Harrison objects to the notion of an American psyche, calling it "silly bullshit" (29). However, this supposedly silly bullshit provides a key to the meaning of this story, instructing me in how to understand—in cultural terms—the story's unpredictable close.

What happens is this: While Amy Kunstler is distracted by a man, probably her ex-husband, who is stalking her in the park, Harrison is suddenly on her own. Watching as the couple swing at each other, Harrison thinks, "A dance," and takes off in her wheelchair. Feeling "free," she suddenly realizes that she hadn't lied: "She was rushing toward something new. The piece flashed into her mind. On stage, moving chairs, and women with strong arms—stronger than hers—spun themselves about, the large wheels making great circles in the eyes of the audience. It all came to her in great circles itself, as she kept moving along the path" (32). But when she has to pee, she calls out to two young boys, mistakenly assuming they will help her find a lavatory. Instead, the boys kidnap her, calling her "Wheelchair Granny" and "Granny Wheelie!" During a battle between two gangs, her purse is stolen by one gang and her chair by the other. At the close of the story, she lies in a hospital bed, sobbing without sound in the presence of her son and his wife. Closing her eyes, she sees "wheels and skates and boards and bikes, bandanas, wheels and wheels and wheels" (36). Yes, it is a cultural dance, but not precisely what she had envisioned.

My initial response to this ending was angry resistance. I attacked the author, whom I imagined (incorrectly) to be a young man because he seemed to imply that an aging woman should not be seen or heard in public. During a calmer, more reflective rereading, I recognized that my response to the story mirrors Harrison's response to aging. I became cranky toward someone younger, an irritability more intense toward someone upon whom I feel dependent. In this case I felt dependent, as a reader, on how a (male) author had envisioned me. Forced to acknowledge Harrison's dependency, her vulnerability, I wonder: Are such feelings inevitable? It is this very question, I conclude, that Cheuse is asking readers to contemplate when he has Kunstler say, "I'm trying to find some connection between a [dance] piece and the American psyche" (29). What is this connection? Harrison finds herself in a brutal dance over which she has no creative control: Wheels and wheels rush by as she herself on wheels is caught in the battles of the young people around her. It is a brutal choreography, one without gentleness toward the elderly, a cultural choreography that allows Harrison no space for dignity or creativity. I comfort myself: Since I am a writer like Amy rather than a dancer like Jane, I need not fear such a loss of creativity as I age. I don't use my body to write; hence, unlike a dancer, I can work until I drop dead. Almost immediately I recognize this thought as a flight from the body. As a writer I may be able to escape (some of) the limitations of aging and embodiment; as a teacher I cannot.

A teacher's choice of metaphors has a powerful effect on pedagogy, according to a young colleague, Deb Marquart. Perhaps the fact that embodiment is inescapable in the classroom helps to explain why I, along with others, think of teaching as dancing. For example, working-class academic Julie Olsen Edwards uses the dance metaphor to describe her teaching of mostly working-class students. She says, "I have the privilege of orchestrating our dance together. I tap into their hope and offer them mine. 'Your families and mine,' I tell them, 'do the work of the world'" (357). Edwards reminds me that, when I define myself primarily as a writer and not as a teacher, I am guilty of trying to leave this labor—this dance of teaching—to embodied others while I as a writer assume the superior life of the mind. Yet it is difficult to resist the widely shared assumption that research is more important than teaching, at least at a university such as Iowa State. Moreover, although parental roles should not be thoughtlessly mapped onto teaching—I do not play the part of mother to my students—the two are dialectically related. Being a parent has influenced my teaching, just as teaching has influenced my parenting. For example, as both a mother and a teacher, I understand that it is important to be available to the young while, at the same time, it is important to set boundaries not only for the benefit of the child, who needs the experience of dancing alone, but also for my own benefit: If I fail to care for myself and if I do not remain generative (creative), I cannot care for the next generation. Recalling Jane Harrison, I ponder a recurring nightmare: a fear of falling in the classroom.

   To examine my fears of aging—an examination that must precede more effective methods of teaching about aging—I decide to focus on English 384, "Twentieth-Century Fiction," a course in which "family" is a recurring topic. Having resolved to stop denying my own aging, I analyze the portrayal of grandparents, however marginal, in the stories I frequently assign. As stated earlier, the course enrolls up to thirty-five students, mostly nonmajors in their late teens and early twenties, most of them white. In the fall of 2000, I begin the course with Willa Cather's well-known story, "Paul's Case" (1902), closing with a story published in the late-twentieth century, David Leavitt's "Family Dancing" (1984). As Leavitt's story dramatizes, it is now possible—as it was not at the time Cather wrote "Paul's Case"—to be explicit about a character's sexual orientation; however, this change does not suggest that the family—a historically heterosexist institution—is any healthier in the late-twentieth century than it was earlier in the century. Since a grandmother appears—in fact, opens the dancing—in Leavitt's story, I begin to explore the question: How will an aging woman respond to a gay man or, more specifically, how is their interaction represented by an openly gay author? This question was prompted, in part, by an invitation from a young gay colleague, just out of the closet in the fall of 2000, to join his proposed session, "Writing the Body," at the Conference on College Composition and Communication the following April (2001). Sadly, the grandmother knows nothing about her grandson Seth's sexual orientation; only Seth's sister, Lynnette, knows that John, a man who happens to be her best friend, is her brother's lover.

But before turning my attention to Leavitt's grandmother, here is a brief synopsis of the story. "Family Dancing" opens as Seth's mother, Suzanne, who is newly remarried, prepares to host a party at which she will encounter her former husband, a man she continues to love, despite the fact that he has rejected her. Ironically, despite the fact that the story's central event is a party arranged to celebrate the son's graduation from prep school, Seth remains a marginal figure in the story and in his family. One obvious explanation for Seth's marginality is that the story is told primarily from the mother's perspective; however, it soon becomes apparent that Seth has also been marginalized by his troubled, heterosexual parents. The question of who is whose partner grows more complex, psychologically and literally, when the party ends with a family dance. John, Seth's secret lover, begins by inviting Seth's grandmother to dance. With my new attentiveness to grandmothers, I note that Pearl "dances with amazing energy" (139) to the applause of sisters, cousins, and grandchildren. Some family members—including the angry Lynnette—try to stay out of the dance, but these onlookers are eventually pulled onto the floor. For example, Suzanne asks her ex-husband, Herb, to dance despite the fact that during their marriage he had shown his aversion to Suzanne by frequently telling his daughter, Lynnette, that she is his favorite partner. Next, as Pearl calls to her granddaughter Lynnette, "Don't be a spoil-sport" (141), John pulls her onto the floor. Given the father's past seductive behavior toward his daughter and her resulting hatred of her mother this experience is frightening for Lynnette.

Initially, following Leavitt's shifting narrative perspective, I analyzed this scene from the point of view of the mother and daughter, sympathizing with each in turn. Lynnette has contained her feelings of abandonment by overeating, displacing the anger she feels toward her father onto her mother. Yet as Lynnette observes, Suzanne has also been rejected and abandoned: "It is not her fault, she tells herself, if Suzanne is still in love with Herb. . . . Perhaps there is something wrong with her taking such pleasure in her mother's sad predicament" (135). As a daughter, I understand Lynnette's anger toward her narcissistic father, and, as a mother, I share Suzanne's sad bewilderment at her daughter's behavior. But as I began to analyze this story from the perspective of a minor character, the grandmother, I experienced this scene differently. Initially I regarded Pearl's dancing as undignified, but eventually I recognized my attitude as a symptom of flight from my body as well as from my changing role in the family. What makes it possible, I wonder, for Pearl to enjoy herself when she may well have accumulated more painful memories than her daughter or granddaughter? Is something positive—perhaps a greater capacity for joy—possible for me as I enter old age?

While rereading Leavitt's story from Pearl's perspective—as I prepared to present a portion of this chapter with my colleague—I reflected on the possibility that Pearl may be the only family member capable of blessing Seth in his new life—in his partnership with John and his planned career in fashion design. As the story makes obvious, Seth's father and mother are too preoccupied with their own lives to nurture their son. For example, both parents are surprised at Seth's request for a sewing machine as a graduation gift. Nor is Seth's sister Lynnette a likely supporter. Unlike her parents, she knows that Seth is gay and accepts him; however, she has been so severely damaged by the family romance—in particular, by a seductive father who has made her, not his wife, his primary emotional partner—that she has little to give Seth. Pearl is, for this reason, Seth's last best hope. Unfortunately, however, despite Pearl's affection toward her grandson, she has not been told that he is gay, and this suggests a lack of intimacy between them. Moreover, because Pearl is described as viewing her daughter's marriage as a move "up" on the social ladder, she begins to sound materialistic. Sadly, although this dancing grandmother seems to enjoy herself, I find little evidence that she has the capacity to bless Seth in his life choices.

Sunday, December 24, 2000. *Would I rather be like Pearl, dancing with the family at times of ritual celebration—at graduations, weddings, birthdays, even funerals—than at home writing, as I am today? Like Jane Harrison, part of me wants to escape family, part of me wants to be an independent, creative woman, not somebody's teacher or mother or grandmother. When my son calls on Christmas eve, we close with "I love you." This year my partner and I give each other "events"—spots of time—rather than gifts. We enjoy the quiet and, because we are both writers, we value the time and the freedom to write.*

Although my search for dancing grandmothers—for generative aging women—yields a greater number than I had anticipated, I find myself resisting some of them. For example, I resist joining the dance of working-class grandmothers that Northrup invokes as an antidote to our culturally inscribed fears of the aging female body. Quoting from "The Dancing Grandmas" by Clarissa Pinkola Estes, Northrup describes "four old women refugees who wore black, had red hands and ruddy cheeks, and whose 'entire history was in their forearms'"—as follows:

> At a family wedding, these four danced beautifully and powerfully, "lifting their skirts to display piano ankles wrapped in Ace bandages." As was their tradition, they danced to exhaustion, all the young men, including the groom, as a way to test their stamina. At the end of the evening "Everyone had been inoculated with the power of age. No one could ever become sick from age, or made ill by the idea that aging was a pathetic time. Everyone knew a good and decent, deep life awaited them in later years." We've been too long without those powerful, honest, wise women of old—too long without images of their beauty, power, and strength. Welcome them back, They are inside each of us. (479)

I appreciate the strength and camaraderie of these women, but I don't want their bandaged ankles. It may be snobbishness—I have been programmed to prefer looking like Jane Fonda—but a deeper source of my resistance is that these aging women remind me of my paternal grandmother. As a Norwegian immigrant, she gave her life to support her five children; as a result she had almost no time for creative self-expression. She was a strong dancer for years, but her legs finally gave out. Like Jane Harrison, she had hip-replacement surgery and, during her final years, could not walk.

I admire working-class women like my grandmother, but I don't want to romanticize their suffering bodies. What might my grandmother have become, I wonder, if she had had a chance for a life of the mind? I also wonder why Northrup, a professional woman, chose working-class rather than middle-class women to function as an image of embodiment in *Women's Bodies, Women's Wisdom?* Is she attempting to dissociate from her own white, professional, middle-class body? Yet Northrup understands that her professional education has alienated her, not only from her body, but also from her feelings. She discloses that, although her father had advised, "Feelings are facts. Pay attention to them," her scientific training quickly taught her "that feelings, intuition, spirituality, and all experiences of life that cannot be explained by the logical, rational parts of our minds or measured by our five senses are ignored or discounted" (12). She describes the practice of medicine as an "addictive system" that "fears emotional responses and highly values the control of emotions because it is so out of touch with them" (12). In an effort to resist such gendered cultural imperatives, Northrup, like Spelman, points out that "female bodies, long associated with cycles and subject to the ebb and flow of natural rhythms, are seen as especially emotional and in need of management" (13). Along with our entire society, the medical model of aging perpetuates this view of the body. As Northrup says, "The experience of aging as we know it is largely determined by beliefs that need updating. Though many people do decline with age in this culture, this decline is not a natural consequence of aging—it is a natural consequence of our collective beliefs about aging" (434).

I have already experienced the painful reality of these collective beliefs. For example, I was once verbally attacked by a young man simply because I was an older woman who happened to be in a place dominated by the young. I was in my early fifties when I arrived, alone, to hear my son who was playing a gig in a bar near the University of Minnesota, the same university where I had earned my Ph.D. some years earlier. Now, a tenured professor, I was returning to campus town to hear my son, the lead soloist and guitarist in a band that played mostly for college students. While I was making my way through the bar to the dance hall in an adjacent room, a young man invited me to dance. I turned him down courteously, but he responded, in a voice filled with contempt, "You're old." "Yes," I answered, "I am. Old." I wasn't yet a grandmother, but I had been pronounced "old." As I listened to my son's music, I imagined cruel retorts I might have made—"I'd rather be old than young and stupid, like you" or "I don't dance with babies"—but I wondered: Am I too old to dance now? Have I already begun the decline into old age? This encounter may have prompted my preoccupation with images of dancing grandmothers, but it also heightened my anxieties about meeting the cruel gaze of some young people. But I remind myself that the gaze of most young people is not cruel. Quite the contrary. For example, when I told Elyse Lord, the first graduate student I mentored at Iowa State in 1987, about my preoccupation with dancing and aging, she told me the following story via E-mail. She was purchasing tickets for a performance by Anna Halprin, an eighty-year-old modern dancer, she said, when the ticket agent warned her that there would be some nudity in the retrospective, which was described as "a meditation on life and death." Feeling the need to forewarn her uncle, whom she had invited, Elyse received in return his comment that "he didn't think he'd like seeing an eighty-year-old woman naked unless he was himself eighty years old." "I wasn't sure what he meant," Elyse remarked, "other than the stereotypical—that naked women exist for the pleasure of men and eighty-year-old naked women aren't as pleasurable to look at to men (who aren't themselves eighty?)" This man's response is similar to that of Marvin Howe in Oates's novel, *Do with Me What You Will:* He does not want to be reminded of his own mortality. As an antidote to this sexist attitude—that the aging female body is repulsive—I remind myself that the aging women in the photographs on the "Ladies of Rylstone" calendar are not repulsive; they are lovely.

December 27, 2000. *In her holiday letter, Elyse writes, "I got to see dancer Anna Halprin's 80th year retrospective performance. She is one of the most brilliant and inspired people I've ever encountered, so watching her dance her 'good-bye' perfor-mance was a once-in-a-lifetime experience, as was participating in the Circle the Earth Dance on Easter." Although I am not sure what the Circle of Earth Dance is, I want to learn more about it.*

I do not wish to deny that I am aging, nor do I want to pretend that I can overcome death. However, as Northrup and others emphasize, patriarchal cul-ture promotes the view that death can be overcome. David Morris reiterates Northrup's argument in *The Culture of Pain,* when he writes: "Tragedy tells us that the body must go down to death. Medicine cannot endure this thought" (264). Yet I remain uncertain, as I confront the eventual demise of my own body, that I will be able to maintain my spirit—my spirited body, my dancing body. Must I differentiate body and spirit? Religion has taught me to do so, making the promise that (spiritual) life can be "everlasting." As a Lutheran I also learned the price of this comforting belief when I asked my minister,

"What is your view of dancing?" His answer, "It's like having intercourse standing up!" was a blunt summation of the attitude of some Lutherans toward the supposedly "lower" pleasures of the body. His answer also implied that in order to have life everlasting, I should engage in sex without pleasure and only for reproductive purposes. Such a view of the body would make me, inevitably, an adversary of dance. As Ann Wagner states in her title, *Adversaries of Dance: From the Puritans to the Present*, Protestants have positioned themselves as "adversaries of dance." However, like many in my generation, the late fifties and early sixties, I refused to obey this command. Hearing the music of Elvis Presley and Buddy Holly, Chuck Berry and Little Richard, I wanted to dance, and I did.

At that time I did not know that I owed the joy of such dancing—the jitterbug, the swing, and the bop—to African American culture. However, I have since learned that "whites have steadily borrowed from African American dance—largely without acknowledgment or appreciation of the source" (Hazzard-Gordon xi). Katrina Hazzard-Gordon also explains that dance was sacred in African culture although, over time, sacred, ceremonial dance and secular dancing were differentiated. "The split began in the middle passage," she explains, "and by the time the first generation of slaves was born on these shores the process was well underway" (15–16). Now, through Toni Morrison's inspired ability to "dance the page," I participate in the sacredness of the dance that Baby Suggs, holy, initiates in *Beloved*. Calling her people to a clearing in the woods, Baby Suggs, holy, begins by calling to the grown men, "Let your wives and your children see you dance" (87). Because Baby Suggs understands, "Yonder they do not love your flesh. They despise it," she invites her people to love and celebrate their bodies. She invites them to dance: "You got to love it. This is flesh I'm talking about here. Flesh that needs to be loved. Feet that need to rest and to dance" (88). My culture has not taught me to love my flesh, particularly my aging flesh. As Morrison demonstrates through the figure of Schoolteacher, fear of death in patriarchal culture leads Anglo-Europeans to project the burden of embodiment onto an "other" whom it then loathes and enslaves.

January 1, 2001. *The New Millenium has arrived. During the past week I have received two requests from students for letters of reference, one due January 16th, the other January 31st. Although I am happy to write these letters (on average I write two such letters a week), they take time. The semester begins on January 8th, but I find it difficult to stop writing. Yesterday, on the television show, "Sunday Morning," Mickey Hart, Curator of American Folk Music, explained that drumming wakes up patients suffering from a range of illnesses, including Alzheimers. Doctors now prescribe rhythm for such patients.*

As I proofread the syllabus for English 345, a topics course in women and literature that my coteacher and I have titled "Changing Our Stories," I reflect on how each author portrays aging women. The course begins with Susan Glaspell's drama of an aging woman who is presumed to have killed her husband. Next on the syllabus is Mary McCarthy's *Memories of a Catholic Girlhood*, which presents two narcissistic grandmothers. Fortunately, strong, aging women are portrayed in narratives by Leslie Marmon Silko, Sandra Cisneros, and Kim Chernin. For example, in *Storyteller*, Silko credits her aging Aunt Susie with teaching her how to tell Laguna stories, stories told not only for pleasure but also for survival. (Fortunately, having thought about aging and ageism before teaching *Storyteller*, I was prepared when a student remarked, "What is this, a geriatrics ward?" In response to this young white woman's comment, I contrasted Laguna Pueblo views of aging women with Euro-American views, explaining that Aunt Susie is portrayed as part of a culture in which women are respected rather than demeaned or dominated.) Like Silko, Paula Gunn Allen explains that she learned the lessons of her culture from an older woman: "When I was small, my mother often told me that animals, insects, and plants are to be treated with the kind of respect one customarily accords to high-status adults. 'Life is a circle, and everything has its place in it,' she would say. That's how I met the sacred hoop, which has been an integral part of my life" (1). Having grown up inside patriarchal stories, stories in which animals, insects, and plants are usually regarded as mere background for human dramas, I find this notion of a circle, a circle in which all are spiritually kin, a powerful alternative.

Because I am not part of a gynocentric culture, a culture that respects aging women, I continue to seek stories that provide images of cultural transformation—a metamorphosis of self and tribe. That is why I am desperately seeking stories of dancing grandmothers. As I reread Kim Chernin's *In My Mother's House*, I am saddened that Rose Chernin, the courageous Marxist revolutionary, refuses to dance. Even after lawyers had successfully prevented Senator Joseph McCarthy's committee from forcing her to testify, Rose refuses to dance, according to her daughter Kim Chernin. Kim writes: "I grabbed her around the waist and danced with her. It was like moving a ton of bricks. 'Come on, Mama, dance,' I kept insisting. She pushed me on the shoulder, took a few little steps, looked over, shaking her head at my father, and finally broke way and sat down on the couch" (246–47). Because Rose had been forced to be a fighter for most of her life, she had perhaps armored her body, making it impossible for her to dance. This was a great loss, in my view, of the body electric. To reclaim this lost poetry, a gift Kim shared with her maternal grandmother, she began to turn away from political life in the 1950s, finally deciding to become a poet, not a revolutionary. Mother and daughter are eventually reconciled, as are poetry and politics, but Rose herself refused to dance.

In contrast to Rose Chernin, Emma Goldman did not consider dancing and revolutionary activities incompatible. According to Alix Kates Shulman, "When her comrades disapproved of her love of dancing as a frivolity unworthy of a true revolutionary, she grew incensed, retorting that a revolution without dancing, without 'beautiful radiant things,' was not worth fighting for" (15). For what is life, as Emma asks, without "beautiful radiant things"? What is life if we cannot see that Anna Halprin, dancing at age eighty, is beautiful? What is life if we cannot see ourselves, at any age, as part of the earth rather than isolated from her or in dominion over her? If we truly engage students in critical thinking, we must ask these questions, creating classroom occasions in which to explore them in depth. My coteacher and I raise such questions each time we teach "Changing Our Stories." Through the study of a range of genres—letters, memoirs, poetry, autobiography, myth, fiction, criticism, and theory—we show that the boundaries between poetry and criticism are not great, despite the fact that, in our class-conscious academy, theory is privileged over poetry, writing over teaching, and mind over body. These hierarchies create jealousy, according to Valerie Miner, who says: "Some scholars are jealous of writers—and irritated they spend so much of their lives writing about writers. Witness the new vogue in literary criticism as veiled autobiography" (83). Miner may be right, but I prefer to think that autobiographical criticism has emerged, instead, out of a desire to transgress and transform hierarchies of genre and class. I yearn to think in terms of an inclusive circle-dance rather than in terms of the familiar choreography of competition.

April 2001. *Shortly after we complete our study of Audre Lorde's* Zami: A New Spelling of My Name, *including a report on* The Cancer Journals, *my teamteacher learns that she has had a recurrence of breast cancer. On a Tuesday, she tells me about her biopsy; the next day she informs me that the tumor is malignant; that Friday she has a lumpectomy. The following Monday I give students the good news; tests results show that all the cancer has been removed. As my colleague begins chemotherapy, she is optimistic.*

The changes that have taken place in our department during this academic year are challenging my ability to evolve into a generative mentor of young faculty. For example, because we have many new, research-active faculty in our department and because we do not have a budget that provides for more course releases for research, tenured faculty must teach an extra course every other year, regardless of their productivity as scholars. This increase in my teaching load will provide untenured faculty with an automatic one-course release during their first five years. Under our old competitive system, I always won a one-course research release, which meant that I taught only two courses each semester. To be blunt: If I am to remain a generative faculty member, I must also have support for my creative work and, in my view, the university should support both young and aging faculty. Sadly, I can do nothing about this problem—except to resist displacing my frustration and anger onto younger members of the department.

An even more severe challenge to my goal of becoming a generative feminist professor has been created by the recent shortfall in the state budget. For our department, the effects of the budget cuts are severe: (1) the number of students in English 339, "Literary Theory and Criticism," has been increased from twenty to twenty-five; (2) one section of "Twentieth-Century Fiction" will be cut, which means, quite possibly, that I will teach first-year writing instead; and (3) all tenure-line professors are now expected to "volunteer" to tutor for two hours a week in the Writing Center. There is also talk of a furlough for all faculty, which means that in December we may not receive pay for one week's work. In a recent meeting on the topic of mentoring, the provost began with a summary of the budget crisis—whose results, since the state legislature remains in session, are still unknown—but he did not address the problems of mentoring that would be created by the budget cuts. "Mentors will have to work harder," he answered when I asked, "What would you recommend that mentors do to address the morale problem that is already beginning to affect retention?" This suggestion is not particularly helpful to mentors who, like me, are already facing the exodus of young, untenured faculty. Moreover, the provost's reply does not acknowledge that departments that do not have strong records of obtaining grants, such as ours, will suffer the most severe cuts. How, under these conditions, do we continue the generativity dance?

Confronted with increasing competition between young and old as resources dwindle, I wonder: Can the dance metaphor be sustained? As the competitive choreography intensifies, I am skeptical as I read Parker Palmer's dance metaphor: "Mentors and apprentices are partners in an ancient human dance, and one of teaching's great rewards is the daily chance it gives us to get back on the dance floor. It is the dance of the spiraling generations, in which the old empower the young with their experience and the young empower the old with new life, reweaving the fabric of the human community as they touch and turn" (25). How, I wonder, is this dance of mutual empowerment to take place under such dire budgetary conditions? Yet it is precisely this kind of crisis—as, for example, when the rains do not come, and the crops are threatened—that prompts the Laguna Pueblo to call on all their members, young and old, to participate in ceremonial dances. Such ceremonial dances, or rituals, are also central to the structure of Laguna Pueblo stories, as Paula Gunn Allen explains, whereas conflict is central to the structure of Euro-American stories. Perhaps, if I can resist viewing myself as competing with younger faculty, if instead I imagine women as mutually empowering dancers, new possibilities might emerge. In this receptive mood, I reflect on the revolutionary dance of feminists, young and old.

My first dance lesson comes from a former graduate student who, as a new temporary instructor, has just learned that she has lost her job as a result of the budget cuts at Iowa State. Despite this crisis and despite my more privileged and secure position, she has expressed no resentment toward me. Although I am powerless to save her job, her remarkable generosity prompts me to take some action on behalf of her and the many women like her. A second lesson comes from a young, idealistic feminist whom I first met during her three-year appointment as an adjunct assistant professor (without tenure) at Iowa State. Although she did find a tenure-line job elsewhere and has since become an assistant dean, she is so frustrated at her lack of administrative power that she is planning to leave the academy. She too inspires me with her generosity when, after hearing of my work on aging and teaching, she sends me a handout on "Teaching across the Generations," prepared for the Fifth Annual Faculty Development Conference (January 8, 2001). In this handout, Illene C. Noppe, whose title is "'I Age but the Students Don't': Musings of a Professor at Midlife," points out that the challenge for aging academics who wish to be generative, as Erikson recommends, is to achieve integrity as opposed to despair. I have felt despair as a result of the budget cuts, but thus far—with a little help from my friends—I am resisting its pull.

Another dancing lesson comes from Elyse Lord, who, although she has yet to find a tenure-line position, continues to collaborate with me. Recently, after reading an early draft of this chapter, Elyse suggested that both teachers and dancers experience the tension between "the novel/the new/the unexpected" and "the routine/inevitable/expected." This tension, she says, "mirrors the 'life art' tension of growing old (certain milestones seem inevitable, like thinking about cancer), yet of staying 'new'/young, by dancing!" Most important, despite the backlash against feminism—ever more apparent in the classroom—the revolutionary dance continues. The new president of our faculty senate, feminist historian Christie Pope, created a new committee on women and minorities, which has been active this past year. This committee has, for example, proposed a family-leave policy that is long overdue. Word has it that our new president is receptive to the plan. At the same time, the university will no longer encourage early retirement. Remarkably, despite the budget crisis, women continue to work, teach, and dance together, taking collective action on behalf of all women and their families.

March 21, 2002. One of my two best friends from high school has died of cancer. I grieve for her. Fortunately, my colleague in English has successfully completed chemotherapy with this "bonus": Her hair is now growing in very curly. Once again, we are team-teaching "Changing Our Stories," and we have added a novel, Gloria Naylor's Mama Day, *in which the major character is a powerful, aging woman. Miraculously, I am more energetic now than in 2000!*

The good news—of generative possibilities—keeps coming: I have been awarded a full year's sabbatical for 2002–2003 to begin a project on photography and women's narratives. Best of all, I am still family dancing, most recently at Cancun during spring break. I used to say: "In my next life, I plan to be a dancer." Now

I see that my wish is being fulfilled in this life. While orchestrating my daily activities, crying, laughing, working, playing, striving for a harmonious tempo of teaching and writing, family and friends, I dance the pages of my life.

WORKS CITED

Allen, Paula Gunn. *The Sacred Hoop: Recovering the Feminine in American Indian Traditions*. Boston: Beacon, 1986.

Chernin, Kim. *In My Mother's House: A Daughter's Story*. New York: Ticknor and Fields, 1983.

Cheuse, Alan. "O Body Swayed." *New Letters: A Magazine of Writing and Art* 66.4 (2000): 9–36.

Circlot, J. E. *A Dictionary of Symbols*. Trans. Jack Sage. New York: Routledge and Kegan Paul, 1962.

Cisneros, Sandra. *The House on Mango Street*. New York: Vintage, 1989.

Cixous, Hélène, and Catherine Clement. *The Newly Born Woman*. Trans. Betsy Wing. Minneapolis: U of Minnesota, 1986.

Daly, Brenda, and Maureen T. Reddy, eds. *Narrating Mothers: Theorizing Maternal Subjectivities*. Knoxville: U of Tennessee P, 1991.

Edwards, Julie Olsen. "Class Notes from the Lecture Hall." *Liberating Memory: Our Work and Our Working-Class Consciousness*. Ed. Janet Zandy. New Brunswick, N.J.: Rutgers UP, 1995. 317–58.

Elder, Arlene A. "'Dancing the Page:' Orature in M. Scott Momaday's *The Way to Rainy Mountain*." *Narrative* 7.3 (October 1999): 272–88.

Erikson, Erik H. *Insight and Responsibility: Lectures on the Ethical Implications of Psychoanalytic Insight*. New York: Norton, 1964.

Estes, Clarissa Pinkola. "The Dancing Grandmas." *Common Boundary* (Mar./Apr. 1993): 38–40.

Fetterley, Judith. *The Resisting Reader: A Feminist Approach to American Fiction*. Bloomington: Indiana UP, 1978.

Hazzard-Gordon, Katrina. *Jookin': The Rise of Social Dance Formations in African-American Culture*. Philadelphia: Temple UP, 1990.

Leavitt, David. "Family Dancing." *Family Dancing*. New York: Houghton Mifflin, 1983, 1984. 117–42.

Marquart, Deb. "Teachable Metaphors: Articulating Metaphors: Articulating Difficult Concepts and Abstract Ideas through Metaphor." *Teaching at ISU* 12.4 (Apr./May 2001): 1–4.

Miner, Valerie. "Writing and Teaching with Class." *Working-Class Women in the Academy: Laborers in the Knowledge Factory*. Ed. Michelle M. Tokarczyk and Elizabeth A. Fay. Amherst: U of Massachusetts P, 1993. 73–86.

Moore, Lorrie. "Dance in America." *Birds of America*. New York: Knopf, 1999. 47–57.

Morris, David B. *The Culture of Pain*. Berkeley: U of California P, 1991.

Morrison, Toni. *Beloved*. New York: Knopf, 1988.

Northrup, Christiane, M.D. *Women's Bodies, Women's Wisdom: Creating Physical and Emotional Health and Healing*. New York: Bantam, 1994.

Oates, Joyce Carol. *Do with Me What You Will*. New York: Vanguard, 1973.

Palmer, Parker J. *The Courage to Teach: Exploring the Inner Landscape of a Teacher's Life*. San Francisco: Jossey-Bass, 1998.

Rich, Adrienne. *Of Woman Born: Motherhood as Institution and Experience*. New York: Norton, 1976.

Shulman, Alix Kates, ed. and comp. *Red Emma Speaks: An Emma Goldman Reader*. 3rd ed. Atlantic Highlands, N.J.: Humanities, 1996.

Silko, Leslie Marmon. *Storyteller*. New York: Arcade, 1981.

Spelman, Elizabeth V. *Inessential Woman*. Boston: Beacon, 1988.

Wagner, Ann. *Adversaries of Dance: From the Puritans to the Present*. Urbana: U of Illinois P, 1997.

Wyatt, Jean. "On Not Being La Malinche: Border Negotiations of Gender in Sandra Cisneros's 'Never Marry a Mexican' and 'Woman Hollering Creek.'" *Tulsa Studies in Women's Literature* 14 (Fall 1995): 243–71.

Enforcing Diversity and Living
with Disability: Learning from
My First Teaching Year

Ray Pence

I enter my eighth year as a graduate teaching assistant carrying two bundles of experiences associated with my first classrooms and students. What I have learned from teaching introductory composition and literature courses at two Midwestern universities, living with chronic illness, and immersion in disability studies grounds this exploration of those experiences. There may be no relationships between the experiences other than chronological ones. Though I am unsure of the presence and significance of connections, I believe that searching for them will be productive for my audience and for me even if it does not result in a seamless statement. Because they have shown me that bodies are as important as minds in pedagogical and scholarly activities, the experiences I address here have made the largest contributions to my identity.

Reflecting on these contributions takes me into territory that should be familiar for many readers (teaching situations complicated by race issues) and to less well known places (daily life with a rare condition that is more felt by the afflicted than seen by the well).

One experiential bundle consists of efforts to enforce diversity that accompanied my interactions with the few African American students in courses I taught during the 1994–1995 academic year, my introduction to teaching and to graduate school. I was pursuing an M.A. in English literature at a public but selective (one could say exclusive) university in a rural corner of the Midwestern United States that lacked the diversity celebrated in my department's common syllabus for composition and literature classes. At that time I saw diversity solely in ethnic and racial terms and believed the syllabus reinforced my perception.[1] When those who I expected to embody diversity in my classes—black male students—showed what I thought was insufficient interest, I panicked. Without them, the inclusiveness and critical bite represented in the syllabus by bell hooks, Cornel West, and similar "Others" would go unappreciated, as would my commitment to an agenda I saw in the syllabus. Though I was uncertain about how much authority I had and uncomfortable using it, I could not curb my desires to reach these students of color and ensure their presence. Predictably, the more I sought to make them part of my project, the more they eluded and resisted me. Under pressure from me, the black male students of my first teaching year—all three of them—finally withdrew from the courses. Their reactions showed more relief than resentment; I was left with no teaching energy but a surplus of frustration.

By displacing race onto "minorities," I made a mistake that Nancy J. Peterson suggests is common among white teachers (39). I wish I had been ready for her argument that whites ought to make racial categories personal and political by recognizing we are people of race even if we are not people of color and by interrogating our privileges. My first students and I would have been productively challenged if the syllabus and situation had fostered critical inquiry into the whiteness most of us represented. Peterson's perspective is compelling because she and I share privileges and problems. Both of us are white, heterosexual, middle-class instructors who ask students on Midwestern (mostly white and conservative) campuses to read multicultural texts. Peterson's recollection in "Redefining America: Literature, Multiculturalism, Pedagogy" of how her pregnancy (with its reassuring heterosexual subtext) may have made Adrienne Rich safe for students is resonant (33). I often think my race allows white students to cope with texts by poets such as Amiri Baraka and Sonia Sanchez, whose anger and agency apparently do not frighten their teacher. If I can withstand the assaults of such work and live to analyze it, perhaps they can, too.

Where Peterson helps me know myself as a teacher, Michelle Fine has changed the way I think about my writing identity and practice. In her essay "Working the Hyphens: Reinventing Self and Other in Qualitative

Research," Fine presents a case that resembles Peterson's in its debt to bell hooks. Many white narrators with college educations and middle class locations—including Fine herself, as she reminds the reader more than once—are committed to "Othering" but not to analyzing their own identities and interests. It is easier to write about or for those whose gender, race, and class identities are associated with subjugation, "banishing them to the margins of the culture." But as its title suggests, Fine's essay looks for ways out of the Othering trap: "When we construct texts collaboratively, self-consciously examining our relations with/for/despite those who have been contained as Others, we move against, we enable resistance to, Othering" (139).

Though I have participated in "the construction and distancing of Others" by writing this version of what happened during my first teaching year (Fine 131), I also have sought the critical self-reflection Fine advocates. Skin privilege and a measure of institutional prestige give me relative freedom to write what I please and the chance to reach an audience. In spite of its focus on my subject position as narrator, observer, and participant, this story reproduces and reinforces unequal power relations between me and student Others in my past. But as Fine insists, stories like this are also occasions for "working the hyphen" that both links and separates the researcher and the subject, the teacher and the taught, and the writer and the written about (135). Eliminating "structures of domination" in this narrative may be impossible (153); searching for their sources in society and in myself is imperative.

Reviewing my campaign to enforce diversity made me return to a question I have avoided for a long time and that may be on readers' minds as well. Were black males the only "problem students" I had that first year? Of course not. Several white students also disregarded my course policies and showed little or no interest in my approach. But as I saw things then, shaped by a pedagogical climate that prioritized diversity, my narrow definition of the concept, and a lack of classroom management skills, I had to intervene to save my African American students from an education without my course.

As I have indicated, the concept and consciousness of whiteness were not part of my thinking. Now that such awareness is central to my teaching, I wonder what difference it might have made during my first year. I am asking better questions that require students to reflect on assumptions they may have about the race of authors and of characters in texts and on their own raced reading responses. Do they conclude that third-person omniscient narrators have no race or create no racially exclusive audiences? Do they see fictional authority figures like doctors, lawyers, and teachers as white men until they learn otherwise? Is it a coincidence that many texts they call "boring"—which usually means that they find the subject insignificant and point of view frustrating—are by or about people of color and women? Without knowledge of whiteness as a default category that dominates but rarely asserts itself, I would not be posing such questions.

Ability is another category that is shaped by a society it structures. Living with disability, the second bundle of experiences I reflect on here, has showed me that ability and whiteness resemble one another in their composition and deployment. Just as people who are defined as white benefit from whiteness consciously and unconsciously, those who meet standards for sound bodies and minds enjoy the privileges of culture and society that practice ableism.

I started learning about ability and disability during my second teaching semester, a time when I pressured myself not to colonize black bodies to serve my notion of diversity. Avoiding that abuse of power while being confident in my ability to teach the fiction and poetry that were part of my spring 1995 syllabus was the key to improvement. However, it soon became clear that I would handle situations involving black male students even less effectively than I had in the fall. This time, my emphasis on African American literature justified paternalistic interventions. Sterling Brown, Langston Hughes, Gwendolyn Brooks, and Toni Morrison were on my reading list for English 112: Composition and Literature. Why weren't my black students coming to class and turning in their work? I tried to answer the question by calling the students, seeking help from their academic advisors, dropping them from the course, and then asking the director of the composition program to "force add" them back into the class after I could no longer live with my decision. Once again, anxieties about the absence and presence of black bodies determined my decisions and priorities.

It took grave conflict with my own body to keep the second semester from turning into a repeat performance of the first. Psoriatic arthritis (PA), a condition I had never heard of until I had no choice but to listen, did not free me from dealing with real or imagined student problems. But the farther I went into territory from which there is no escape—chronic illness—the more I realized the need for new strategies to face difficulties that would, like students themselves, come and go. The first part of this chapter was about what went wrong with my teaching while I was preoccupied with the bodies of certain students; the rest addresses what happened when PA arrived to bring my body into my teaching. To tell the story I must take on the role of a patient who needs to define his illness experiences not for doctors but for himself.[2]

The first symptoms showed up on my scalp. What I assumed was stubborn dandruff turned out to be psoriasis—more of an annoyance than a concern, I thought then.[3] Later, the red and scaly spots spread to my arms, buttocks, legs, and lower back. Psoriasis changed the nails on my fingers and toes, which developed pits, thickened, and crumbled. Before that, I detected other symptoms beneath my skin. Their randomness made them especially disturbing. Though I was feeling progressively worse, there was nothing linear about learning I was sick. Stomach pains that woke me up before sunrise were the first alarming symptoms. After I got out of bed and moved about, with difficulty but determination—I had to meet my class on time and with a sense of purpose—the pains would subside. This would have been reassuring were it not for the persistent soreness and stiffness in my right foot and ankle, and eventually in my lower back, that made getting dressed, walking, and using stairs into struggles. Fortunately I had health insurance for the first time in my life, so I made full use of the campus clinic.[4] Initially doctors were confident I had tendonitis, which did not scare me, and then ankylosing spondylitis, which did. I had never heard of this condition with its name like a poisonous insect, nor did I know of Reiter's syndrome, which is known today as reactive arthritis, until a doctor used it to label my symptoms. The search for a name for what I was feeling marked the beginning of a process of redefining myself in an unequal collaborative relationship with physicians.

Confused and upset as I was, calling these assessments misdiagnoses would not have been fair to those who made them. Like PA, the three conditions I turned out not to have are systemic rheumatic illnesses covered by the umbrella term *spondyloarthropathies* (Shiel 1). When people ask what my disability is (a common occurrence because it is obvious to others only during flare-ups), I usually tell them I have arthritis. This does not mean much because it can mean *too* much: There are more than one hundred kinds of rheumatic disease (Theodosakis et al. 207). Saying that I have PA is more accurate and specific but still insufficient. PA takes five different forms: asymmetric polyarthritis, symmetric polyarthritis, arthritis mutilans, distal interphalangeal joints (DIP), and ankylosing spondyloarthropathy (Birks 1–2). Because my symptoms correspond to four of these five variants, I still am unsure of the PA category I belong to. Though I have help from medical authorities and loved ones, learning the truth about PA is a solitary process because it is a rare condition that affects fewer than three million people in the United States (American College of Rheumatology 1; Birks 1). My health condition is marginalized even if I am not. There are no best-selling books offering cures or prevention of PA; I have never met a fellow "sufferer" (though I have found friendship with people who have other forms of arthritis, all of them women).

I would not begin learning all of this information until I received a definite PA diagnosis in the summer of 1998, more than three years after initial symptoms. To find out what the symptoms meant I made several disorienting visits to a local hospital whose specialists took over when the campus clinic could do no more. A gastrointestinal doctor looked for explanations of my stomach problems and anemia with upper and lower GIs and X rays.[5] Many of the procedures took place during the midmorning hours, just after I had finished teaching. In spite of the pain of my symptoms and the fear that went with the tests, I missed just one day of teaching and one seminar meeting and was proud that I had upheld the Protestant work ethic my father embodied.[6] The gastrointestinal specialist was also working hard but could find nothing wrong for all of his effort. Though my perception was clouded by sedatives that helped me through the lower GI, I can recall with clarity his frustrated tone when he told me I must go to a rheumatologist.

This was a turning point. My stomach pains had faded away, but my joints were worse than ever, and more of them were falling prey to the unknown assailant. While teaching sometime in April 1995, I tried to turn my head to face the students who sat to either side of me in our discussion circle but could not do so without agonizing effort. Other movements I had taken for granted brought unwelcome surprises. I learned to dread dropping things because I had to squat slowly and stiffly to retrieve them; bending from the waist became a faint memory. Plugging in an overhead projector or VCR triggered pain that shot from my elbow to my shoulder. Rising from a chair after just a few minutes created "locking" sensations in my lower back and ankles, which often did not feel as if they were there to support my decreasing weight.

Talking about these symptoms with my peers was an activity I usually avoided, in contrast to my compulsive discussions of problems with enforcing diversity (especially when the topic was "our" African American students). As for revealing to my students what I saw as physical and emotional weaknesses, this was out of the question. Our classroom environment, tense from the beginning because of the demeanor I adopted in reaction to the fall semester, had no camaraderie or trust. As the end of the semester neared, my symptoms intensified, and I struggled to be a minimally effective pedagogical presence. Students were less enthusiastic with each assignment and more willing to challenge me rudely. In bitter moments I told myself—and believed—that some of them would be happy to know I was ill.

Another side to being sick and scared helped me through the semester and revealed a new direction for the future. Jane Tompkins has written of times when teachers must let go and stop wanting too much from themselves and their students (659). Such a time arrived for me in the late spring of 1995. Chronic illness pushed me toward the goal Tompkins describes with remarkable simplicity and awareness of what keeps teachers from caring for themselves. My perfectionist expectations were dominating my teaching and living until PA altered my reference frame. Illness imposed limits on me in some ways; in others it freed me to identify and address pedagogical difficulties that immobilized me even more than my most painful symptoms did. With PA, there were more important things to worry about than whether students adhered to my course policies. Hard as it was, I had to allow students to be responsible for problems they created for themselves. The stress of taking on the burdens of students was a luxury I could no longer afford.

Readers may wonder whether this stress, along with the anger, fear, and despair brought on by enforcing diversity during my first and second semesters, had anything to do with the onset of my PA. I have thought and worried about possible links and still do, though no clinical evidence suggests that stress triggers or increases the chances of getting PA. Now that I have lived and taught with PA for more than six years, I know from experience that emotional turmoil intensifies whatever symptoms I have, especially when that turmoil is associated with or generated inside the classroom.

But what interests me more than probable or certain connections between my reactions to teaching situations and my PA is the way my illness experiences are situated, culturally and socially. The postmodern theoretical context Arthur W. Frank uses in his study of the emerging genre of life writing about illness in *The Wounded Storyteller: Body, Illness, and Ethics* was also a setting for my initiation into the world of PA. Though I knew almost nothing about critical inquiries into whiteness and disability that were starting to attract widespread attention at around the same time I was getting ill, I was aware of the postmodern thought that influenced those inquiries. My first year of graduate school was an immersion in antifoundational philosophy that showed me the importance of Michel Foucault's analyses of institutional power and medical and clinical discourses. At the time I resisted much of what I read because it challenged my investment in humanism and Marxism. Later I realized that this difficult, disorienting thought had prepared me to interrogate the medical model of disability, which locates defects in individual bodies and their remedies in modern scientific practices. Chronic illness helped me find something useful in postmodern philosophy; postmodern philosophy made me want to assess my illness and myself as a life writer.

Acknowledging that PA has made me see things in postmodernism I did not notice before becoming ill is hard to do without turning this story into a variation on the theme of disability as a character builder. My main interest as a narrator is relationships between my body and mind, whose cohesion has been made clear to me by feminism, postmodernism, and PA. With its emphasis on postmodern critical theory, my first year of graduate school showed me sites for exercising agency and asserting identity I had not known. Becoming ill that same year was the beginning of moving toward such a site as a person with disability. Discovering disability studies was finding the site itself, a place where I can begin to make sense of how PA contributes to my social position, relationships, and responsibilities. Few concepts are more important to disability studies than the medical epistemology that the field challenges but cannot escape any more than people can be outside capitalism, heterosexism, patriarchy, and racism. Knowing about that model and its critique is one of the many empowering benefits of knowing about disability studies. In sum, disability studies manages my symptoms as much as Naproxen pills and Methotrexate shots do,[7] and this is a story of converging factors, not of causes and effects.

I have not always been as eager to share my story as I am now and wish I had kept a journal during the onset of PA. Comparing my initial reactions to PA with the perspective I have as a participant in two interdisciplinary fields, one dedicated to bringing disability to the attention of the humanities and the other committed to explaining change and conflict in the United States, would be useful. With its emphasis on life writing by people with disabilities who also theorize disability as scholars, disability studies is a community and context for stories like this. Fortunately, the flexibility that American studies and disability studies share should make the former field an additional space for disability narratives and help overcome past inattention to disability. My own required coursework as a Ph.D. student in American studies, which began in 1997, included no courses that addressed disability. What bothered me more than this exclusion at a time when disability studies was emerging was my failure to notice it sooner, especially considering my PA. That American studies would include class, ethnicity, gender, race, and sexuality seemed natural to me. When I thought of disability as a subject of scholarly interest I confined it to applied fields such as occupational therapy and special education. Bound by medical model thinking, I had trouble seeing that American studies was not as inclusive as I had assumed.[8] But American studies was also where I found peers and teachers who pointed me toward Simi Linton and Rosemarie Garland-Thomson, who urge dialogue between disability studies and American studies (Linton 2–3; Garland-Thomson, "Incorporating" 1).[9] Now I work on making the bulk of my reading and writing contribute to that conversation.

In the months between the end of my first and start of my second year in American studies, another convergence of factors served as catalyst for change. My PA was flaring up after what I had thought was a long remission, making getting up from sitting positions and walking hard. I was sorting through the social constructionist ideas about categories such as ethnicity, gender, and race that were woven throughout my first year of seminars. Then came news of one of 1998's pivotal U.S. Supreme Court decisions. The majority opinion in Bragdon v. Abbott held that HIV-positive persons are covered by the Americans with Disabilities Act (ADA). Learning that disability was, more than anything, a definition—in this case, people who were often perceived as living under a death sentence became people with disabilities, finding agency in national policy—made me want to continue thinking about disability in relation to my personal and professional identities.[10] Far from being the well informed citizen I wanted to be, I knew next to nothing about what being HIV-positive means and was conscious of the ADA for the first time, eight years after its passage. I would learn later that the ADA definition is more in harmony with the minority and social models of disability than with the medical model because it acknowledges both official documentation and interpersonal perception of disability. Knowing about this definition made me want to redefine myself as someone seeking to eliminate his ignorance of disability, its social construction, and its relevance to his own experience.[11]

I was struck by how the definition fits what I have known with PA, which does indeed substantially limit one or more of my major life activities. But while the ADA defines me as a person with a disability, I rarely do. Cultural and social emphases on striking visual disability markers are part of the reason. Only by stopping my medicine and making special effort to reveal my psoriasis can I make my PA known in a public way. There are no obvious signs—such as a cane or wheelchair—of authentic, official disability on or associated with my body. However, the absence of these markers has helped me avoid discrimination and prejudice along with making my disability identity ambiguous. I have never attended an academic conference devoted to disability studies and worry about how my claim of disability would be perceived and received. As a white heterosexual man who is far more comfortable than most of the planet's people no matter how much he complains about his wages as a teacher and tutor, perhaps I am not one of James I. Charlton's "us."[12]

Being oppressed and silenced is an experience I have not known and do not expect to know. But it is better to recognize my reservations about my identity and make them part of this narrative than to let them keep me from writing. If I do not, I cannot feel like a member of the support group I have found in disability narrators or add my voice to what Frank calls "testimony" (137). Though I never anticipated that analyses and stories from scholars of disability in Canada and Britain would be useful or even acceptable within American studies, their influence is something I value. For example, debates over social model theory within disability studies in Britain address questions about impairment's definition and value as a critical concept. Because I often think of PA more as an impairment than a disability for reasons explained earlier, this debate helps me interrogate my own definitions and rationale for separating disability and impairment and taking the former more seriously than the latter.[13] Another compelling element of dialogues on impairment within British disability studies is how they appear to be split along gender lines. Liz Crow, for instance, advocates a resurgence of interest in impairment, which she connects with a feminist emphasis on the personal as political. This is an alternative to the exclusive concern with materialist critiques of social structures and how they disable impaired people that Crow finds in Michael Oliver's work.[14]

Susan Wendell is another feminist scholar interested in challenging materialist emphasis on social structure over personal experience. Her book *The Rejected Body: Feminist Philosophical Reflections on Disability* also challenges feminism by proposing "transcendence of the body" (165). Wendell, who writes candidly about her chronic illness, is not always clear and consistent in defining and arguing for transcendence. But her exploration of the paradoxes of pain and its consequences is original. "Experiences of the body," Wendell observes, "can teach consciousness a certain freedom from the suffering and limitations of the body" (172). The critical stance we take toward our bodies cannot be separated from our bodies, but this does not mean we cannot perceive them with the objectivity materialists bring to their critiques of disabling social structures. Acknowledging the social contexts within which pain is intelligible, Wendell refuses to concede that pain requires a context. She suggests that some bodily conditions are difficult no matter what the context, and her point reached me because few people ever see the pain in my joints or, to be accurate, its consequences.

Reading Wendell and others with a feminist location in disability studies helps me know the gendered character of my PA experience, just as reflective writing reveals that my teaching body is as raced as the Others in whom I saw little but race. Years of the privilege not to think about how my own body was situated within constructions such as able, male, and white shaped my perceptions of and reactions to my problems as a new teacher. This freedom from something was perhaps the greatest of the benefits that accompanied my subject position. Dealing with race was easy for me as an undergraduate English major who could feel as good about his absence of prejudice toward black people as he could about his abilities to analyze their literature. I did not have to think about the realities of who and who is not empowered until I had, and had to use, institutional power. Nor did I have to think about PA—or other forms of arthritis, or chronic illness in general—because I did not fit the cultural profile of people who are affected by such conditions. The only arthritis narrative I had before becoming ill was made up of images and messages from television advertisements. Commercials featuring little old ladies who complained of not being able to knit and who eventually were rescued (to the relief of their families) by various pills with reassuring brand names represented my knowledge and ignorance of arthritis. It was not my problem, nor would it be.

Giving up the privilege of involuntarily ignoring arthritis has meant gaining valuable new perspectives. I admit that I would rather not be chronically ill, but I also do not want to return to the thinking that was changed through living with PA. Definitions of diversity and identity that I brought to my pedagogy were not quite real to me until I began acting according to them in the classroom. Understanding diversity solely in ethnic and racial terms, and mostly in black and white, was no understanding at all. Now I recognize that diversity embraces as many categories as there are people and that disability is among them. This has been good for me and for my students—instead of enforcing diversity, I am interested in exploring it. The course I currently teach, an introduction to the methods and goals of American studies, lets me do that by offering the life writing of disability narrators Helen Keller and Lewis B. Puller, Jr., along with the autobiographies of Frederick Douglass and Maxine Hong Kingston.[15] Acknowledging disability must be part of any course titled "Understanding America."

An inclusive syllabus is a simple way to avoid returning to the narrow diversity definition of my past. Being attentive to the presence and absence of students with disabilities is more complicated and crucial. Over the past seven years my courses have been those that degree-seeking students take because they must and consequently are excellent sites for assessing campus diversity. As the reader knows, students of color are vastly outnumbered in the institutions where I have worked. Students with disabilities are usually not represented at all. Though a small handful of my students have had learning disabilities such as dyslexia, not one blind student or deaf student or wheelchair-using student has come through my door.[16] People with disabilities and topics related to them were as invisible in the classes I taught as they were in seminars I took. In both cases I was too slow to recognize these disturbing realities, which showed me just how much I was a part of ableism.

There will always be one person with a disability in any classroom where I am teaching, but I anticipate retaining control over visibility of my PA, which seems to have stabilized, well into the future. On the few occasions when I have revealed my condition I have done so out of curiosity about how the news will be received and not because I have been all that comfortable doing so. One reason is the limits on how much of myself I will share with students who for the most part would rather be other places than my class. Perhaps things will change when I teach graduate students. Another reason is my reluctance to present myself to anyone as a person with a disability because I do not meet unofficial, informal, but nevertheless powerful public criteria. When I stand before my students I am passing as an able-bodied person, one who knows he should not reinforce social standards for competence and control. This says more about how I perceive my students than about the students themselves, but I feel I must avoid speaking of or showing my disability lest I lose authority. There have, of course, been exceptions to my silence. Sometimes I will give my perspective as a person with arthritis (not PA) when we encounter characters with a form of that condition. Just as it was crucial for me to overcome my ignorance about arthritis and whom it does and does not affect, it is important for students to see that many people who appear to be healthy do not always feel that way. In general, however, I have incorporated disability into my courses not by talking about myself but by making sure it is a category and a subject that deserves attention in its own right and in conjunction with other topics.

Like my understanding of diversity and disability, the way I think of identity has become more complex during my seven years of graduate study, teaching, and chronic illness. Knowing that my social roles are made possible within and on the terms of institutions is the key to that change. As a new teacher I was interested in African American students mostly because I wanted to confine them to a constructed category they apparently fit. An educational institution legitimized my efforts, and institutionalized medicine sanctions my doctor's interest in me as a PA patient. To put it another way, black students were important to me because they were not white and I am important to my doctor because I am not, in his words, normal. There are dramatic differences between situations involving my students and me and those involving my doctor and me. But his authority and mine occupy a similar space. Neither one of us always knows the people we deal with professionally as whole persons. If we could learn to do that while reflecting critically on our own authority and how disciplines make it—and us—possible, I am sure there would be many benefits for us and those we say we serve. Maybe the only significant difference between my doctor and me is that I have opportunities to make assessments of my professional identity part of that identity—by writing this essay, for example. I am also writing for purely personal, even selfish reasons: to convince myself that even though I was not ready for teaching or chronic illness, what matters more are my reactions to those transforming experiences. I want to know that I am currently doing the right things in the classroom and in my scholarly work. But my uncertainty, like my PA, will remain a chronic condition.

NOTES

1. The syllabus for English 111, College Composition, had five units: reflective narrative, institutional knowledge, argument, discourse analysis, and cultural texts. Two course goals were demonstrating that language is value-positive and actively shapes experience and subjectivity and showing that the human subject is not the humanist subject: autonomous, integrated, and rational. The English 111 syllabus was, to use terms I was learning at the time, a social-constructionist rather than an expressivist syllabus.

2. This self-definition is a key concern of narrators such as Nancy Mairs, Robert Murphy, and Irving Kenneth Zola. Their stories have provided me with invaluable examples of how to explore roles of the teacher and of the scholar with disabilities. I am particularly impressed with how these writers explore disability's intersections with class, ethnicity, gender, race, and sexuality.

3. At that time I did not know that psoriasis precedes arthritis symptoms in most PA cases, sometimes by years.

4. My health insurance plan expired when my time at the university where I earned an M.A. ended. I have been unable to purchase a new plan because of prohibitive costs associated with my preexisting condition and my age (thirty-eight).

5. Upper and lower GIs are procedures in which doctors search for evidence of gastrointestinal disease: polyps and tumors, for example. The procedures involve inserting long, thin apparatuses resembling hoses into patients orally (upper GI) and anally (lower GI).

6. Since that time I have not missed a teaching session because of my illness, though there have been times when doing so would have been better for my students and for me.

7. Naproxen is a type of nonsteroidal antiinflammatory medicine, a more potent form of over-the-counter products such as Aleve. Methotrexate is a toxic drug that was

developed to treat cancer but has been effective against arthritis and psoriasis. I have taken Naproxen since May 1995 but began Methotrexate in 1998. The lack of dramatic results with Methotrexate in my treatment may validate what physicians suspect is true: The medicine is most effective when prescribed during the earliest stages of PA and other forms of arthritis.

8. George Lipsitz's address to the 1994 American Studies Association, titled "No Shining City on a Hill," is an example of this neglect. Lipsitz argues energetically that his field should align itself with various social movements but emphasizes ethnicity and race to the exclusion of people with disabilities and their cultures.

9. I am also intrigued by Linton's and Garland-Thomson's inclusive disability definitions. For Garland-Thomson disability is "the attribution of corporeal deviance—not so much a property of bodies as a product of cultural rules about what bodies should be or do" (*ExtraordinaryBodies* 6). Linton avoids Garland-Thomson's stress on physical disability with a broader definition. Disability is "a marker of identity [that] has been used to build a coalition of people with significant impairments" and a category open to those with "behavioral or anatomical characteristics marked as deviant, and people who have or are suspected of having conditions . . . that make them targets of discrimination" (Linton 12).

10. My experience of being tested for HIV antibodies at the order of my first rheumatologist also made me attentive to the Bragdon v. Abbott decision. He explained his order by telling me that some of my symptoms, particularly joint soreness and stiffness, were common in relatively young men during the onset of AIDS.

11. The ADA covers people with physical and/or mental impairments that substantially limit one or more life activities, have a history or record of such impairment, or are perceived by others as being impaired (Illingworth and Parmet 3). The minority and social models locate disability in discriminatory cultural and social practice and structure.

12. The reference is to the title of Charlton's book *Nothing About Us Without Us: Disability Oppression and Empowerment.*

13. I have reservations about Oliver's disability definition, which he borrows from a British organization called the Union of Physically Impaired Against Segregation (UPIAS) but do acknowledge its influence. Quoting from the UPIAS definition, Oliver calls disability "the disadvantage or restriction of activity caused by a contemporary social organization" that acknowledges people with impairments only to exclude them from the mainstream (11). According to this definition, I am exempt from such exclusion because society does not know I have a serious impairment.

14. Crow argues that social model exponents such as Oliver "disable [themselves] by tackling only one side of [their] situation" when they focus on disability at the expense of impairment (211). According to Crow, impairment and disability need to be understood through an examination of their interdependence. The model of disability that is dominant in British social sciences reduces impairment to something that triggers disability and is not a priority for critical analysis, she maintains. Crow calls for a "renewed" social model that goes "beyond grand theory and into real life" by addressing personal experiences of impairment (223).

15. Keller's 1903 autobiography *The Story of My Life* exemplifies the "overcoming disability" narrative. The Pulitzer Prize-winning *Fortunate Son: The Autobiography of Lewis B. Puller, Jr.* may be better known as a Vietnam War memoir than as a disability narrative. Puller, who lost both legs and parts of both hands in combat, also struggled with alcoholism and committed suicide after his book won the Pulitzer Prize.

16. My language in this paragraph reinforces a false binary opposition between "students of color" and "students with disabilities." This is difficult to avoid but raises provocative questions about language's limits. In disability studies we need always to be sure our audience knows that addressing disability involves accounting for class, ethnicity, gender, race, sexuality, and other imperfect but still indispensable identity categories. It is especially important to remember that in many cases people of color are more likely to be people with disabilities than are whites.

Feminist scholars have taken the lead in raising incisive objections to uncritical acceptance of the categories I have mentioned. Barbara DiBernard draws an analogy between how the terms "person with a disability" and "woman" have been used to "falsely universalize" diverse groups of people (135).

WORKS CITED

American College of Rheumatology. "Psoriatic Arthritis Fact Sheet." <http: www. rheumatology.org>, 2000.

Birks, Kristen. "What Is Psoriatic Arthritis?" Missouri Arthritis Rehabilitation Research and Training Center. <http: www.muhealth.org>, 2001.

Charlton, James I. *Nothing About Us Without Us: Disability Oppression and Empowerment*. Berkeley: U of California P, 1998.

Crow, Liz. "Including All Our Lives: Renewing the Social Model of Disability." *Encounters with Strangers: Feminism and Disability*. Ed. Jenny Morris. London: Women's P, 1996. 206–26.

Denzin, Norman K., and Yvonna S. Lincoln, eds. *The Landscape of Qualitative Research: Theories and Issues*. Thousand Oaks, Calif.: Sage, 1998.

DiBernard, Barbara. "Teaching What I'm Not: An Able-Bodied Woman Teaches Literature by Women with Disabilities." *Teaching What You're Not: Identity Politics in Higher Education*. Ed. Katherine J. Mayberry. New York: New York UP, 1996. 131–54.

Fine, Michelle. "Working the Hyphens: Reinventing Self and Other in Qualitative Research." *The Landscape of Qualitative Research: Theories and Issues*. Ed. Norman K. Denzin and Yvonna S. Lincoln. Thousand Oaks, Calif.: Sage, 1998. 130–55.

Francis, Leslie P., and Anita Silvers, eds. *Americans with Disabilities: Exploring Implications of the Law for Individuals and Institutions*. New York: Routledge, 2000.

Frank, Arthur W. *The Wounded Storyteller: Body, Illness, and Ethics*. Chicago: U of Chicago P, 1995.

Garland-Thomson, Rosemarie. *Extraordinary Bodies: Figuring Physical Disability in American Culture and Literature*. New York: Columbia UP, 1997.

———. "Incorporating Disability Studies into American Studies." <http://www.georgetown.edu/crossroads/interests/ds-hum/thomson.html>, 2000.

Illingworth, Patricia, and W. E. Parmet. "Positively Disabled: The Relationship between the Definition of Disability and Rights under the ADA." *Americans with Disabilities: Exploring Implications of the Law for Individuals and Institutions.* Eds. Leslie P. Francis and Anita Silvers. New York: Routledge, 2000. 3–18.

Linton, Simi. *Claiming Disability: Knowledge and Identity.* New York: New York UP, 1998.

Keller, Helen. *The Story of My Life.* 1903. New York: Macmillan, 1964.

Lipsitz, George. "No Shining City on a Hill." *American Studies* 40.2 (1999): 53–70.

Mairs, Nancy. *Waist-High in the World: A Life among the Nondisabled.* Boston: Beacon, 1996.

Mayberry, Katherine J., ed. *Teaching What You're Not: Identity Politics in Higher Education.* New York: New York UP, 1996.

Morris, Jenny, ed. *Encounters with Strangers: Feminism and Disability.* London: Women's P, 1996.

Murphy, Robert. *The Body Silent.* New York: Holt, 1987.

Oliver, Michael. *The Politics of Disablement: A Sociological Approach.* New York: St. Martin's, 1990.

Peterson, Nancy J. "Redefining America: Literature, Multiculturalism, Pedagogy." *Teaching What You're Not: Identity Politics in Higher Education.* Ed. Katherine J. Mayberry. New York: New York UP, 1996. 23–46.

Puller, Lewis B., Jr. *Fortunate Son: The Autobiography of Lewis B. Puller, Jr.* New York: Grove Weidenfeld, 1991.

Shiel, William C. "Psoriatic Arthritis." SmartMed Site. <www.focusonarthritis.com>, 2001.

Theodosakis, Jason, Brenda Adderly, and Barry Fox. *The Arthritis Cure.* New York: St. Martin's, 1997.

Tompkins, Jane. "Pedagogy of the Distressed." *College English* 52.6 (1990): 653–60.

Wendell, Susan. *The Rejected Body: Feminist Philosophical Reflections on Disability.* New York: Routledge, 1996.

Zola, Irving Kenneth. *Missing Pieces: A Chronicle of Living with a Disability.* Philadelphia: Temple UP, 1982.

A "Sisterly Camaraderie" and
Other Queer Friendships:
A Gay Teacher Interacting
with Straight Students

Jonathan Alexander

In an insightful discussion of teaching, Michel Foucault tells us what almost every gay, lesbian, and bisexual teacher has come to know: "The fact that a teacher is homosexual can only have electrifying and intense effects on the students to the extent that the rest of society refuses to admit the existence of homosexuality" (144). And when the love that dare not speak its name opens its mouth in the university- or college-level classroom, things really start to get interesting. Indeed, putting aside our fears of personal and professional retaliation, as well as our own internalized homophobia about teachers recruiting students, many of us have decided to step out of the closet and into the classroom. And I think I can safely speak for the majority of my fellow queer teachers when I say that the experience has never been anything less than "electrifying and intense"—for all parties involved.

The stories we could tell.

And in fact the stories are being told. As we've thrown ourselves into the often-boiling cauldron of the classroom, many of us have had the presence of mind to reflect on what has occurred in the pressure-cooking process. Just a few years ago, in 1995, queer scholar and teacher Harriet Malinowitz could say, "Unfortunately, lesbian and gay studies, in my experience—and perhaps because it's still relatively new—has seemed the least interested in connecting its theoretical work and research with issues of pedagogy and student consciousness" (107). But we've come a long way since then. Numerous articles and books, from Toni McNaron's *Poisoned Ivy: Lesbian and Gay Academics Confronting Homophobia* to Rita M. Kissen's *The Last Closet: The Real Lives of Lesbian and Gay Teachers* and Malinowitz's own *Textual Orientations: Lesbian and Gay Students and the Making of Discourse Communities*, have traced the contours of the interactions between students and their openly queer professors. They also often detail the ways in which queer teachers can challenge the prejudices and bigotries of homophobia and heterosexism in their classrooms.[1]

Indeed, many queer scholars and teachers are beginning to realize that there are multiple pedagogical advantages to coming out in the classroom. For instance, in a recent article in *Feminist Teacher,* social psychologist Karen Yescavage and I reflect on our own experiences as openly queer professors, and we discuss how important it is for les-bi-gay teachers to come out—not just to foster gay visibility and become role models for les-bi-gay students but also to invite *all* students to "cast a critical gaze on . . . configurations of the sexual within our culture" (120). Specifically, in marking our sexual orientation, we encourage straight students (and faculty) to mark *their* sexual orientations and become aware of the ways in which sexuality is labeled, codified, and politicized in our society. At the simplest level, we postulate that, if the unexamined life is not worth living, then the unexamined heterosexual life, with latent homophobic attitudes left intact, could be lethal—as it has been, for instance, for Matthew Shepard and many other gays and lesbians.

Such theorizing, of course, speaks to a high level of personal investment in queer issues, and my initial publications about queer pedagogy coincided with my official coming out in 1996 at the University of Southern Colorado (USC) in Pueblo, where I taught English composition and literature from 1994 until 1998. In the intervening years I have frequently meditated on my own first steps out of the closet and into the classroom, with Foucault's words—"electrifying and intense effects"—coming to mind again and again. Specifically, I have marked the effect of my open queerness as a series of *bodily* sensations. Indeed, for nearly half a year after I first came out on campus, I would wake up every morning, a slight tension in my back and shoulders, and wonder, "What have I done to myself?" Surely part of my concern arose out of a very real fear for my body, particularly as openly gay men are frequently the objects of assault; indeed, before I left Colorado in September 1998, I had been the victim of a death threat, which made the murder of Matthew Shepard the following month all the more frightening.

Beyond such obvious fears for my physical well-being, though, I have begun to reflect on other ways in which my embodied queerness had some "intense effects" on my teaching and my relationships with my students. As higher educators we often think that our tasks are (or *should* be) purely mental ones, and we subscribe almost by default to the Cartesian split between the mind and the body. But recent scholarship about teaching has begun to articulate and explore the insight that pedagogy is never just an affair of the mind but also one of the body and even the heart. For instance, in *Vice Versa: Bisexuality and the Eroticism of Everyday Life*, Marjorie Garber puts forth the controversial notion that "It is [the] very potential for loving, and for falling 'in love,' that makes education possible" (324). Suggestively, her comments come in the middle of a chapter discussing bi-eroticism in the classroom, claiming that some subconscious erotic interest underlies most student/teacher interactions—across genders.

Although I have no accounts of students falling in love with me (or vice versa) to offer here, I *have* become increasingly aware of how bodies, and not just minds, are intrinsically a part of the student/teacher milieu in which I have worked and taught. Specifically, I am more and more conscious of how I use my body to move through the classroom, gesturing, touching students on the shoulder, and even jumping up and down or dancing to make a point. More personally, at USC I used my youthful body to connect with students—to dress in ways that would show them I was in touch with their generation and to shake hands in ways that they taught me—all in an effort to bond with them. Many of my students were first-generation college students, and they frequently felt uncomfortable in the classroom, unsure of what was expected or even how they should behave. To counter this, I tried (not always consciously) to approach my students in such a way that suggested that I was comfortable inhabiting their "space" and that I wanted them to be comfortable in my classrooms and as part of a collegiate student body. In the process I was often thought of as the "cool" teacher, one sensitive to and in tune with students' needs, interests, and concerns.

Interestingly, such appreciation from the student body was also at times focused more directly on *my* body—and what I was or was not doing with it. Most notably, before I came out of the closet, students would speculate about my romantic and sexual affiliations, while almost completely ignoring (in the realms of shared classroom discursive space at least) the possibility that I might be queer. Indeed, they often performed an amazing set of epistemological acrobatics, coupled with any number of rhetorical contortions, to resist seeing my potential queerness. For instance, students would at times make comments about how attractive certain female students were, or they even suggested that *I* found such and such a female student attractive; such discourse, I think, continued efforts to bond with me not just as a teacher but also as a potential friend, and although no student ever tried to "hook me up," their conversation was clearly intended to foster greater camaraderie. Male students in particular would often physically reach out to me, touch my clothing, shake my hand, and comfortably inhabit my personal space—all as an expression of their comfort with me. My public disclosure of my queerness, however, *shifted* responses to me—and my queer body—in some interesting ways. When students were faced with acknowledging the possibility that I am indeed queer, then their use of touch in communication changed in several ways, and the use of physical proximity to communicate (acknowledgement? comfort? respect?) generally ceased.

Other reactions, interestingly forming along gender lines, steadily became apparent to me. For instance, several of my male students were almost inevitably more distracted or problematized by my coming out, whereas very few female students revealed or displayed concern or consternation. According to studies of homophobia, this isn't particularly surprising. At the 1998 Joint Annual Meeting of the Society for the Scientific Study of Sexuality and the American Association of Sex Educators, Counselors, and Therapists, Steve L. Ellyson reported that homophobia among male college-age students has continued to be far more prevalent than that among female college-age students. Perhaps in an attempt to address their discomfort, many more of my male than female students pursued the subject of my queerness with me outside of class time. I had practically innumerable conversations with young male students desiring to talk with me about my queerness or homosexuality in general, but few female students have ever approached me to do the same. Certainly, many young women I taught probably *were* uncomfortable with homo- and bi-eroticism, and I'm sure many sought others out, including teachers, with whom to share or talk about their discomfort. But they generally did not process their reactions with me, leading me naively and prematurely to believe that my straight female students, for the most part, had little reaction to my queerness.

However, many of my young and middle-aged female students *were* reacting and responding—just differently. For instance, I was forming some fairly intense relationships—both professionally and personally—with several of my straight female students. After the students had taken the required courses I taught, many of them sought me out for coffee, dinner, beer, and then movies, parties, and other social events; when I asked why, many of these students reported that my friendliness, and to some extent even my queerness, made me interesting and "worth getting to know." Even though I'd navigated the transition from professional to personal relationship with several male students, the transition seemed to be occurring with greater rapidity with my female students. The shift in relationship also seemed fairly natural and unforced.

So, to explore this dynamic a bit more, I began a discussion about straight student/gay teacher friendship with several former students (three women and two men) and one former colleague—all of whom I had worked with at the University of Southern Colorado during the academic year 1997–1998. I had had each of the students in various writing classes, and in each case we had navigated the transition from student/teacher to friends. We E-mailed one another for several months (November 1998 to February 1999), and the discussion was very personally (and professionally) enlightening, prompting me to speculate about the way my openly acknowledged queerness played itself out in (and out of) the classroom.[2]

Almost immediately my students and I noticed some distinct trends generally common to both male and female students. First, there are many male and female students who found my queerness completely unremarkable. Allyn, a straight male student with whom I've maintained E-mail correspondence, reported that "I wouldn't say that your presence affected me. I had my thoughts after a few classes that you might be 'playing for the other team'[;] it didn't bother me then and once I found out for sure it still didn't bother me. I'm not some lame piece of shit homophobe." Interestingly, I remember Allyn being pretty "touchy-feely," very willing to engage me physically by shaking my hand, touching my shoulder, bumping up against me with a friendly push—as though he were letting me know that he is indeed "not some . . . homophobe." Similarly, Michele, a straight female, compared me to several straight teachers and noted that we "are similar in most ways"; many other students I've spoken to have corroborated her feeling.

Inevitably, though, there were students—both male and female—who wanted to keep their distance from me. For these students the openly queer teacher seemed too much of a proselytizer seeking potential converts. One of my former students reported what she felt was a typically—and regrettably all too common—homophobic response, replete with images of recruitment:

> Before I even had my first classroom experience w/you, I heard a lot from other people, though. When I compared classes w/my friends they told me quite a bit of stuff. Someone told me "Oh, that guy's a fag!" An older student told me that you were out to convert everyone. He told me to "watch out" for you. He also said if he ever had a class w/you he would be arguing w/you all of the time because he didn't agree w/your lifestyle.

In general I experienced this kind of reaction much more from my male students than my female students, as though my queer body contained homocontagions that had to be quarantined lest they infect others. I distinctly remember, however, one female student who rushed from my classroom after making a snide comment about homosexuals; one of her friends leaned over and told her that I, the teacher, was gay—which precipitated her hasty departure. But she came back next class and completed the course, eventually writing a paper about homophobia in women's sports. I'm sure other straight women wanted to rush from my classes and may even have avoided taking my courses in the first place, but in my experience this was much more likely to be the response of a (generally) young straight male student. Notice that I say "(generally) young"; age was definitely a factor since almost every one of my older, nontraditional students—both male and female—seemed all but indifferent to my sexual orientation.

Finally, some students treated my open queerness as an opportunity to become more familiar with and even more comfortable with diverse individuals. A male student, Timmy, said,

> I find myself increasingly considering, and trying to be respectful about considering, people's lifestyles. This is a direct result of getting to know you, and knowing that you are gay . . . your sexuality pushed my unconscious bias to the forefront of my mind, and forced me to acknowledge it as prejudice.

Such comfort generally occurred only as students resolved their cognitive dissonance about my queerness—a dissonance that arose, I think, out of the conflict between, on one hand, their identification with nonsexual features or aspects of my personality or life and, on the other hand, the troubling unfamiliarity of my open queerness.

Resolving such cognitive dissonance seemed to be handled slightly differently by men and women. For example, Michelle initially found my announcement of my queerness to be distracting, but she also began noticing how straight teachers mark their straightness. She says,

> Generally, the instructor isn't there to discuss his sexual orientation though there are certainly times when it will come up. In comparing you [Jonathan] with Robert Burns—an English teacher, [who is] straight, . . . both of you were willing to discuss your sexual orientation.

Michelle noted, however, that I was more willing than others to discuss sexual orientation:

> Robert, for whatever reason, didn't seem to feel as compelled to do that and often refrained from discussing his personal life. I realize that there are probably some extenuating circumstances—things like personality and the content of personal relationships, but I think that Jonathan was more open about his sexual orientation because his "queerness" became the political platform that he used to move his career.

Two aspects of her comments interested me. First, she marked Robert's, the straight teacher's, discussion of his personal life as a discussion of sexual orientation—a move that acknowledged a diversity of sexual orientations and thus queried heteronormativity, or the automatic assumption of heterosexuality. I can't help but wonder whether my openly queer presence helped sensitize her to the fact that the discussion of one's personal life is a form of self-marking; it is in fact an assertion, even if not acknowledged as such, of sexual orientation identity. Second, Michelle viewed me as a "professional queer"— my queerness becoming perhaps a vehicle for my job and career. I think she is wise to intuit my "outness" as job related since such outness was (partly) intended to query the automatic assumption of heterosexuality in public realms such as the classroom.

Let me offer another example, drawn from my interactions with the male student who pursued out-of-class discussion with me because we were both born and raised in New Orleans. In general he thoroughly enjoyed reminiscing about our hometown—that is, until I came out in class. He still sought me out after class and visited during my office hours but not to reminisce. Instead, he attempted to convince me that homosexuality was caused by demons and that my mortal soul was in danger. I do not know how he resolved the dissonance he must have felt about me, but I do know that he went out of his way on several occasions to greet me in public, chat with me, and even shake my hand. The bodily contact seemed particularly important to him, perhaps because it was his way of demonstrating continued interest in me despite the troubling specter of my queerness. Although I don't think I prompted this student to change his notions about the demonic origin of certain sexualities, at the very least I think my willingness to talk with him and even treat his position with consideration prompted a civility all too rare in such discussions. And even though he and I, unlike Michelle and I, did not become good friends outside of the classroom, I am confident that he was learning to cope with diversity—and that is enough. I did have one similar experience, in terms of religion, with a female student—one whose Christianity troubled her attraction to me as a teacher. We had a long discussion about how I negotiated my queerness with the dictates of her Bible, but, once that was done, she felt free to associate with me publicly and even socially; she E-mails me to this day, pursuing a very cordial friendship.

Although it would be easy to explain such preoccupation with discussing my *queer* sexuality as an essentially homophobic response, other possible explanations are more telling and suggestive. Specifically, I have come to think that it is imperative for most students to suppress the teacher's sexuality—especially if it is particularly salient, as queer sexualities often are in our culture—in order to successfully accomplish the task of using us as surrogate parents or transferential figures in their ongoing family romances. Because we are, in many cases and to varying degrees, in loco parentis and thus continuing the roles that our students' parents or guardians held for them in their families of origin, our embodied sexualities must remain eclipsed, much as

Freud suggests that knowledge of parents' sexualities must be backgrounded in order for people to enter into sociality as it is constructed in our culture. Even though I wouldn't advance a purely Freudian reading of the pedagogical site, there is an insight here that is worth pondering; specifically, just as many of us do not enjoy thinking of our parents as sexual beings, our students do not usually enjoy thinking of *us* as sexual beings. I think the parallel exists because of the parental nature of many of our interactions with students—guiding them into adulthood and nurturing their progress toward maturity. In thinking along these lines, I am reminded of my work for our human relations committee at the University of Cincinnati, where, in considering policy about fraternization, we have more quickly moved to craft policy regarding consensual relationships between students and teachers as opposed to those between, say, senior and junior faculty; the assumption here of course is that our students are both in need of more protection and are generally less likely to be mature enough to understand the full consequences of their actions. Although we could be accused of patronizing our students, many other universities have entertained similar discussions (and enacted policies similar to the ones we are considering) primarily because we figure ourselves as somehow responsible for our students, perhaps even as wanting to protect them just a little bit longer from the brutalities of the real world.

All in all, these experiences and responses—indifference, repulsion, and the opportunity to become more comfortable with sexual orientation diversity—don't seem substantially different among the straight men and women I have had the opportunity to teach. Beyond the similarities we identified, however, it quickly became clear to my E-mail correspondents and me that many of my female students were thinking about and understanding my queerness in some unique ways—ways not shared by the vast majority of my male students. And we speculated that gender was at the heart of the difference.

Namely, my female students were much more likely to suggest that I, because of my open queerness, was someone whom they could speak and work with at a personal level—resulting in the formation of bonds that often enhanced, albeit in complex ways, the professional interaction between them as the students and me as the teacher. Female students frequently requested independent studies with me, workshopped their work with me, and took advantage of my office hours for both professional and personal development in ways that few straight males did. Eventually, such close work together resulted in the steady development of friendships with these students, many of whom I still correspond with or see frequently to this day.

At this point I can only speculate about what might account for the development of such friendships—but I think such speculation both provocative and informative, particularly as I feel that my queerness was the catalytic element in forming these extracurricular bonds. Louann, for instance, made the following observation: "I do think females are more accepting of a male being gay and discussing it. A lot of my guy friends shuddered when I told them I was in your class. Most of the females said[,] 'Oh, he's a pretty cool guy, huh?'" In response to a follow-up question, Louann explained one possible reason for this gender divergence:

> I think the only thing that I found different about you was that you were more open to discussing your feelings. For example, when you talked about something like "kill all fags" being scrawled on the bathroom wall along w/your e-mail address.

Louann refers here to an incident in which I discussed, in class, a student's discovery of a bit of bathroom graffiti that showcased my campus E-mail address scribbled under the injunction to "Kill all fags." I discussed this as an example of homophobia and commented about my personal and emotional response to the graffiti. Several students suggested that I shouldn't worry about the graffiti and should ignore it as an expression of ignorance, but I argued that such hateful messages have an emotional toll—and even a physical impact on both the victim and the perpetrator—that cannot be ignored. Apparently my willingness to discuss my emotional response was something that Louann, at least, had not encountered before in a male instructor—and it was an experience that interested and attracted her.

I'm a bit leery of stressing this particular point, though, primarily because it is so stereotypical for women to be portrayed and perceived as more in touch with their feelings, so I'm resisting the conclusion that women will be more drawn to a "touchy-feely" gay teacher—a comment that risks both banality and bigotry. For that matter, suggesting that gay men are more "touchy-feely" is problematic since certainly not all gay men will openly discuss or share their feelings in front of their classes. However, several students suggested that gay male teachers and female students might share bonds of empathy—bonds that don't always exist between women and straight men. One student, Lisa, jokes about the "sisterly camaraderie between women and gay men," itself a Hollywood stereotype. And in a way, such friendships often feel natural, primarily because they are given cultural legitimacy in movies and on prime-time television, as in the movies *My Best Friend's Wedding* and *The Object of My Affection* and the television sitcom *Will and Grace*. All of these revolve in large part around the mutually fulfilling and emotionally supportive friendships that can arise between gay men and straight women. Although the two don't always do their nails together, they seem to be able to discuss intimate aspects of their lives that are more difficult to share with others—such as the men they love.

But Lisa also (more seriously) wondered whether such camaraderie "might translate into the classroom": "Perhaps when a class does turn hostile, as I've seen my classes do to a degree, the women are more likely to come to the defense of a gay teacher (certainly [more so] than the men, but also it seems [the women are] less likely to attack)."

I myself had certainly encountered this. At my current institution, the University of Cincinnati, I discussed the murder of Matthew Shepard with a group of first-year students. During the discussion, several male students, referring to rumors that Shepard had flirted with the men who eventually murdered him, unashamedly asserted that they didn't see anything wrong with assaulting a gay man for making a pass at a straight man; Shepard's attackers, they said, just went a "little too far." Immediately after making these comments, several female students responded vehemently that such comments were completely out of line. I do not know whether they were attempting to defend me; I had not come out to this class at this juncture, which is probably why the young men felt free to express their homophobic positions. But it was evident that the majority of the women in the class were not going to condone or tolerate violence against gays in this case. So perhaps Lisa is right; these women were "clearly less likely to attack." Indeed, they seemed ready to defend—perhaps because many of them know what it is like to fend off unwanted suitors and *not* have violent action as a readily available or culturally encouraged means to do so; many of them probably have to put up with unwanted advances on a regular basis, so their sympathy for Shepard's attackers, particularly the attackers' response to something that many women have unfortunately grown accustomed to, was probably pretty low.

Again, though, such speculation seemed fraught with potential stereotypes, and Lisa herself inserted a caveat into our discussion, fearing that she was generalizing a bit too much:

> I seem to be dealing in stereotypes a great deal here, which makes me uncomfortable. But is there perhaps a ["]we're-in-this-together-I-know-what-its-like-to-be-on-the-receiving-end-of-this["] thing going on there? Is the supposed connection between gay men and women a relation to shared interest as it is often represented or more a camaraderie or empathy for shared experience[?] Too much reliance on a victim stance to make good theory, but . . .

Even though Lisa hesitated, I still think there might be more to her musings than she was willing to commit to. A shared sense of experience and even of victimization may have created empathic bonds that allowed these students and me to form supportive and nurturing relationships with relative ease.

Of what, specifically, might this bond consist? Michelle boldly proposed a commonality of sexual object choice or desire:

> I think it's easier for me to identify with gay men—though I like men just because they aren't women. I like the way men think, I like the way

men/males look, physically—even in other species. I like the sound of the male voice . . . I just like men. With the gay men I know, it gives us something else in common. So, of course there is that with a gay teacher.

She immediately qualified her comments, recognizing that "There are other female students who don't react that way[,]" citing Shawna, the Christian who thoroughly enjoyed my courses but who shuddered nonetheless at any thought of my lifestyle.

Our initial discussion of these issues prompted Michelle to discuss the intricacies of the student/teacher relationship as it is sometimes impacted by erotic interest, stemming from either the teacher or the student. Interestingly, Lisa, unaware of the discussion Michelle and I were having, also talked about this in her E-mails to me, and both students suggested that the relative absence of the possibility of sexual interest coming from the gay male teacher might be a key factor in fostering productive working, as well as emotionally intimate and trusting relationships. Michelle explained thus:

> I guess what it comes down to is that there is a comfort zone with gay men that isn't there with straight men. I think when you stop and think about it, teaching is a very intimate thing . . . you are influencing (generally) young people, or at least, people who are open to new ways of thinking. If sexual tensions get in the way, some of the trust in the teacher/student relationship (or even in platonic relationships) dissolves.

To make this point clear, Michelle related how such "sexual tensions" negatively affected her instruction from heterosexual teachers:

> In dealing with several heterosexual male teachers/professors, too, in my experience, there has been that tension of heterosexuality to contend with. There was at least one teacher in high school who openly hit on me and there was one that did the same while I was earning my degree as a draftsman. Of course, that is lacking in my experience with gay professors . . . (Yes, it should have been lacking in my experience with hetero professors, but . . . isn't that almost an accepted part of mainstream heterosexuality?) I was able to "like" Jonathan and express my comfort with him as an individual without the worry of heterosexually linked extenuating circumstances.

What's fascinating—albeit a bit disturbing—was this student's rueful acceptance of an institutionalized heterosexuality that positioned her to expect sexual advances from teachers, even at the high school level.

And there are consequences affecting the pedagogical environment; Michelle suggested that "When they succeed in making me uncomfortable with their behavior, things can rapidly escalate to situations bordering out of control in the classroom." Michelle never remembered anything remotely comparable happening in one of my classes. Lisa, corroborating Michelle's experiences, explained why:

> I think a key difference lies in the power structure. A gay male teacher is often viewed by the female student as less threatening sexually. Having a gay male professor destabilizes the standard dynamic of male/female, teacher/student with which we are so used to dealing. The relationship of female student to male teacher is often sexually charged and [the gay teacher's] queerness deflects some of that energy.

The language used here is revealing. For Lisa, like Michelle, the classroom often seemed a combat zone, composed of a "power structure" of "threatening" teachers. With the introduction of the openly gay teacher into this zone, the possibility (probability?) of sexual threat was perhaps destabilized and even deflected. The classroom seemed less combative and, for some, more cooperative. Lisa reported that

> . . . simply acknowledging your own homosexuality in a classroom seems a far more personal gesture than acknowledging a spouse or girlfriend. Because of [our culture's] sexualization of homosexuality, students find that extremely personal information to disseminate. However, that might work to the advantage of a female student uncomfortable with a formal academic setting. Perhaps it also helps create a more cooperative classroom (you seemed to have a much freer style with the class [I saw in which you openly acknowledged your queerness]).

And, as a former colleague, Margaret Barber, commented, "With openly gay teachers, suspicions of sexual harassment would be unlikely—a plus."

Ironically, however, this same lack of sexual interest might also have proven problematic for some. Louann put it bluntly: "The only thing I think a lot of females have trouble accepting is that they can't 'impress' you." Hoping for some clarification, I talked about this with Margaret, who has been teaching for over a decade; she told me, "The way that female students learn from men depends on how the men teach and on so much else. Are they attractive? Are erotic elements present?" To explain this point, as well as the relevancy of her questions to the pedagogical situation, Margaret discussed her experience as a female teacher instructing female students:

> I'm sure I have female students who learn better from males than from me because they're willing to work for a male they see as attractive, whereas at my age [midfifties] for women I may seem to be a mother image, and younger women are still attempting to establish psychological independence from their mothers. Nonfeminist young women tend to be much

more critical of female teachers than of males, I am convinced, since they've been conditioned to see all women (regardless of generation) as competition in some way.

Provocatively, Margaret suggested, like Louann, that some female students respond better to male teachers, especially if they find such teachers attractive. This is difficult and murky material to consider, and, according to Margaret, few have been willing to do so:

> I don't think feminists have been very willing to look at this. It would be repugnant to them to believe that a female student might learn *better*—because of applying themselves more—when there are erotic dynamics in the teacher-student relationship.

However, it *is* the case, as Margaret pointed out, that erotic elements can creep into the classroom, and, as noted earlier, some education is inevitably motivated by erotic or transferential erotic interest.

Of course, if the male teacher discloses his queerness to a class, then the situation shifts a bit; Margaret explained: "Whether the erotic element would be there for a female student and an openly gay male teacher, I would doubt." Some of the potential erotic motivation might be lost. Indeed, all bragging aside, the coordinator of the writing lab at my former institution reported to me that a chorus of wailing from her female tutors greeted my self-disclosure as queer. But these same grieving students still took—and, judging from their reports and student evaluations—enjoyed my courses. Margaret offered an explanation for this response: "There would also be an element of safety that might compensate for anything that might be lost with the possibility of believing oneself possibly attractive to the teacher." Indeed, I could see this dynamic taking place with several students from the writing lab, which was located just around the corner from my office. The frequency with which these students visited my office actually increased *after* I came out of the closet. One student in particular, Amy, formed a very collegial friendship with me after taking several of my courses, and after she graduated she and her boyfriend would double-date with me and my partner; in this way, any erotic interest she may have had for me was most likely deflected into friendship. And I would argue that my queerness was the ground on which that friendship could be built since the perceived possibility of reciprocating her feelings was negated, but in a way that didn't reject her as a person; if I, as queer, was perceived as *generally* not interested in women romantically or sexually, then I could not reject Amy *specifically*. In other words, I suspect she found my queerness a safe way to negotiate a friendship—and just a friendship—that would allow us to get to know one another without the prospect of having the relationship develop into a romantic one, with the various threats of rejection that such relationships often entail.

In a related vein, however, both Lisa and Margaret implied that the openly queer male teacher might "put off" female students who perceive the teacher as too male focused or male centered. Both correspondents were very concerned with thinking through how the female student can become comfortable in the traditionally male-dominated world of the academy, assuming (correctly for the most part, I think) that many of their male teachers may not be trained sufficiently to understand or appreciate women's experiences. In this regard, I, as the queer male teacher, might have had an advantage in that I was thought of as probably more attuned to recognizing, from personal experience, systems of oppression and prejudice; at the same time, though, the seeming naturalness of the connection between gay teacher and straight female student might also have been illusory. Margaret explained:

> Unless a gay or any other male teacher deliberately cultivates "feminist" teaching styles, I would presume that they are considered to be at risk of falling into traditional modes as much as any other male—or female, for that matter, since many female teachers of older generations have seen only "male" styles consistent with patriarchal attitudes modeled. Also, the degree to which women students felt that the gay male teacher "liked them" or, conversely, "didn't like women," might be a factor worth exploring.

Lisa's concerns were almost identical in this regard: ". . . [A]s a woman, it is . . . hard to know where you fit into the world of a gay teacher. Many women hope to break free of a male-centered academia and are leery of a teacher they may presume to be exclusively male oriented or antiwoman." To explain her point, Lisa used the scenario of the lesbian instructor/straight male student:

> I want to say that it's similar to the reaction a straight male student would have to a lesbian teacher. He would be faced with someone whom he perceives as extremely woman centered and find it difficult to place himself within her sphere. [. . .] Female students come into academia often as silenced voices used to a system which ignores them in the classroom and gives them very little to study that seems familiar. I wonder if she might feel even more alienated when faced with a man she might perceive to be even more male oriented than usual (most men ignore her experiences and her mind, *you* don't even want her body). From a very cynical power perspective, she might perceive that a gay male academic has no use whatever for a female student.

We cannot assume, then, the easy Hollywood-style connection between gay men and female students—primarily because, I think, the dynamic between teacher and student creates a power imbalance. Note how Lisa talked about the queer teacher: A "gay male academic" may have "no use whatever for a female student." Lisa is acknowledging that attraction, even in small ways, plays an important role in who gets attention and who doesn't. And this, unfortunately, is corroborated by many studies that point out how males and more attractive individuals are likely to receive greater social attention in classrooms. So, if a teacher is already perceived to be more interested in men than women, it seems only logical that the female student might feel as though she has little use-value (i.e., potential to attract pedagogical attention) in the marketplace of ideas.

In contrast, I was often surprised by how infrequently my queerness negatively affected students' perceptions of me as an instructor. Their evaluations of my courses may actually have slightly improved after I came out of the closet. On these evaluations, which asked students to rate on a scale of one (low) to five (high) both the course's effectiveness and interest level and the teacher's knowledge and approachability, I generally scored mostly fours and fives—both before and after my disclosure. Student narrative comments continued to be positive—"This teacher is too good to lose." Invariably, a comment or two has been made on such evaluations about my sexuality—but these, in the past five years, have amounted to only that—a comment or two. One in particular is worth noting. Responding to the question, "What is the one thing you would change about the teacher?" a student wrote: "The fact that he's gay." In response to the question, "What is the one thing you could have done to improve your chances for success in the course?" the same student wrote: "Not care if the teacher is gay." Certainly one could read such a comment in a number of ways, but I prefer to see in it an initial consciousness of the student's own homophobia—and a consciousness that suggests to the student the need to grapple with that homophobia lest it cut off meaningful work relationships with others.

Of course, in thinking about this subject, I've considered only one openly queer man—me. How would the pedagogical interactions and responses change if the teacher happens to be an "out" bisexual? What new issues, if any, are added to the mix in that case? Might a female student feel a bit more "threatened" by such a teacher, especially considering our culture's stereotypical portrayal of bisexuals as disease-carrying sex maniacs? Actually, the most interesting issue related to an openly bisexual male teacher might be whether his bisexuality is acknowledged at all. Most of my students knew my ex-wife, who taught part-time at the same university, but the possibility of my bisexuality never seemed to register. I was marked only as gay—an interesting deployment of biphobia, perhaps.

Finally, let me stress the need to consider how these dynamics play themselves out in terms of ethnicity and class. Indeed, little thinking has been done about the impact we are having across class, racial, and ethnic lines—variables that might have significant effects on how our queerness is perceived and how it affects the pedagogical environment of the classroom, as well as the individual student/teacher relationship. These considerations may be crucial since homosexuality and bisexuality have varying social meanings and positions from culture to culture, leading me to suspect that my open queerness may be engendering different reactions by members of varying racial or ethnic subcultures, especially where such groupings are supported by substantial subcultural formations.[3]

There are many other factors that determine how well a student—any student—will learn from any given teacher. I must admit that my situation— and my students' interest in me—may be unique. Personality, I think, counts for a lot. As one of my female students put it, "In high school, I met a cool teacher and I still keep in touch w/him from time to time, but other than him, you are the only other teacher I keep in touch w/because you're cool too." Another student, Michelle, reported that "All the women that I know [who] had you for classes, really enjoyed the experience with you—but I tend to think you're a unique experience." Does my queerness make me unique? Or is there another, unaccounted attraction in my performance of the higher educator, such as my relative youth when first stepping out of the closet? Regardless, I contend that my openly queer presence signaled something that several straight women understood—or at least were not threatened by. That shift, from viewing the male instructor as threatening to perhaps empathic, is a key difference in how men and women responded to me—and perhaps to other openly queer male teachers. Only further research will show us for sure.

Ultimately, I cannot control how my openly queer presence will be perceived or interpreted. As we have seen, my performance as an openly queer male instructor, intended to challenge homophobia and heterosexism, might be read as enabling a different kind of sexism—a male-centered or at least male-directed interest that (yet again) marginalizes women in the classroom. Even though I may not be able to prevent such interpretations from forming, I know I have become more sensitive to the number and variety of interpretations produced by the many different subjectivities, with their different histories and expectations, at play in the classroom. As this greater sensitivity has led (and continues to lead) me to engage in dialogues about educational needs and expectations, then I feel I am—with my students—moving one step closer toward creating the kind of classroom in which all of us are educated, nurtured, and respected.

NOTES

1. And, if you're queer or otherwise courageous, you can even find detailed directions for putting together your own courses with substantial les-bi-gay content. For more studies of queer visibility in the classroom, see the recent collection *Inside the Academy and Out: Lesbian/Gay/Queer Studies and Social Action*, edited by Janice L. Ristock and Catherine G. Taylor. This anthology also contains an excellent and fairly comprehensive bibliography for those looking for additional information.

2. Each student has given me permission in writing to use his or her comments in my discussion.

3. For more information about and examination of cultural differences in the understanding and perception of homosexuality, see *Coming Out: An Anthology of International Gay and Lesbian Writings*, edited by Stephan Likosky.

WORKS CITED

Alexander, Jonathan, and Karen Yescavage. "The Pedagogy of Marking: Sexual Orientation in the Classroom." *Feminist Teacher* 11.2 (Summer 1997). 113–22.

BlackBoard On-Line: The Website of the Gay, Lesbian, and Straight Education Network. June 25, 1999. <http://www.glstn.org/>.

Ellyson, Steve L. "The Interaction of Homonegativity and Gender: Fifteen Years and Four Samples." The 1998 Joint Annual Meeting of the Society for the Scientific Study of Sexuality and the American Association of Sex Educators, Counselors, and Therapists: "Sexuality and the Media: Hooray for Hollywood?" Los Angeles, November 14, 1998.

Foucault, Michel. *Ethics: Subjectivity and Truth*. Ed. Paul Rabinow. New York: The New Press, 1997.

Garber, Marjorie. *Vice Versa: Bisexuality and the Eroticism of Everyday Life*. New York: Simon and Schuster, 1995.

Kissen, Rita M. *The Last Closet: The Real Lives of Lesbian and Gay Teachers*. Portsmouth, N.H.: Heinemann, 1996.

Likosky, Stephan. *Coming Out: An Anthology of International Gay and Lesbian Writings*. Pantheon Books: New York, 1992.

Malinowitz, Harriet. *Textual Orientations: Lesbian and Gay Students and the Making of Discourse Communities*. Portsmouth, N.H.: Heinemann, 1995.

McNaron, Toni A. *Poisoned Ivy: Lesbian and Gay Academics Confronting Homophobia*. Philadelphia: Temple UP, 1997.

Ristock, Janice L., and Catherine G. Taylor, eds. *Inside the Academy and Out: Lesbian/Gay/Queer Studies and Social Action*. Toronto: U of Toronto P, 1998.

.

Teaching Pregnant:
A Case for Holistic Pedagogy

Amy Spangler Gerald

When I first learned I was pregnant, it was very early in the morning on the day my husband and I were leaving for my first academic conference where I was to present a paper. Greg was running on the treadmill when I walked in with the pink stick. He hasn't exercised since!

We both had all of the usual reactions to a first pregnancy: excitement, fear, laughter, tears, and uncertainty, but I had one feeling that I think is unique to academic women or at least unique to women whose careers are important to them. It was a sinking feeling. As I sit at my computer composing this chapter, I realize that my daughter may read this some day, and I have a twinge of guilt knowing that she might feel bad about herself to learn that her mom had a sinking feeling about her imminent birth. Somehow, though, I think she will understand.

179

The sinking feeling was not related to actually giving birth to and raising a child, because being a mother is something I always felt I would be and wanted to be at some point in my life. Instead, it was a physical reaction to the realization of the sacrifices to my career that I would inevitably make. I was thirty years old and in the second year of my Ph.D. program, almost finished with my coursework but not quite ready for my comprehensive exams or dissertation. I had just gotten back on track in academia, having worked in the "real world" for five years after I had earned my master's degree. I was worried about how being pregnant and being a mother of a young child would affect my opportunities within the department, such as teaching summer school, teaching a literature course, being considered for various awards or service positions, being observed by faculty, and simply being around the building—having a presence. I knew that in seeking my degree I still had a long row to hoe, so to speak, and having a baby (and raising her in the quality manner she deserves) would make that row even longer and much rockier.

My worries, then and now, about balancing an academic career and a family without causing damage to either mirror the concerns of many women academics because the years in which women attend graduate school and work toward tenure often coincide with the years in which many of them have babies and raise young children (AAUP). In *Coming of Age in Academe: Rekindling Women's Hopes and Reforming the Academy,* Jane Roland Martin finds that this particular brand of work-family conflict is "one of the main dilemmas [women faculty] face," but that they are "loath to speak to others about this problem" (170–71). Because universities have traditionally focused on objective knowledge, shunning the subjective or personal, they often do not "consider the world of the private home their business" (170). The resulting separation of the life of the mind and the life of the body and heart creates a wall of silence between faculty and students. Martin reports that this silence "troubled [a female undergraduate] because she was trying to decide whether or not to work for a doctorate and was wondering if it was possible to combine an academic career and children" (170). Martin's vision for reforming the academy calls for women faculty to reconnect with one another to share their stories. She describes a scenario in which "the women faculty agree that students need a realistic picture of academic life so that they can make informed decisions about the future. One scholar says that they need to know that a woman can be a professor and the mother of young children" (171). By deciding to present themselves as people with lives outside of the academy, women faculty can become models and mentors and can give strength to each other and their students.[1]

Although I certainly was not a full-time, tenure-track faculty member, I was in training to be one, and I knew that the difficulties of balancing motherhood and my career would not end once I earned my degree. My child would still be small when I entered the job market and began the tenure process, all realities that I knew would demand intensive attention and time. Luckily, the faculty, my cohorts, my husband, family, friends, and neighbors were all supportive and encouraging. I cannot speak highly enough of the largely female faculty in my department, many of whom are also mothers, and their positive attitude about my pregnancy. Very much like Martin's models and mentors, my professors were sympathetic, but more important, by sharing their own stories they helped me realize that I could also be a professor and a mother. I could teach, study, write, be pregnant, and be a mother—and they were right. Here I am writing at the computer with my daughter taking her afternoon nap in the next room.

I am fortunate to be living this period of my life at a time when a growing number of university faculties are comprised of many professional and often influential women who help support their younger sisters. But before I paint a completely rosy picture of this situation, I must explore a familiar shadow in the scene—my students. During the semester when I was pregnant, I sensed a lesser level of respect in them and a lower level of authority in me. Although the teacher's authority is often a subject of feminist and poststructuralist scholarship in that its misuse can be oppressive, particularly to "marginal" students such as women or cultural minorities, the need to develop some sense of authority is also a valid issue for new, young, and/or women teachers in many academic settings.[2] Even though my teaching philosophy recognizes the need to de-center my authority as a teacher in order to encourage students to accept responsibility for their own education, it also depends on an unspoken and probably naïve understanding that the teacher has a certain amount of expertise in her field and in teaching and that students have something to gain from that expertise. This approach seems to have worked for me for years because I had not had issues with student behavior since I taught ninth-grade summer school six years before.

Trying, then, to understand the change in classroom dynamic, I naturally wondered whether the increased noise level and sometimes uncooperative behavior of my students had anything to do with my pregnancy. Whether this was so may have depended in part on the influence of two new variables in the teaching equation (other than my growing belly). The semester I was pregnant I taught English 101 and 102, composition courses with which I am extremely familiar, but the English 102 section (Advanced Composition) was to be a themed section, meaning the focus of the writing done in the course was to center around a unifying theme. This was new to me, as was the fact that the English 101 class (a required composition course) was a Learning Community section made up of first-year students who all lived in the same dorm and who were all interested in exploring teaching as a career. Most of the English instructors who have taught Learning Communities in my university say that the fact that these students are so familiar with each other makes them rowdier than a regular class of writing students. But was their rowdiness in my section truly based on their familiarity, or was it tied to a perceived lack of authority in me because of the state of my body? At the start of the semester I was six months pregnant, so my physical state was unavoidable. I was happily full of energy, still taking the stairs and walking the campus, backpack on my back, yet I was developing that pregnant waddle, I had to visit the restroom more often, and I needed to sit down during the course of the class period. Did all of these factors, plus the obvious evidence of my sexual activity, cause my students to look at me differently? Was there a lower level of respect (or did I command a lesser level of authority) teaching pregnant?

Eileen Schell explores the issues of authority in the classroom as it relates to gender in her essay "The Costs of Caring: 'Feminism' and Contingent Women Workers in Composition Studies." She reports, "Ethnographic studies and surveys of feminist classrooms demonstrate that students, both male and female, expect their women teachers to act as nurturing mother figures" (78).[3] At the same time, however, "if women teachers give challenging assignments and exams and follow rigorous grading policies, students are more inclined to give them lower ratings" (78). She concludes that if an instructor wants high student ratings, she must be both competent *and* nurturing, whereas a male instructor must simply be competent. My course evaluations for that semester, especially from the 101 class, were indeed lower than the evaluations from previous semesters; without my calculating percentages it is accurate to say that my ratings shifted from mostly "outstanding" and "good" to "good" and "average." If my students wanted nurturing, what image could invoke more nurturing tendencies than that of a pregnant woman? Then again, because my due date was about two weeks before the end of the semester, I was forced temporarily to abandon the portfolio/process-based teaching method (I would normally be basing their grade on a final writing portfolio turned in at the very end of the semester). Instead I evaluated their four papers as the semester progressed, so that by the end they could approximate their final grades and the load on me in my first few weeks of motherhood would be relatively light. As a result, the climate of the classroom was more focused on performance, not process and progress, and may have been perceived as more rigorous. Could the more challenging evaluation system have been the reason for the lower evaluations? Was it the conflict between the stricter course structure and what they hoped was (and probably should have been) a more nurturing teaching approach?

A look at some of the comments from the 101 students indicates that the problem may have had more to do with my physical and emotional state than a pedagogical issue.[4] Out of seventeen responses, five students had something to say about my pregnancy. When asked, "What changes would you recommend the teacher make next time s/he teaches the course?" they responded with "Don't be pregnant" or "not have another baby." Although these hurtful comments are obviously the sign of an immature group of first-year students, they still are clear enough evidence of students' difficulties with a pregnant teacher. Students often have difficulty with the idea that a teacher, especially a female teacher, has a life away from school, much less a sex life. As Hélène Cixous writes in "The Laugh of the Medusa," the pregnant woman "acquires body and sex," but "the unsurpassed pleasures of pregnancy" have been repressed in women and denied in general society by the dominant culture, resulting in the creation of "the taboo of the pregnant woman" (90). As with any taboo subject, people feel uncomfortable being confronted with its manifestation, and even though pregnant women are certainly not an anomaly in my city, they are an unusual sight on the campus of this university, which reinforced the discomfort my students and I felt. In retrospect, it is also disconcerting that ninety percent of my class that semester was female, not unusual in the midsized, public university and former women's college where I teach and study, where enrollment is sixty-six percent female. One might expect a class full of young women to be more sympathetic to one of their own, yet even though I did not consider this then, the race, class, and age differences between me and my students certainly contributed to the distance I failed to overcome that semester.[5]

As Susan Bordo explains in *Unbearable Weight,* the female body has always presented problems, especially for academics. She recalls a time when she lost an important job "because (as I was informed later by one of the members of the committee) I 'moved my body around so much' during my presentation." Here, her body "disqualified [her] as a serious philosopher" (284). Academics are expected to be all *mind* and no *body;* instructors, administrators, and students have been taught, through largely male example, to deny the body. A pregnant body in its later stages is impossible to deny, and therein lies the problem for the pregnant teacher.

Clearly, as seen in their written comments, some of my students had issues with my pregnancy, yet could their difficulties have been a response to my behavior, rather than to my physical appearance? Always the conscientious perfectionist, I had vowed to conduct myself in a manner that would not make the pregnancy an issue. I did not want to let down the director of composition, the department, my students, or myself, so I never made excuses, never cancelled class for being tired, and very rarely discussed the pregnancy during class. Perhaps I went overboard and became too distant. In past courses and in teaching evaluations from professors, some of the more common comments are that I develop a good rapport with my students, that I am understanding, helpful, and approachable, and that I genuinely care about them as students and as people. Students have also said of me in past semesters, "she knows what she's talking about." So imagine my surprise when I read some of the more specific negative comments from last semester: "She did a great job considering her pregnancy—I know that pregnant women have stressful days so sometimes they don't want to hear students' side comments," "due to pregnancy sometimes she was a little short," and "she was alright, but her pregnancy was a problem." Maybe I should have talked about the development of the baby, how I was feeling, or even how they felt about me. If I had discussed the pregnancy with them, would they (and I) have been more comfortable in the class? Would that more open, embodied, and feminist approach have resulted in better evaluations and, more important, a better learning experience for both the students and me?

In *Teaching to Transgress*, bell hooks discusses Buddhist monk Thich Nhat Hanh's idea of "a pedagogy that emphasizes wholeness, a union of mind, body, and spirit," saying that Hanh's "focus on a holistic approach to learning and spiritual practice enabled me to overcome years of socialization that had taught me to believe a classroom was diminished if students and professors regarded one another as 'whole' human beings, striving not just for knowledge in books, but knowledge about how to live in the world" (14). hooks's socialization is somewhat like mine as a student from kindergarten through my master's degree. Rarely did my teachers give their students a glimpse into their personal lives, so why would I take a more open approach, never having seen it happen in my own schooling? hooks continues, "During my twenty years of teaching, I have witnessed a grave sense of dis-ease among professors (irrespective of their politics) when students want to see them as whole human beings with complex lives and experiences rather than simply as seekers after compartmentalized bits of knowledge" (15). Perhaps my students really wanted to see me as a whole person, especially when evidence of my life away from the university was so apparent. I felt uneasy about sharing information and experiences about my pregnancy with my students because I thought it was an inappropriate subject to bring into a writing classroom. But how hypocritical is that attitude when I assign journal entries and paper assignments that ask students how they *feel* about race, gender, family, and other personal subjects?! A principle of effective feminist pedagogy that I did not realize then is that students shouldn't risk what the instructor won't do.

Looking back on not only the classroom dynamic but also the course structure and assignments themselves, I now see that I worked counter to several feminist pedagogical principles that semester. hooks says, "One of the central tenets of feminist critical pedagogy has been the insistence on not engaging the mind/body split. . . . To subvert the mind/body split . . . allows us to be whole in the classroom, and as a consequence wholehearted" (193). I very much fostered the mind/body split that semester in an effort to appear professional. Ironically, my student, colleague, and faculty evaluations from semesters when I was not pregnant tell me that I usually have a more holistic approach with my students. hooks also states, "progressive, holistic education, 'engaged pedagogy' is more demanding than conventional critical or feminist pedagogy" (15)—and it is. To care about students is to give of yourself, and as a new mom, wife, student, daughter, sister, and neighbor I find myself always giving until there is almost nothing left of me. Yet teaching well is part of what makes me whole, and I grow as a teacher and as a person with each new semester. When the walls are torn down between students and teachers, learning and growing can happen in both directions—making teaching exciting year after year.

Although poststructuralist relativism tells us that there is no pure, scientific truth, an objective analysis of this problem is especially impossible in my situation because I cannot compare apples to apples, so to speak, due to the different courses I taught while pregnant. Also, I cannot ignore the fact that I *was* more tired and my hormones really were raging. Still, I found the student course evaluations helpful—and disheartening—in my research. And I must go by my instinctual perceptions with relation to my lack of connection with the students. As a result of this experience, I have determined that if I am teaching when and if I have a second child, I will try to plan the due date a little better, but more important, I will pay more attention to the rhetoric I use with regard to pregnancy. I have discovered that it is important for pregnant teachers to talk about what is always looming in front of them, both figuratively and literally. Two principles of feminist pedagogy and women's rhetoric are to speak from experience and to tear down the wall between the mind and the body that is so pervasive in academia. If I had brought my pregnancy into classroom discussions instead of hiding or ignoring it, the classroom climate may possibly have been more relaxed and therefore more productive. I had created what Helena Michie calls "the transparent pregnant body" (68), denying myself as the person going through the pregnancy, trying to maintain a nonpregnant persona. In her work and through example, bell hooks teaches us to find a way not to separate the personal from the theoretical, to be who we are and to use it—I plan to find a way to maintain my more approachable, caring persona the next time I find myself teaching pregnant.

NOTES

1. The 2001 AAUP "Statement of Principles on Family Responsibilities and Academic Work" may help women more successfully integrate family and work responsibilities by recognizing that "the conflict between work and family obligations that many faculty members experience is more acute for women faculty than for men" and advocating "stopping the tenure clock" and other suggestions to no longer make women's choice to have children a career liability.

2. Elizabeth Ellsworth discusses the problematic nature of authoritative voice in the classroom in "Why Doesn't This Feel Empowering? Working through the Repressive Myths of Critical Pedagogy," *Feminisms and Critical Pedagogy*, ed. Carmen Luke and Jennifer Gore (New York: Routledge, 1992), 90–119. For several essays on

authority from the perspective of new, young, and/or female teachers see *In Our Own Voice: Graduate Students Teach Writing,* ed. Tina LaVonne Good and Leanne B. Warshauer (Boston: Allyn and Bacon, 2000).

3. Schell cites studies by Susan Stanford Friedman, "Authority in the Feminist Classroom: A Contradiction in Terms," *Gendered Subjects: The Dynamics of Feminist Teaching,* ed. Margo Culley and Catherine Portugues (New York: Routledge, 1985) 203–8 and Neal Koblitz, "Bias and Other Factors in Student Ratings," *Chronicle of Higher Education* Sept. 1, 1993: B3.

4. Course evaluations from my English 102 class during my pregnancy were also slightly lower than evaluations from previous semesters, but possibly because 102 students are older, more mature, and not members of a learning community, they made no comments at all regarding my pregnancy or behavior.

5. At my school, the University of North Carolina at Greensboro, undergraduate African American enrollment is fifteen percent. Thirty-six percent of my class was African American, only one of whom was male. All of the students were of traditional age, and all of them lived on campus. Although I cannot speculate about socioeconomic class, it was clear that my life situation as a thirty-year-old, married, pregnant, white woman was very different from their own.

WORKS CITED

American Association of University Professors. "Statement of Principles on Family Responsibilities and Academic Work." *American Association of University Professors.* Sept.–Oct. 28, 2001. <http://www.aaup.org/re01fam.htm>.

Bordo, Susan. *Unbearable Weight: Feminism, Western Culture, and the Body.* Berkeley: U of California P, 1993.

Cixous, Hélène. "The Laugh of the Medusa." 1976. *The Women and Language Debate.* New Brunswick, N.J.: Rutgers UP, 1994. 78–93.

hooks, bell. *Teaching to Transgress.* New York: Routledge, 1994.

Martin, Jane Roland. *Coming of Age in Academe: Rekindling Women's Hopes and Reforming the Academy.* New York: Routledge, 2000.

Michie, Helena. "Confinements: The Domestic in the Discourses of Upper-Middle-Class Pregnancy." *Feminisms: An Anthology of Literary Theory and Criticism.* Ed. Robyn R. Warhol and Diane Price Herndl. New Brunswick, N.J.: Rutgers UP, 1997. 57–68.

Schell, Eileen E. "The Costs of Caring: 'Feminism' and Contingent Women Workers in Composition Studies." *Feminism and Composition Studies: In Other Words.* Ed. Susan C. Jarratt and Lynn Worsham. New York: MLA, 1998. 74–93.

A Vessel of Possibilities:
Teaching through the
Expectant Body

Kimberly Wallace-Sanders

> In pregnancy I literally do not have a firm sense of where my body
> ends and where the world begins.
>
> —Iris Marion Young

Where do our private lives as teachers end, and where does the public world
of the academy begin? In *Teaching to Transgress*, bell hooks's candid and
inspiring book about her life as a teacher, hooks makes this observation about
the teacher's body:

> No one talked about the body in relation to teaching. What did one do with
> the body in the classroom? Trying to remember the bodies of my professors,

I find myself unable to recall them, I hear voices, remember fragmented details, but very few whole bodies. The public world of institutional learning was a site where the body had to be erased, go unnoticed. When I first became a teacher and needed to use the restroom in the middle of class, I had no clue as to what my elders did in such situations. (191–92)

The academy largely insists on the body's erasure because the body is the undeniable reminder of our private selves. Our bodies betray truths about our private selves that confound professional interaction. Fatigue, stress, injury, illness, and disability reveal something about our lives through the body in ways that joyous celebrations do not. For academic women, the pregnant body emphasizes gender in an unsettling way. The visibly pregnant body reveals itself as more than a whole body—as additional body, doubled body—as the female body multiplied. At the same time, the pregnant body is fragmented; the emphasized abdomen obscures the rest of the body—often eclipses the woman behind it as it refuses to be ignored. Regardless of how a teacher became pregnant, students will see her as both sexual and maternal, which complicates and can undermine her authority. She is the embodied evidence of sexual reproduction; suddenly the teaching body is fragmented into the sexual and reproductive parts of its whole. Pregnant teachers find a way to excuse themselves from class in order to use the restroom because the body demands it, thus asserting its own undeniable authority.

In "Pregnant Embodiment," feminist philosopher Iris Marion Young eloquently reminds us that there is a startling fluidity to the pregnant body, a "compromising of corporeal integrity." Young writes, "the integrity of my body is undermined in pregnancy, not only by this externality of the inside, but also by the fact that the boundaries of my body are themselves in flux. In pregnancy I literally do not have a firm sense of where my body ends and where the world begins" (163). This chapter takes up ways in which faculty encountering pregnancy and parenting challenge the boundaries of private and public life. What happens when this corporeal compromise of pregnancy meets with authoritative presence in the classroom? What can one learn from examining how the academy responds to pregnancy and motherhood? How does the pregnant teacher or graduate student confound, challenge, or subvert the intellectual environment by blending the public and private spheres?

Earlier I quoted bell hooks telling us that in her youth, no one talked about the body in relation to teaching. The question arises, what is there to say about the teacher's body? The teaching body is not supposed to matter because it is merely the vessel for the mind at work in the classroom. What do we say about our own bodies as teachers? We say that teaching makes our pulses race or leaves us fatigued. We say that our students exhaust or energize us, and we say that we worry about what our faces betray about us in the classroom and in student conferences. Race and gender play a crucial role here: My white colleague who teaches Asian American literature senses her Asian students' discomfort with her presence at times but is unsure of how or whether to address it. A white graduate student in my department who teaches a course on African feminism says that she spends most of her first day of class assuring students of her credentials because she knows that her body surprises them when they walk into the room. When one male student enrolls in an introductory Women's Studies class, he confides to me later that he has never felt more aware of his gender.

Faculty of color, and female faculty of color in particular, are often very self-conscious of their bodies in the classroom. They are aware that their bodies bear the ontological markings of race and gender difference as opposed to the typical authoritative bodies of white men. Erasing those differences does not end these tensions. When I taught at Spelman College, a historically black college for women on the West Side of Atlanta, I shared both gender and race with the vast majority of my students. Yet I worried about undermining my authority with them by relating to them too often. It is an extremely powerful experience to be able to say "We as Black women" in a classroom. At the same time I feared this sentiment would encourage my students to see me as a peer rather than an authority figure. Eventually I learned the complex steps to the dance I call "draw them in but not too close."

Iris Marion Young reminds us that "We should not be surprised to learn that discourse on pregnancy omits subjectivity, for the specific experience of women has been absent from most of our culture's discourse about human experience and history" (161). I take up Young's challenge in this chapter about my own experience as an African American feminist, teaching women's studies while pregnant. My visibility on a majority white campus was magnified in triplicate: I was black, female, and pregnant in a sea of white male professors at Emory University. In addition to my being the only black untenured female in both of my departments (I am in a joint position between Women's Studies and an Institute of Interdisciplinary Studies), my husband also teaches at Emory. Unlike most pregnant professors, whose spouses or partners are invisible, my baby's father was very visible on campus as the current chair of African American studies. Suddenly we were no longer two African American professors who many people did not know were married; we were becoming a family—in public.

Located in Atlanta, Georgia Emory University is a large research institution (ten thousand students, predominately white), with several affiliated professional schools and very southern roots. My second year on campus, 1999, I was slated to teach "Introduction to Women's Studies," a first-year seminar. This class was composed of twelve first-year students, all female. The class was a collage of New Yorkers and Southerners; there were ten white students, one African American, and one student from India. We met twice a week in a classroom two floors away from my office. The students sat in a semicircle in front of me, and I walked back and forth across the room occasionally stopping to stand behind a table at the front of the room where I reviewed my notes or referred to a text. I called on my students by name as often as I could, except that I had a tendency to confuse two students whose only similarity was the length of their hair. "If one of you would just cut your hair and dye it purple, I'm sure that would end the confusion," I joked.

I discovered that I was pregnant early in the fall semester. Instead of gaining weight, however, I began to lose weight because the prenatal vitamins made me sick. The early months of pregnancy are a time of corporeal secrecy while the pregnancy is not yet visible. I remember a moment early in November when I was standing at the whiteboard writing with large brightly colored markers. I wrote the words: "feminist critiques of patriarchy" and asked students to give me some examples based on the reading assignment. The strong smell from the markers suddenly left me dizzy and so nauseous that I had to lower my head for a moment. The students were responding to my question, but I could not focus enough to write their comments on the board. I looked at the clock; we were ten minutes into class. I called on a student and reached for a small bottle of water nearby. I took very small, slow sips and nodded vigorously even though I knew that I had not heard one word that she said. The water was a bad idea; instead of its settling my stomach I realized that I would have to leave the room in a hurry. My body threatened to reveal my secret and make my private life public.

I remember that when I returned I simply apologized for the interruption and asked students to remind me of where we had left off in our discussion. I decided that I could manage without writing on the board for the day. As the conversation resumed, I recall thinking that if anyone held a Regurgitation Olympics, I would be a finalist for distance and accuracy. The students didn't seem to notice that I sat on the table for the remainder of class, something I rarely did. The class went quite well after the interruption; the discussion was lively and interesting. I knew that my students would not suspect that I was almost twenty weeks into gestation and growing an invisible new life inside me.

> Not only have I made mother issues the main focus of my scholarly work, but by widely spacing the arrival of my three children I have been actively mothering across three decades and up the academic ladder as I climbed from graduate student to full professor.
> —Barbara Katz Rothman

Like Barbara Katz Rothman, I find motherhood, more specifically, nineteenth-century African American motherhood, and body theory to be the main foci of my scholarly work. Having researched and written about, taught courses about, and presented conference papers about the black female body and/or about African American mothering has been intriguing preparation for pregnancy and motherhood. Much of my scholarship on race, gender, and the body involves pushing my colleagues and my students to ask different questions about the body, questions that move African American women to the center of the discussion as a way to encourage a fresh perspective on body theory. When I became pregnant, a new layer of questions revealed themselves to me. I wondered what role my own body plays when I teach the course I designed called "The Black Female Body in American Culture." How is the pregnant body viewed in the women's studies classroom? What if that pregnant body is also African American? How did my teaching change, and how did my interaction with students change? How did that interaction change again once the pregnancy was visible?

When I shared my pregnancy with my undergraduate students on the last day of class in the fall semester, they were shocked. I was aware of them staring at my body—trying to see the pregnancy—searching for proof of what I was saying. They were so surprised that they hadn't known that my restroom interruptions and the one rescheduled class were indications of my being pregnant.

My students were the first to ask the questions that I was to hear repeatedly for the next five months. They wanted to know if I knew the baby's sex. Had I picked out a name? Was I going to have natural childbirth? Would I return to teaching after the baby was born? In answering their questions, I surprised myself by confessing that the pregnancy was a surprise. I hadn't planned to say that, and yet I felt almost compelled to assure them that I wasn't trying to get pregnant.

This compulsion proved to be the most intriguing aspect of my pregnancy and my professional life. I had the same compulsion when I told both of my department chairs that I was expecting. I found myself repeatedly assuring them that the pregnancy had come as a complete surprise. I joked that I had every intention of sending the contraceptive company a picture of my baby. I suppose I wanted them to know that I didn't mean to let them down on purpose.

I am fairly guarded about my private life. Why did I feel such a need to reassure my students and colleagues that I hadn't been trying to get pregnant? Was I less culpable because I had been caught off guard? Was it a way for me to say, "Don't blame me! I didn't do this on purpose; I didn't do it at all. Mother Nature did this to me!" In the body vs. career schema that I mentioned earlier, I represented myself as a victim of my body's reproductive inclination. The more significant question here is: Why did I think I was going to be blamed for becoming pregnant? I seemed to know almost intuitively that if I could invoke my department chairs' sympathy, I stood a better chance of gaining their support. I knew that I needed their support in order to request the following semester off for parental leave.

The body resurfaces in an uncomfortable way when women faculty reflect on telling their department chair that they are pregnant. A philosophy professor confides:

> I remember when I was pregnant with the second child, I was a teaching fellow and at the beginning—he was born in June—at the beginning of the spring semester I figured I better tell my professor and it was a horrible experience. When I think about that now, it is sort of retroactively shocking because I was very embarrassed to tell him. . . . I mean it was quite legitimate, I was married and there was nothing wrong with being pregnant, but *I felt this sense of embarrassment and shame and I think it was partly, clearly the woman thing, that this is this whole kind of admission of yourself as a sexual being* that I felt very uncomfortable about. (emphasis added)

This professor adds an important final comment, "Everybody was very nice about it, but it's true that it wasn't something that you expected of your male students, and so it was an irregularity" (Aisenberg and Harrington 110).

Again the female body is presented as aberrant when pregnancy marks women as sexual beings in a "shameful" way. This professor's admission that her pregnant body embarrassed her is not an unusual sentiment for women in this position. But the shame they experience is not because they are women ("the woman thing") but because they are not men. When this professor says that pregnancy "wasn't something that you expected from the males," she has clearly articulated how our standards of professional behavior are continually based upon the normative experience of men.

> "What can one do without one's own body?"
> —Waheenma Lubiano,
> Black Female Body Conference, Duke University, 1996

> What did one do with the body in the classroom?
> —bell hooks

My course on the black female body in American culture examines many of these themes. I have taught both undergraduate and graduate versions of this course. I also taught it at very different institutions, first at Spelman College and later at Emory University. At the beginning of this course I ask the students to introduce themselves by saying something about their bodies, something that they are comfortable sharing. In this course we talk about how every scar on our bodies tells a story about us and about how the body holds our autobiographies through scars and birthmarks, the moles and oddly placed freckles.

When I taught this course at Spelman College, my students talked about their own skin color, hair texture, and body shape in relation to that of other family members. A memory that many students shared was one of white high-school classmates showing off their deep tans by comparing their new *tempo-rary* color with the complexions of African Americans. Students reported: "They put their arms up against mine and say 'see—we're almost the same color!' What does it mean that I am the same color as a white girl with a tan—is that good?—is that supposed to be a compliment?" My Spelman students also told me that they were proud of not having high incidents of eating dis-orders such as bulimia and anorexia when compared with young white women. At the same time they were often frustrated by their weight, body shape, and size, and many of them wanted to look like popular African Amer-ican actresses or models who are very slim. The effects of racism and sexism are most apparent when Spelman students speak candidly about their body image. Young African American women are very much aware of mainstream standards of beauty that exclude them and the perplexing beauty standards projected by African American men.

At Emory University I taught "The Black Female Body in American Culture" to a graduate seminar of mainly white students. In that environment students talked about childhood memories of feeling that they were too tall or too short and about struggling with weight issues and self-esteem. These stu-dents spoke of people treating them differently when they cut their hair very short (are you a lesbian?) or when they dyed their hair unusual colors (have you joined a cult?). A Japanese woman in my graduate class spoke poignantly about being called "black" as a child because she tans darkly and has hair that is unusually curly for a Japanese woman. Her hair was so difficult for her mother to comb that she eventually had to have it chemically straightened. The student's childhood experiences led her to study Japanese attitudes toward "blackness" as a graduate student. Two of the African American women in the class found that they were able to connect their own corporeal narratives with this student's story because they also felt that their bodies—their hair in particular—had marked them as outsiders in mainstream Amer-ican culture.

In the introduction to this volume, Diane Freedman finds that no teacher's body goes unobserved. I know that I have this in mind when I intro-duce myself in these body classes. As part of my introduction I tell my stu-dents that I have finally reached the conclusion that my body is perfect for my particular journey in life. This is different, I explain to them, from being happy with my body or even accepting it. I was asking different questions about my own body. Instead of asking "do I like it?" or "can I accept and love it?," I began to ask, "what is my body's function?" I developed a new relationship with my body—not by seeing it differently—but by asking different questions about its function in my life. As a result I came to the conclusion that my body worked perfectly; this was a revolutionary change in perspective for me that I wanted to share with them. I often tell my students that how they feel about their bodies determines whether they go through life as a question mark or an exclamation point. I tell them that I want to move through the world feeling both powerful and peaceful and I want to know how my body can help me with that.

Throughout the course I carefully select what I reveal about myself as a way of encouraging my students to re-view their own bodies. All of this is done as a means to more fully understand the body theory. For example, when I tell them that I am considered "paper bag brown," I do so in order to introduce discussion about the old paper bag test done by middle-class African Americans in the early twentieth century as a way of discriminating against dark-skinned African Americans.

As the introduction notes, "if the teacher's body fades from awareness in the course of many classes, it always shows up on the first day of school." When I walk into the classroom on the first day of the school year, I am acutely aware of my body because my heart is pounding and my pulse is racing. I carry a small bottle or cup of water because my throat is so dry. I dress up for class, a practice I began in my very first teaching job. I have been told that the way I dress emphasizes my ethnicity. I braid my own hair, often adding extensions that I take great pride in arranging in elaborate styles. I wear colorful scarves, an oversized jacket made of African cloth, and Indian dresses with elaborate embroidery. I take three deep breaths as I get to the room. I push the door open, and a miracle of corporal alchemy occurs: Fear turns to excitement and adrenaline. When I am in front of my students I am "on"; I talk quickly, gesture grandly, and laugh often. I almost always mention my race and gender in the first classes. Why do I feel that I must articulate the differences that are written on my body? In many ways my body becomes a tool that I use to assert my authority.

How did my teaching change while I was pregnant? I have already relayed an experience with teaching during my first trimester in the fall. By the beginning of the spring semester I was showing and waddling. I could no longer wear my favorite Indian dresses because the drawstring slipped out of place once my waist disappeared. Simple, boring, maternity clothes replaced my colorful wardrobe. I was convinced that wide elastic was the most wonderful thing in the world. Soon I found it liberating to think less about what I wore to class. I learned to dress for comfort instead of drama and found that I was more relaxed in class. My wardrobe was less impressive, but it was also less intimidating.

My son was very active in utero; he often kicked me while I was in mid-sentence during class. I learned to talk through these jarring moments, yet they were constant reminders of the blurring between inside and outside that Iris Marion Young addresses in the first epigraph to this chapter.

I had a teaching assistant for my spring undergraduate class, a course called "Women and American Identities." That class was the most diverse class I have ever taught. Out of sixteen students, eight were white and eight were students of color. There were four male students in that class, an unusually high number for a course cross-listed with Women's Studies. I ask my teaching assistant what she remembers about how my pregnancy affected the course. She tells me that she remembers my bringing crackers to class and apologizing for having to eat in front of the students. She adds, "I rarely saw you eat anything; you were so discreet. I would see you put something in your mouth while a student was talking, but by the time you made a response, the food was gone." In the introduction Diane Freedman shares her similar experiences of having to eat small snacks during class. The pregnant body's hunger can't be denied and serves to remind students that something is happening to their teacher's body that requires more fuel.

My teaching assistant does remember me having to leave class for restroom breaks, and she reports that there was utter silence in the room while I was gone. Even if I had encouraged the students to continue with their discussion they just stopped and waited for me to return. She says, "They did not talk to each other. They sat in silence; it was as if your presence animated them, and without you they didn't know what to do."

My strongest memory from that semester was how nurturing my students were to me. They asked periodically about my health, my energy, and the baby. They volunteered to carry my slide projector, large piles of books, folders full of graded papers, and stacks of videos. My favorite memory is one where my unwieldy body both amused and embarrassed me. Late in my third trimester as I was preparing my materials for class, I stood up and knocked a pile of folders off of the table with my belly. When I bent over awkwardly to retrieve them, I knocked over a stack of video boxes with my rear end. This was at the very beginning of class, and there were few students in the room. One student said, "Wow, that was pretty impressive" in a way that made us both laugh.

Throughout the semester my pedagogical style evolved along with my pregnancy. When my energy was low, I relied on the students to increase their own participation. I was more patient when there were long silences in class, and as a result of having more time to think, the students were more thoughtful in their responses. I asked students to write on the board when it was difficult for me to stand for long periods of time. This move reminded me of how much the students enjoy sharing the teacher's authority in productive ways. The more I stepped back from "driving" the class, the more the students took the lead.

I recently spoke with a colleague who taught several courses while she was pregnant. Sandra Sims-Patterson is an associate professor of psychology at Spelman College. Sims-Patterson said that her teaching style changed because she is usually very active in the classroom, moving around the room and writing on the board a great deal. When she was pregnant, she had to sit down more often to conserve her energy. "So I learned to take more risks in the classroom, I learned to pace myself during a class, something that I wasn't good at before." Students asked a lot of questions about her pregnancy, and because she was teaching child development courses, she found ways to make the discussion relevant. Her baby was due before the end of the semester, and she says that she did double time to prepare for the classes she would miss by videotaping lectures and making extra handouts. Sims-Patterson admits that she did far too much in an effort for her students not to feel her absence. "I did much more than I needed to do. They were able to do more on their own than I gave them credit for." She stresses that her experience of teaching while pregnant was positive because she worked in a cooperative environment; she felt that she was well supported by her department and the institution. We agreed that feeling supported is crucial for pregnant faculty and that the experience had changed our teaching in positive ways.[1]

> What, after all, is more personal than the life of the body? And for women, associated with the body and largely confined to a life centered on the body, . . . culture's grip on the body is a constant, intimate fact of everyday life.
>
> —Susan Bordo

There is no shortage of studies, reports, articles, and books about motherhood and the academy. I received a call for submissions for a new book called *Alma Mater: Narratives of Motherwork and the Academic Culture* as I was completing this chapter. The Center for Mothering at York University in Toronto sponsored a conference called "Teaching Motherhood, Being a Mother-Teacher and Doing Maternal Pedagogy" just a few days before this chapter was submitted. When I reviewed the program for this conference the breadth of the topics that were addressed astonished me. This sample of the paper titles reaffirms much of what I have argued here: "Throwing the Baby Out with the Bath Water: The Marginalization of Motherhood in Women's Studies," "The Intersection of Mothering, Research and Teaching: A Maternal Feminist Pedagogy?" "Mother/Student/Money Memoirs: Class and Motherhood in the Academy," "Motherhood and Feminist Academics," "Dr. Mamma: The Resiliency of African American Graduate Student-Mothers," "The Construction of Mother Identity by College and University Professors," and "Professor/Mother: The Uneasy Partnership."[2]

As an academic community we are clearly taking up the most significant themes and issues about faculty women and motherhood at this moment. A recent AAUP statement on family responsibility and academic work proposed that new parents be given additional time to apply for tenure. My home institution reviewed its parental-leave policy some years ago; the new version is one of the more progressive and parent-friendly policies available. This policy grants twelve weeks of paid leave to parents of newborns, newly adopted children, and children under five years of age. Parents are transforming the academy, but it is a slow and often rancorous shift. The obstacles to transformation strike at the very core of the academic profession as a community of scholars, teachers, writers, researchers, and administrators. What kind of community will we be if we continue to devalue parents? The infusion of more white women and men and women of color into the academy continues to have a profoundly positive impact on our institutions at every level. I propose that the pregnant teacher's body is a vessel of pedagogical possibilities with similar potential.

NOTES

1. Personal interview, Sandra Sims-Patterson, April 10, 2002.

2. For additional sources of reading about motherhood and tenure, see *Shattering the Myths, Women in Academe* by Judith Glazer-Raymo (Baltimore: Johns Hopkins UP, 1999), "The Trouble with Equal Opportunities: The Case of Women" by Jackie West and Kate Lyon, *Gender and Education* 7.1 (1990): 51–68, and "Marital Status and Academic Women" in *Academic Women: Working Towards Equality* by Angela Simeone (South Hadley, Mass.: Bergin & Garvey, 1987), 119–40.

WORKS CITED

Aisenberg, Nadya, and Mona Harrington. *Women of Academe: Outsiders in the Sacred Grove*. Amherst: Massachusetts UP, 1988.

Freedman, Diane, and Martha Stodddard Holmes. Introduction. *The Teacher's Body*. Ed. Diane Freedman and Martha Stoddard Holmes. Albany: SUNY P, 2003.

hooks, bell. *Teaching to Trangress*. New York: Routledge, 1994.

Rothman, Barbara Katz. "Back to the Classroom, without the Kids." *Chronicle of Higher Education*. Sept. 3, 1999: A112.

Young, Iris Marion. *Throwing Like a Girl and Other Essays in Feminist Philosophy and Social Theory*. Bloomington: Indiana UP, 1990.

At Home at Work:
Confining and Defining
Pregnancy in the Academy

Allison Giffen

In the epistolary novel, *The Coquette* (1797), Hannah Webster Foster explores the gendered binary of confinement and freedom in the context of women's roles in the New Republic. I teach this work almost every semester and consistently must explain to students the historical application of the term "confinement" to pregnancy and birth. Students are often irate over the fact that when upper-class American women became visibly pregnant they were expected to hide their pregnancy from public view and remain inside the home. I typically use this moment to begin an explanation of "separate spheres," historicizing the gendered binaries of private/public, static/mobile, domestic/professional, and feeling/thinking. Last year I conducted this classroom conversation while I was visibly pregnant. Standing in full view with my belly protruding, I had the gratifying and powerful feeling of offering my students a positive role model, one that collapsed those gendered binaries and suggested that "pregnant professor" was not an oxymoron. Yet I couldn't help feeling that there was something suspect about my sense of power and gratification and something potentially problematic about the model I offered my students. When I discussed the experience of teaching while pregnant with colleagues who had also taught through their pregnancy, almost everyone commented that, like me, they liked the message that the visibility of their pregnancy offered within the classroom. Yet I think we need to consider the potential fault lines of such modeling and to consider how we might be subtly, and not so subtly, endorsing sexual scripts in the ways in which we perform our professional identities while pregnant.

I can trace those competing feelings of gratification and unease related to my work and my pregnancy to professional encounters outside the classroom as well, and I want to focus on the role of pregnancy within the academy at large before turning my attention specifically to what happens in the classroom. On more than one occasion, once my pregnancy became more visible, senior colleagues complimented me on how well I was "managing the whole thing." Of course, I initially felt deeply gratified by such comments, particularly since I had taken special care to put on a happy face through the nausea and exhaustion and to show up at meetings smiling and ready, even if I had been retching on the side of the road not fifteen minutes earlier. But what these compliments really said was that I had been successful at controlling, or confining, my pregnancy, successful at making it as invisible as possible. These (well-intentioned) comments reflected a larger institutional invisibility—that particular state university has no maternity policy, and women faculty are expected to manage their pregnancies individually. In my case I was relying on the generous support of other faculty members to step in and cover my classes.

My efforts to appear professional to my colleagues reflected my anxieties about the ways in which my pregnant body might play into incumbent essentializing tendencies about womanhood on the part of senior colleagues. With my tenure review just a year and half away, I feared giving senior colleagues and administrators the opportunity to see me as an outsider, someone who did not belong to this life of the mind. It seemed important that I appear effective, professional, and competent—essentially, as good as a man. In her essay "Transgression and the Academy: Feminists and Institutionalization," Val Walsh rightly reminds us that "'competence' and 'good behavior' are not neutral terms, but contextually specific and gendered" (89). In my case competence seemed related to the degree to which the exigencies of my body did not obstruct my work. To this end I repeatedly made assurances that my pregnancy would not get in the way and that I would teach right up until the day of delivery. However, because of a condition called preeclampsia, I stopped teaching a week before the delivery, and the reality is that I should have stopped sooner. My midwife put me on modified bed rest, and, at my insistence, my only activity was to lug myself into the classroom each day. Of course, no one ever told me that I had to keep teaching. My decision was motivated by my own internalized ideas about professionalism, though I also feared that if I didn't teach for the majority of the semester, I might not be paid during the time I was out. In addition, I didn't want to impose too heavily on those colleagues who were kindly teaching my classes for free.

Despite assurances to my department chair, I couldn't control my body so that my labor would occur conveniently at the end of the semester, just one example of the way my unruly, pregnant body seemed antithetical to a professional identity in académe. Feminist theorists have long called attention to the ways in which the ideological foundation of the academy comes from a specifically gendered notion of the life of the mind.[1] In an examination of the place of the body, specifically the disabled body, in académe, Tracey Potts and Janet Price offer an eloquent articulation of this idea:

> The western Academy has been held as the site, par excellence, for the expression of Cartesian logic. During the Enlightenment era, it was the site where the universal subject came most fully into "his" own, the arena in which rational thought, predicated on a transcendence of the body, could be most fully sought. In this life of the mind, bodies were a constant threat, for they were held to contaminate reason, to interfere with the "view-from-nowhere." Women's bodies, with all their associations with childbirth, menstruation, and the "natural," unreasoning, instinctual world, were seen as particularly dangerous. (103–4)[2]

A pregnant professor offers a highly visible reminder of the woman academic's body and all of its historical associations with the natural and the nonrational that locate it outside of the western academy. Certainly my own experience testifies to the way that, on the institutional and individual level, pregnancy occupies a vexed site within académe. Yet my sense is that these binaries such as mind/body and private/public are not clear-cut, and, in particular and qualified ways, the pregnant professor is actually "at home" in the academy. Indeed, the private realm of home and family with all of its normative sexual scripts and uneven power relations inundates the profession, often acting as an organizing metaphor for an array of work relationships.

In much of my own work, I explore the effect of the family model on the construction of a professional identity for nineteenth-century American women writers.[3] Posing the question, "What does it mean to be figured as a daughter when building a professional career?" I am interested in the often debilitating effects of the father-daughter model on women when it shapes their professional relationship with male mentors. Historically, professional literary mentor-mentee relationships were structured by a model of fathers and sons, and as increasing numbers of women entered the writing profession in antebellum America, not surprisingly, this model shifted to fathers and daughters to accommodate them. But the contours of the father-daughter relationship are radically different from those of the father-son relationship. For example, daughters don't have access to the same privileges of inheritance as sons, and when they grow up, they don't displace and become fathers. They become mothers. As an organizing metaphor, the family exerted a powerful and limiting force upon women seeking to act in the public realm, effectively putting them back in their place.

These models continue to have relevance today. In my own professional life, I have found that, first as a graduate student and later as an assistant professor, senior men often related to me paternally, with a kind of genial condescension, a response that changed very little once I became pregnant. Senior (male) colleagues, for the most part, were quite interested in sympathizing with "my condition," often by recalling their wives' experiences. In these amiable exchanges, rather than marking me as an outsider, my pregnancy made me comfortably recognizable and gave me access to the social world of marriage and family that structured much of the discourse of collegiality. As long as I did not disrupt power relations or the current economic arrangements (in other words, as long as my pregnancy remained institutionally invisible), I would be at home within the academy. Such encounters left me uncomfortable, feeling like a "good girl" and wondering whether women who did not fit the white, hetero, middle-class model would receive the same solicitude. My bulging silhouette against the wall may have comforted my colleagues, but had a different woman stepped into it, say someone who was a lesbian, of color, or artificially inseminated, what would the nature of these social exchanges have been? Would they have even occurred? More than twenty years ago, both Adrienne Rich and Audre Lorde not only warned us of "the pitfall [for white women] of being seduced into joining the oppressor under the pretense of sharing power" but also counseled us to attend to the ways that this qualified status occurs at the expense of lesbians and women of color (Lorde 118).[4]

In a recent and important essay, "On Being Married to the Institution," Robyn Wiegman examines the exclusionary effects of this collapse of the private and public in the academy. Specifically, Wiegman is interested in "opening the academy's social and collegial forms to the prospect of a queer sexuality that does not reproduce intimacy's disciplined horizons of monogamy, marriage or the family form" (73). Given my own interests, I had always been suspicious about being positioned in the role of the daughter and, once pregnant, anxious about the effects of being perceived as a mother, an identity that seemed to stand in contradistinction to that of scholar and professor. Wiegman's work allows us to see the kind of privilege that accrues to such identities within the academy and to critique these social dynamics by taking into account the outsider, the invisible or excluded queer identity. Consequently, her work opens up a critical space for a more nuanced examination of preg-

nancy within the academy and leads us to question the ways that the visibility of pregnancy on the interpersonal level might implicitly endorse what she
calls the "the overarching and indeed oppressive atmosphere of heterosexual
marriage, family, and reproduction that structures the interpersonal codes,
affective economies, and social practices of the academy"(71).[5] While pregnant, I rarely felt as though I occupied a position of power and have even seen
the ways that motherhood directly effected negative tenure decisions. But to
stop there is to risk what June Jordan calls a "temporary, short-sighted, and
short-lived advancement for the few" (2239). We cannot begin to redress the
institutional "confinement" of the pregnant professor until we broaden our
view and articulate with greater specificity the ways that pregnancy also
potentially partakes of the privileges of a larger nexus of raced and gendered
power arrangements.

Wiegman's warnings are applicable to interactions not only with colleagues and administrators but with our students as well, and how pregnant
women faculty "manage the whole thing" has a direct effect, both positive and
negative, on the classroom dynamic. My son was born in March of the spring
semester, and during that previous fall semester I handled the fact of my pregnancy differently in two different classes. These choices were in part a consequence of the differing level, size, and demographics of the particular classroom. The class in which I taught *The Coquette* was a large, 200-level survey
of American literature required of English majors. With its ambitious curric-
ular agenda and its composition of new majors with very little background in
literary and cultural history, the survey required some lecturing and a greater
efficiency in working through the material. In this class I spent very little time
talking about myself and downplayed the visible fact of my pregnancy. That
semester I also taught an upper-level seminar on Early American women
poets. This small class of mostly women was cross-listed with women's studies and was composed of both graduate and upper-level, undergraduate students, many of whom had taken other classes with me and whom I knew well.
Here I often allowed my pregnancy to occupy center stage in our discussions.
Though this choice turned out to be pedagogically more productive, I want to
explore in some detail the effects of my choices in each class.

In the large survey of American literature class, I performed a kind of
implicitly gendered professionalism similar to that in my interactions with
senior colleagues. I didn't immediately tell my students about my pregnancy
until it became obvious, at which point I briefly informed them, then moved
on to the day's topic. Though I offered students a visual example of the ways
that I could embody both a maternal and a professorial identity, my "business
as usual" approach suggested that I performed my job *despite* my pregnancy.
I was presenting what I think of as the "exceptional woman" model: someone
who can be "one of the guys" and have a family. This model contributes to
the idea that pregnant bodies, with all their leaky, awkward vagaries, must be

carefully controlled and are in effect out of place in the professional sphere. More dangerously, it is a fiction that establishes impossible expectations for women. I may have been able to offer a smooth performance in which the needs of my body did not interfere with my work, yet I could sustain it for only short periods of time (the fifty minutes of class, for example).

After my initial announcement about my pregnancy, I rarely discussed it, though of course the visible fact of it shaped our discussions in all kinds of subterranean ways. Not allowing my pregnancy explicitly to enter the conversation produced missed opportunities for a critical examination of an array of cultural assumptions. My treatment of *The Coquette* was perhaps one of the most glaring of these occasions. For, as we discussed the socially enforced invisibility of pregnancy in the eighteenth century, my pregnant body seemed to flaunt itself against the blackboard, upon which I was dutifully scratching out neat columns of binaries, and served to visually assert the (facile and indeed erroneous) idea: "You've come a long way, Baby." Students could then indulge in a comfortably self-righteous indignation for the sins of America's past. This is the kind of easy and complacent response that I typically work against in my classes, encouraging students to examine their own assumptions by making links to those in earlier historical periods. By not explicitly engaging the realm of the personal, my own pregnant body, I found myself working at cross-purposes.

Such was not the case in the seminar on Early American women poets. The material for this class came directly out of one of my current research projects, so before I even walked in the door, my engagement in this class felt personal. In addition, the room was filled with familiar faces, students who regularly stopped by my office and were familiar with my teaching style. In many of my classes, I explicitly engage the personal, drawing on my life and those of students in order to validate and empower student voices and to encourage them to develop ways to value and make meaning out of the lives and work of groups typically underrepresented in académe. Consequently, it was an easy decision to resist that distancing model of professionalism. I allowed my students to see that I wasn't always smoothly juggling the competing requirements of my maternal body and my professional work. And, yes, talking about my swollen feet, my aching back, or the way that nausea was making it difficult to concentrate at times may have made me feel vulnerable. But it also provided students with a more realistic model of professionalism and offered a useful opportunity for thinking about social expectations and women's roles in our culture.

In this seminar several of the class members were returning students, older women who had raised families and who still felt unsure of themselves as college students. These women, especially, demonstrated an interest in my pregnancy, and opening up a space for some exchange on the topic, asking advice and confirming various symptoms, gave them the opportunity to speak with a degree of authority I hadn't heard before. To some small degree, allowing myself to become vulnerable by allowing students to see the ways I was not always in control of my body perhaps de-centered the authority, creating an environment in which these students could speak more readily. The sense of personal urgency and engagement that we brought to these conversations then extended into our discussions about the poetry. The issues of motherhood, reproduction, and family are central to many of the women poets we were investigating, and our class discussions seemed animated with a greater urgency and relevance because I didn't try to confine the obvious fact of my pregnancy to the sidelines.

Before I paint too rosy a picture of this classroom, I want to return to some of my earlier observations about the ways that the pregnant professor is at home at work in order to think about the potential fault lines of this teaching practice. My experience has been that, as a rule of thumb, successfully introducing one's personal life into the classroom requires some discrimination. As teachers, we need to attend to our motives when talking about ourselves and to avoid the temptation to indulge in a captive and usually fascinated audience at the expense of what is most pedagogically productive. Even more important is the necessity to avoid universalizing our experiences—to avoid relying on assumptions about home and family. And so, I want to think about the other students in that classroom, the ones who weren't participating in those personal disclosures. To what extent was that discourse of heterosexual motherhood and reproduction excluding certain kinds of experiences? Here Robin Wiegman's analysis again becomes helpful:

> For the queer subject, whose lack of status as a mother or spouse marks her eccentricity to the codes of institutional sociability, there is no recognizable "outside" to her work or workplace identity; she is in this regard without a public narrative of her own private life, since it is paradoxically the family form that enables professional women today to claim a private life that can have legitimacy in the public sphere of academic labor. (78)

Though Wiegman is interested here in discourses of collegiality among faculty, her ideas are equally applicable to the classroom. Invoking the public/private dichotomy, Wiegman reminds us that only certain kinds of private lives—those that conform to heterosexual models—have the legitimacy to enter into the public narrative. Though I may have felt as though something liberatory was occurring in that classroom, I also need to ask to what extent the "baby" talk was further codifying the legitimizing centrality of heterosexuality within the classroom and the university and consequently excluding queer identities or even those men and women for whom having children was either not on option or not a desirable option.

I am not suggesting that my decision to allow my pregnancy to play an active role in the classroom was a bad one. Indeed, I felt that both classes were to a large extent successful. Students appeared to be having a satisfactory experience, and their evaluations were strong for both courses. I am suggesting that regardless of whether we like it, students are acutely aware of their teachers' bodies, and pregnancy only heightens this awareness. We can use this information to make choices that are informed not only by the needs of the particular class but also by an understanding of how pregnancy operates to potentially empower or exclude students. Finally, I want to be clear that I am not diminishing the difficulties for pregnant women working in the academy. My experience was largely positive, but I certainly don't presume it to be typical, and in fact I know of women whose careers have been seriously derailed as a consequence of institutional responses to pregnancy and child-rearing responsibilities. But to effectively address problems such as the institutional invisibility of pregnancy or the way that professionalism is gendered masculine requires that we attend to how pregnancy lends itself so readily to the normalizing scripts of heterosexual marriage and family. We all wish to feel welcomed, comfortable, and at home when we are at work. Pregnant professors, in particular, need to think about the often oppressive, historical implications of home both for those inside its doors and those outside.

NOTES

1. For an early landmark work on feminist pedagogy that explores this idea see *Gendered Subjects*, especially essays by Rich, Maher, and Bezucha. See also essays by Walsh and Evans in *Feminist Academics*.

2. Recent scholarship on disability and pregnancy is especially productive for thinking through issues of pregnancy and the academy. However, we would do well to remember that although pregnancy, like disability, may call attention to the materiality of the body, it differs significantly from disability because it occupies a site of privilege within the discourse of the heterosexual family and reproduction within the institution.

3. See, for example, "Savage Daughters: Emma Lazarus, Ralph Waldo Emerson and *The Spagnoletto*" in *ATQ*. Of late, scholars of nineteenth-century American literature and culture have begun to investigate the ways that critics have relied too heavily on an overarching paradigm of gendered public and private spheres, suggesting that the boundary between these spheres is more permeable than it has been previously represented. See especially a special issue of *American Literature* titled *No More Separate Spheres!*

4. See also Rich's essay "Disloyal to Civilization."

5. Wiegman is careful to make clear that she is not dismissing the challenges that confront women who are negotiating the often competing demands of family and work. She writes: "Rather, I am seeking to foreground the way that even the feminist articulation of reproduction has been less nuanced in its rendering of the complexities of heterosexuality's normative modalities in the daily life of the institution" (77).

WORKS CITED

Culley, Margo, and Catherine Portuges, eds. *Gendered Subjects: The Dynamics of Feminist Teaching*. Boston and London: Routledge, 1985.

Davidson, Cathy, ed. *No More Separate Spheres!* Special issue of *American Literature* 70.3 (1997).

Evans, Mary. "Ivory Towers: Life in the Mind." *Feminist Academics: Creative Agents for Change*. Ed. Louise Morley and Val Walsh. Bristol, Penn., and London: Taylor & Francis, 1995. 73–85.

Giffen, Allison. "Savage Daughters: Emma Lazarus, Ralph Waldo Emerson and *The Spagnoletto*." *American Transcendental Quarterly* 15.2 (2001): 89–108.

Jordan, June. "A New Politics of Sexuality." *Norton Anthology of African American Literature*. Ed. Henry Louis Gates, Jr. New York and London: Norton, 1997. 2238–41.

Lorde, Audre. "Age, Race, Class, Sex: Women Redefining Difference." *Sister Outsider*. Freedom, Calif.: Crossing, 1984.

Potts, Tracey, and Janet Price. "'Out of the Blood and Spirit of Our Lives': The Place of the Body in Academic Feminism." *Feminist Academics: Creative Agents for Change*. Ed. Louise Morley and Val Walsh. Bristol, Penn., and London: Taylor & Francis, 1995. 102–15.

Rich, Adrienne. "Disloyal to Civilization: Feminism, Racism, Gynophobia." *On Lies, Secrets, and Silence: Selected Prose 1966–1978*. New York and London: Norton, 1979.

Walsh, Val. "Transgression and the Academy: Feminists and Institutionalization." Ed. Louise Morley and Val Walsh. Bristol, Penn., and London: Taylor & Francis, 1995. 86–101.

Wiegman, Robin. "On Being Married to the Institution." *Power, Race, and Gender in Academe: Strangers in the Tower?* Ed. Shirley Geok-Lin Lim and Maria Herrera-Sobek. New York: MLA, 2000. 71–82.

Coming Out Pedagogy:
Risking Identity in Language
and Literature Classrooms

Brenda Jo Brueggemann
and
Debra A. Moddelmog

Most scholarship about coming out in the classroom has focused on the act of making visible an identity that has been largely invisible, discredited, or actively ignored in the academy. For example, gay and lesbian teachers have talked about how, when, and why they come out to students, arguing that such disclosures are necessary for pedagogical as well as political reasons.[1] As Harriet Malinowitz puts it, "By coming out to my students and inserting a lesbian and gay discourse into the class, I am divesting those students of their ignorance and their entitlement to prejudice, and am investing them with responsibility to negotiate meanings" (qtd. in Elliott 706).

Similar conversations about "outing" oneself have recently begun in the field of disability studies within the humanities, as scholars-teachers have begun to talk about how and why to claim a disability identity rather than remaining silent about one's body and ability in the classroom.[2] Although the coming-out conversations in gay and lesbian studies and disability studies have their obvious differences (a gay identity and a disability identity are not ultimately analogous), they share a number of points, not the least of which is their interest in exploring the connection of traditionally discredited identities to a larger historical and political picture of the "fit" citizen and thus the "fit" teacher. Besides opening up space for teachers to reverse a societal process of silencing and shaming that often haunts gays, lesbians, and disabled people, these two conversations also reveal a reciprocal relationship between the bodies of scholarship (gay and lesbian studies and disability studies) and the body of the teacher (gay, lesbian, or disabled). In other words these conversations demonstrate how a field of study provides knowledge, discourse, recognition, and a political context for expressing particular identities in the classroom; at the same time, the expression of those identities produces knowledge, discourse, recognition, and a political context for a field of study.

The act of disclosing a historically abject identity in the classroom has had significant pedagogical consequences as well. It has questioned the traditional expectations for the kind of knowledge that can be shared with students, thereby redrawing the lines between the intellectual and the personal, the sanctioned and the taboo, and the academic and the experiential. It has also given the teacher a body, and not only a performing body but one that functions (or doesn't) in physical, erotic, passionate, and sensual ways. Of course, teachers have always had bodies, and with the advent of feminist studies, ethnic studies, and race studies, it has been increasingly easy to acknowledge and discuss the teacher's body in the classroom. The work of gay and lesbian studies and of disability studies around the body has obviously benefitted from the previous and ongoing work of feminism, critical race studies, ethnic studies, and multiculturalism. However, the work of gay, lesbian, bisexual, and now queer studies and the work of disability studies has also extended, complicated, and enriched the ways in which we now think about bodies, including the teacher's body.

One of the ways in which both queer theory and disability studies have extended thinking about teachers' bodies is by challenging essentialist notions of the body and identity. Drawing upon poststructuralist ideas about subject formation, queer theory and disability studies proposes that the body and identity are not synonymous and underscore that both are socially constructed. Such an approach consequently confounds the act of coming out in the classroom. Without a coherent, foundational, and permanent sense of identity, how does one "come out"? What exactly would one come out as? In other words, how does one disclose an identity that is always conditional and that exists only in relation to other conditional identities? We focus on this troubling of identity and the conditional body onto which identity is read in this chapter as we explain how we simultaneously "come out" and "pass" and how we present and perform our identities in the classroom. To put this another way, we are concerned here with how identities that we have been socially assigned but that are paradoxically largely invisible and provisional—in Brenda's case, a deaf identity, and in Debra's, a lesbian identity—might be troubled and troubling for both us and our students.

Pamela Caughie proposes that "all subjectivity is passing, even the subject position of the teacher-scholar who is engaged in the deconstruction of identity" (2). By this she means that if there is no prediscursive subject position from which one acts and speaks, then all identity is performance. We are always already passing even when we are not consciously attempting to pass as something. To consider subjectivity in this way requires that we read a performance "rather than reading through it to expose the 'real' identity behind it" (5–6). Moreover, from this perspective, passing marks the site of an ethical choice. We can perform our identity in such a way that it seems to match a norm, while resisting being read as deviant. Or we can perform our identity in such a way that it seems to match a deviancy and, in the process, resist being read as the norm. This latter performance has often been referred to as "coming out," but if all identity is a presentation attained through repeated performance, then, as Caughie suggests, both kinds of performances are forms of passing. Thus we propose a pedagogy centered around the tension between the concepts of passing and coming out, a pedagogy in which identity disclosures initiate a process of consciously performing but also complicating a particular identity.

For Caughie, the term "passing," even more than the analogous term "performativity," signifies the "*risk* of identity in that the practice has social, economic, and even physical consequences" (5). However, it seems prudent to acknowledge that the risk of identity differs from performance to performance, in part because the performance of an identity is always read in relation to a body that might itself be read as either normal or deviant. For example, people who use wheelchairs, leg or arm braces, guide dogs or white canes or who have physical "disfigurements," such as limbs missing or shortened, will almost always—at least when encountering people face to face—be read as "disabled" regardless of their attempts to pass as able bodied. Even this reading, though, can be a misreading of the complicated terrain of disabilities and disability identities. For example, the person in the wheelchair might be temporarily disabled, a condition that does not ordinarily mean that he or she has a disability identity. Similarly, many women whose bodies look masculine or men whose bodies look feminine will be read as gay. This, too, can be a misreading, of course, but our point is that not all performances are created equal because passing involves a complex negotiation of presentation and reading that can result in an impasse, a passageway, or a pass for gaining social acceptance.

In our own cases, we have both been able to—and still can—perform normalized identities; we can pass in the usual sense of this word. And it is in part this flexibility in performing our identities that we seek to theorize. For ten of her eighteen years of teaching, Brenda passed as able bodied in the classroom, never publicly or pedagogically disclosing her hearing loss. Similarly, for seven of her fifteen most recent years of teaching, Debra passed *as* heterosexual (for seven years before that, Debra passed *for* heterosexual, meaning that this was the way she identified her sexual "orientation"). However, at about the same time in our teaching careers, we both decided to make the ethical choice that Caughie refers to by seeing subjectivity as a "practice and a responsibility," not a "position" (247). We began performing our identities as disabled (Brenda) and lesbian (Debra) but also situated those performances *as* performances, compelling our students to engage not simply with our performed identities but also with identity formation itself.

Our process of coming out—or in Caughie's formulation, our practice of passing—consists, then, of presenting our identities as both real and claimed, stable and fragile, permanent and temporary. This is a shifting frame of reference that doesn't fit the way most students have been taught to think about disability and/or sexuality. As we've said, this shifting frame owes a debt to the reconception of identity promoted by both disability studies and queer theory. In particular, it challenges the notion of stable identity categories, which, as Judith Butler notes, tend to be used as instruments of regulatory regimes (see *Gender Trouble* and "Imitation and Gender Insubordination"). Without the direct route of recognition, the most common frame of reference used to name identity, our students are inspired to ask about origins and affinities. They ask three questions in particular, sometimes spoken directly and sometimes only implied: (1) How did you get to be that way? (2) What does being "that way" mean? and (3) Is it possible for me to be that way, too? Although these questions, especially the first two, might arise in response to any gay, lesbian, and/or disabled teacher who comes out in the classroom, our presentation of our identities as conditional compels our students to ask them. As a result of this presentation and the questions it raises, our identities pose risks: that the academic might explode into the personal; that students might project their fears and desires onto us as they become more aware of their own performances of identity; and that the classroom might become a series of coming outs and coming undone, as students confront (the possibility of) their own disabilities and/or their own queer desires.[3]

COMING IN, COMING OUT, PASSING

In the beginning (which isn't always the first day of class), naming oneself as deaf or lesbian can seem like a confession. We've found that no matter how we might reframe identity and its meaning, our initial declaration still has the look and the feel of a coming out, as if we are disclosing a taboo secret. Moreover, making this disclosure about our identities often causes us to feel as if we've transgressed the moral boundaries of behavior expected of the teacher. Even our recognition that naming our disability or lesbian identity will improve the functioning of our classes—"I must do this in order to carry out the 'normal' functions of classroom communication," "I must do this in order to establish an atmosphere of openness and honesty"—is not enough to completely eliminate our discomfort and worry about how the information will be received, processed, and returned. In particular, Brenda worries that students will read her disability identity with pity or question, at the outset, her intellectual ability or authority based on their perception of missing faculties; Debra is concerned that students might react to her lesbian identity with vitriolic, even violent, homophobia. Moreover, this act of naming our invisible and supposedly private identities can seem to turn the classroom away from knowledge and toward intimacy, and this can be troubling for both our students and ourselves because we have been conditioned to see the classroom as only an intellectual space. As bell hooks states, "Once we start talking in the classroom about the body and about how we live in our bodies, we're automatically challenging the way power has orchestrated itself in that particular institutionalized space" (136–37). However, besides resisting the notion that intimacy has no connection to knowledge and thus no place in the classroom, we are also aware that this necessary moment of disclosure is just that: a moment.

In the classroom we head toward the continual rather than the momentary, turning the naming of our identities into a process that is linked to a theory about identity rather than a one-time confession. Within this perspective, our coming out is not so much a functional disclosure as it is an embodied performance. We subsequently situate our *named* identities as *claimed* identities and explore the relationships, both oppressive and enabling, between what has been named (a positioning of identity as an absolute) and what has been claimed (a positioning of identity as contingent). As a result of this presentation of our identities, the moment of coming out turns into a movement, a bidirectional process of communication in which we and our students must do more than simply encounter a "secret": We and they must relate to it. That relationship is sometimes comforting, sometimes discomforting, and sometimes both at once.

For Brenda, for example, the act of identifying myself as deaf during that first day of class (and having to find the right moment to do so) is a necessary discomfort. Although I can pass as hearing for a while, especially when I'm doing most of the talking (as I usually am on that first day), I feel a responsibility to disclose my disability in order to create the conditions for effective classroom communication. Part of what is so uncomfortable for me, and one of the reasons I passed as hearing for so long, is the potential for those who've just learned of my deafness to turn me into some wondrous (freaky?) marvel—as a journalist recently did when she visited one of my classes in order to do a story about the development of disability studies at my university. At the end of the two-hour class, right in front of my students, she stood in the center of the room with me and asked, with that incredulous tone sometimes used for discussions of Olympic excellence, "but you aren't *really* deaf, are you?" Another great source of discomfort in this coming-out practice is my fear of the almost opposite but equally possible response: that my students will perceive me as incompetent, the echo of "deaf and dumb" ringing in their heads. *My mother doesn't think it's right that my English teacher is deaf,* a student once wrote in a paper he turned into me. So I'm trying to make it right here on this first day, trying to establish the limits of my abilities and the role they will play in expanding and enhancing those (in)abilities.

I start with a little auditory context, explaining the kinds of things I can and can't hear: how I've never heard a bird or bell or the last three notes on the piano; how I can't hear whispers or even soft-spoken folks; why I tune to lower-pitched male voices easier than female ones; why I struggle with consonants; how I can't hear the phone ring but can sometimes talk on it. I also tell them about strategies I use to listen: how I use a special "Clarity" phone for conversations and have to ask callers to identify themselves several times and then give a context for who they are and why they are calling; how I patch together the sense of what they are saying in class by watching their body language and expressions, by lipreading carefully, and by building from contextual clues around what has already been said; how my hearing aids help me in controlled classroom situations; why I love E-mail; how I have a tendency to move in on their space—to go toward them when they are talking; and finally, how they'll often have to repeat what they say in class and maybe, too, be asked to repeat or paraphrase what someone else has said. "So hey," I joke, "you gotta pay attention in this class!"

Now that I have their attention, I move from identifying functional reasons for naming my disability to ethically claiming a disability identity. I replace "deaf"—a term I used initially because I am aware that students have some familiarity with it if only as the antithesis to "hearing"—with "hard-of-hearing." To some extent this repositioning is an effort to claim an identity that more accurately fits me, but at the same time it troubles my identity because it represents a hyphenated existence, a position unclear in hearing culture (since it is a term outside the binary of deaf/hearing and usually assigned to a "special class" of senior citizens) and likewise, it is a position equally ambiguous in Deaf culture (since it is a term again outside the binary of deaf/hearing that doesn't align itself clearly with one's position in relation to sign language). I am not (that) old; I do use (some) sign language, although not here in an Ohio State University English classroom; I clearly am speaking (and don't deaf people have trouble speaking?); I look (pretty) normal; and I am, after all, the teacher (the voice and body of authority), am I not? With these parenthetical positions and the questions posed from them, students begin the process of relating to my identity; they are already starting to ask "How did you get to be that way?" "What does being 'that way' mean?" And eventually, as they become aware of the temporality of all abilities, the (temporarily) able-bodied among them might begin to wonder, Is it possible for me to be that way—if not deaf, then "disabled"—too?

For Debra, the act of coming out does not always happen on the first day, although it has. No matter when it occurs, I typically tell my students that I "identify as lesbian," a positioning that many of them find confusing. Besides the fact that few students expect their teacher to declare her sexual identity in the classroom, they are more familiar with the kind of coming out in which one names oneself, without qualification, as lesbian or gay. If they happen to miss my emphasis on identifying as lesbian, I ensure that they get it by then revealing that I identified as heterosexual for twenty-five years of my life. This claiming of a previous heterosexual identity might be seen as a move that creates comfortable space for both the heterosexual students and for me. However, because it is a claiming that comes *after* the claiming of a lesbian identity, my announcement actually raises the level of discomfort as well as the questions that Brenda and I have established as an effect of our coming out in the classroom: Well, if you were once heterosexual, how did you get to be lesbian (there's a nice double entendre in the way this question is worded, as if becoming lesbian were a promotion or a reward)? What does it mean to be lesbian? Is it possible for me to have sexual desires that contradict my proclaimed sexual orientation? This latter question seems to be especially prominent for some of the younger students since they are still settling into a sexual identity but haven't confronted the possibility that such an identity might be fluid, fragmented, or even transitory. As one of my gay students told me, "The idea that desire might be fluid scares me since I've worked so hard to accept myself as gay."

Our coming out as hard-of-hearing and lesbian-identified, respectively, opens the door for other identity presentations, such as our race (white), class status (middle), feminist identification, and body image (we both have struggled with anorexia at earlier times in our lives). Some of these presentations do not seem that momentous to our students because they name what students think they can see (racial and gender identity), what they believe they know (what a feminist is), or what is accepted in our society (middle-class status). However, we believe such namings are important because they help to articulate and complicate the sexual and disability identities we have revealed that are apparently invisible, discredited, fragile, and fluid.

For example, for Brenda, the particular kind of "hard-of-hearing" I am (even that this is the term I now use instead of "deaf") has everything to do with intersections of class, race, and educational privilege. That I was success-fully mainstreamed—even in a time right before the Individuals with Disabil-ities Education Act (IDEA) took effect in 1975—gaining literacy far beyond the national third-grade reading average for deaf and hard-of-hearing people, was directly related to being raised as a middle-class white child in a rural area where education was well supported in both revenues and community values. I have often quipped that I was not so much mainstreamed as "jetstreamed." Others, I know, couldn't get in the stream to begin with. In places such as the rural south or within immigrant communities in some of our largest cities, deaf and hard-of-hearing children (and adults as well) sometimes go virtually uneducated and remain largely alingual.[4] In Debra's case, I am aware—and I make my students aware as well—that the privilege I have as a white person living in a historically racialized society and teaching at a predominantly white Midwestern university gives me a kind of automatic authority the moment I enter the classroom. This authority might be compromised in a number of ways, including by telling students that I identify as lesbian or through poor pedagogical performance, but it is an authority given to me rather than one I must earn.

We now stand before our students as embodiments of the idea that iden-tity is both credited and discredited, essential and fluid, a nexus of intersect-ing and contingent social positions. As we have said, this approach to coming out makes our classrooms places of comfort and discomfort because it encour-ages both our students and us to share our stories, to investigate our identities, and to name our passions. This collective engagement turns our classrooms into spaces of intellectual and personal discovery as we explore the ways in which identity can ground and trouble us and seek to understand how we come to know what we think we know about ourselves and others. Indeed, the risk of discomfort and the concurrent possibility of discovery arise repeatedly in our classrooms because the social constructionist theory through which we present our disability and sexual identities also permeates our pedagogy. We find ourselves returning again and again to the scene of identity as we go about the usual business of investigating texts, formulating and responding to writing assignments, and leading class discussions. In short, identity becomes a dense transfer point of knowledge and discovery in our classrooms.

TAKING RISKS AND ACTING OUT:
THE CASE OF "SPECIAL TOPICS" COURSES

Although risks and possibilities are always present in all of our classrooms, they are enhanced in those courses that focus specifically on the subjects of sexuality and (dis)ability. In these classes students typically have a vested interest in promoting their own sense of identity, be that identity disabled or able bodied, gay, bisexual, or heterosexual. For the disabled and gay (and sometimes bisexual) students, a class in disability studies or gay and lesbian studies, respectively, is often perceived as a place where they can be themselves, read about others like them, and increase their feelings of self-worth as disabled, gay, or lesbian. It is a place they can come out and into. But it is also a place that can threaten the power or comfort they might have felt in passing. For the able-bodied and heterosexual students, such classes are places where they can learn about disabled and/or gay "others" (often others who are family members or friends), present themselves as sympathetic allies, and in the process publicly reaffirm their identities as able bodied or heterosexual. Yet these classes can also push these students to resist this learning and to oppose yet another diversity or political correctness shove they might feel they are being subjected to.

Because these student agendas are so prominent and compelling, our presentation of our identities as provisional and fluid disrupts almost everyone's expectations, which can lead to other kinds of disruptions.[5] Moreover, in these classes our own identities and bodies are so thoroughly contextualized—by the literature and theory we read as well as by the experiences and understandings that students bring with them—that they become overdetermined texts upon which students project their fears, anxieties, and desires. In short, the stakes over identities and bodies are very high in these classes, and this is also where we find the greatest possibility for transformation to occur.

For example, one of the first undergraduate courses in which Debra presented her sexual identity as conditioned and conditional was a Women in Literature class offered in the spring of 1996. I focused this course on female desires and sexuality, with an emphasis on lesbian sexuality, in twentieth-century literature. The class was so successful that I have used it as a model for my pedagogical practice ever since, even though there were certain unrepeatable variables. The most important of these variables was two graduate teaching assistants who had signed up as "apprentices" in order to hone their skills in teaching an undergraduate literature course. Significantly, both of these women knew about my approach to coming out and performing identity, and they were eager to situate their own identities similarly. So on the first day of class, the three of us talked about how important this literature was to us on both a personal and an intellectual level, and we informed the class of thirty students that we would express this personal relationship in a number of ways. The first way was by coming out. I went first, presenting my white, middle-class lesbian-identified identity as I described earlier; then one of the graduate students came out as a white, middle-class radical s/m lesbian who used to identify as bisexual and before that as straight (I'm not sure all the students in the class knew what she meant by this, which of course increased the ambiguity—and the students' curiosity—surrounding her identity); and the other one came out as a white, middle-class, partnered heterosexual woman who had sexual fantasies about women. There we stood, the three of us, all on some kind of borderline: that between gay and straight, between one kind of lesbian and another, between experience and fantasy, and between "normal" and "abnormal or queer."

The three of us performed along these borderlines as well as others throughout the quarter, and we introduced the students to characters who did the same. One of the first texts the class read was Nella Larsen's *Passing*, in which racial and, arguably, sexual identities fluctuate between instability and stability. On the first day of discussion the students professed their bewilderment over this choice of texts for the course. "The novel has no sex in it, and there are no lesbian characters," they complained. "How can it be about women's erotic experiences when the characters don't have any?" Their questions, of course, opened the door to discussions about what is erotic, how we come to know the sexual identity of someone else or even of ourselves, the role that social conditions and constructions play in our ability to claim an identity, and what it means to "pass." For the next class period the students read Deborah McDowell's introduction to *Passing*, in which she argues that the main character, Irene Redfield, has sexual feelings for her friend, Clare Kendry, and attempts to extinguish these feelings by pushing Clare out the window. The class debate about sexual identity subsequently intensified. I lectured briefly on the time period in which Larsen's novel is set, discussing the medicalization of desire by early-twentieth-century psychoanalysis and sexology and explaining the emergence in this literature of supposedly identifiable homosexual and heterosexual identities and bodies. I also compared Irene's situation to my own. When, I asked, do desires add up to a particular sexual identity? Must one have a heterosexual experience to be heterosexual, or a lesbian experience to be lesbian? Should we presume that our earliest heterosexual desires are false desires that I, or possibly Irene, misread until the true lesbian desire surfaced from the depths of repression? Or can desire take a new form, turning from heterosexual into lesbian? How do we know that one kind of desire will remain dominant and the other kind won't reappear one day? Who says the other kind has disappeared? And is "lesbian" the right identity for someone like me or Irene? Wouldn't bisexual or perhaps even queer be more accurate? Can our sexual categories adequately represent our sexual desires? Do these identity categories actually create the very desires they purport to simply describe?

Other texts on the syllabus, including theoretical works by Carole Vance on the construction of sexuality and by Elizabeth Grosz on the relation of language and female desire, continued our investigations of these questions. For instance, we read Jeanette Winterson's *Written on the Body*, which contains an unnamed, ambiguously gendered narrator who has a history of relationships with both men and women. We also read Carol Anshaw's *Aquamarine*, which follows the same white female character through three storylines, one in which she is heterosexually married, another in which she is involved in a lesbian relationship, and the last in which she is divorced. Both of these novels inspired the students to confront their own assumptions about gender and sexual identity as well as their assumptions about the stability of either. Some students, for instance, tried to prove that Winterson's narrator is female because she is observant in a way, they argue, that men are not, or because Winterson is a lesbian and must therefore be writing from that perspective. Others refuted these arguments by insisting that they rely on stereotypes and prove only that our judgments stem from our biases. "You're reading your own fantasy and assumptions into the novel," they stated, which is, I pointed out, part of what Winterson expects us to do.

Animated discussion also arose over the issue of whether we are more accepting of the violence in Winterson's novel if we imagine the narrator, who hits at least one woman and one man, as female rather than as male. Discussion also was lively over the question of whether we are more sympathetic to the narrator's adulterous relationship with Louise if we envision the narrator as female. A high point came when some students wondered whether the word "adultery" can be used to refer to a sexual relationship between two women, a musing that encouraged the class to think about the heterosexist language and politics of relationships and to consider how language shapes our understanding of desire. In short, like *Passing* and *Aquamarine,* this novel made the students aware of how much we want to know a person's identity, even when that identity might be intentionally ambiguous or ultimately unknowable.

Even some of the course texts in which the narrators are more clear-cut about their lesbian identity, for example, Cherríe Moraga's *Loving in the War Years* and Audre Lorde's *Zami,* were powerful reminders to the students of the social construction of identity. Both Moraga and Lorde are, after all, eloquently aware of how institutions shape us, of the identity possibilities that are and are not available to us given the way our bodies are read in American culture,[6] and of the way that our understanding of identity can shift over time or in different contexts. During these discussions the two graduate students and I were constantly performing our own understanding of the slipperiness and constructedness of identity. We even used our clothing to reinforce our performance. On the day that she was to lead class discussion on transgenderism, the graduate student who identified as a radical s/m lesbian came to class in a stunning, tailored pants suit. This outfit made her look feminine, in contrast to her previous androgynous appearance, until the graduate student who identified as heterosexual entered the classroom with her long blonde hair flowing, wearing a bright sundress. Some days I would dress in a skirt and heels; other days I came boyishly dressed in a jacket and straight-legged pants. Through these sartorial displays we were constantly attempting to engage and deconstruct fixed assumptions about lesbians and heterosexual women.

The changes we witnessed in the students were measurable, especially in the personal ways in which they began to respond to the three of us, the literature, and the theory. Early in the quarter, class discussion was brought to a halt when two students disagreed about the ethics of Moraga's intimate relationship with her mother in *Loving in the War Years,* and one of the students subsequently walked out of class. "I don't like classes where we talk about things," she declared as she left the room, "Teachers should impart information, not expect us to discuss issues." As she was leaving, I asked whether she was all right but decided to wait until later to find out what was going on with her (we talked in my office, and although she did not drop the class, she remained visibly uncomfortable throughout the quarter). As I attempted to return the class to the business of discussing Moraga's work, the other students responded in loud support of my teaching, and I had to caution them against this kind of intervention because it pitted students against each other and made it seem that only one individual was struggling with the implications of the material, which obviously wasn't true.

Later in the quarter a different kind of eruption occurred when several female heterosexual students openly acknowledged their lesbian desires. One of the outspoken lesbians in class challenged their joyful celebration of postmodern fluidity and their efforts to adopt a queer identity (a concept we were starting to discuss), arguing that these students were naïve if they believed they could publicly act on such desires without repercussions.[7] "I dare you to walk across campus holding another woman's hand," she declared, pointing out that their admission of lesbian desire did nothing to alter their privileged positioning within a heteronormative society. This discussion moved us into an exploration of the ethics of identity. I reminded the students that my own positioning of identity was a negotiation of a modernist paradigm of identity as fixed and absolute (I have been socially assigned the identity of "lesbian") and a postmodernist paradigm of identity as fluid and constructed (I am self-conscious about the limits of that identity). I present myself as lesbian-identified not only to be politically responsible to the world in which I must live, which also makes me vulnerable to the homophobia of that world, but also because a fixed lesbian identity doesn't accurately describe my erotic history or even its present. The straight students who were acknowledging their lesbian desires were, in many ways, following my example. However, they had not fully reflected on how their primary positioning within a normalized identity had different ethical implications than did my own primary positioning within a deviant identity. Although their acknowledgement was the kind that I wish more straight-identified people would publicly make, I agreed with the student who argued that it can go only so far in challenging the status quo. This question of ethics is one that I have subsequently foregrounded in my classes in order to address the sense of hopelessness that many students feel when they confront, many for the first time, the effects of their conditioning by a racist, sexist, heterosexist, and ableist society. Given that some identities are privileged in our society (white, heterosexual, male, able bodied), how, I ask students, can individuals who assume or are assigned these identities do so ethically? We don't always fully answer this question—any answer must be complicated since no particular identity is in and of itself subversive or reactionary, since we must all negotiate many intersections of identity, and since that identity can fluctuate—but at least we begin the conversation.

By the end of the quarter, several students in this class had switched their sexual identification from heterosexual to lesbian, and many of the others who identified as heterosexual were much more attuned to the privileges and limits of that identity. As one student put it, she had learned "not to assume and always accept the 'norm' but to examine the idea of a norm and its consequences." A number of the students confessed that they were simply confused about their desire and identification, not yet completely able to process the information they had taken in: "I was forced to think," one student related, "to use my brain even if it complicated and confused the whirlwind of gender and sexuality around me." On the final day of class, I learned that a number of students were having trouble communicating their new understanding of identity and sexuality to their friends and family. One student said that her father was a Christian minister, and she no longer believed what he had told her about the "sins" of homosexuality, but she also didn't know how to challenge him about his beliefs. This concern was echoed by other students in the class, and I realized then that some of these students wanted to be directed to materials that referred specifically to biblical interpretation and how homosexuality might be reconceived within a Christian context. Perhaps the biggest change came in a student who had entered the class identifying as a white heterosexual woman. The racial positioning of a light-skinned woman of color that Moraga examines in *Loving in the War Years* had deeply affected this student as she realized that she had denied her Asian American identity throughout high school, reading herself as white and asking others to do the same. She was also starting to recognize her desires for other women, and this recognition moved her into difficult territory with her strict Filipino parents. This student took two other classes with me, and in the third one, she introduced herself to her other classmates as a Filipino American bisexual woman. She even asked whether her boyfriend could attend a few classes so that he could see for himself what went on in my classes and why they had had such a profound influence on her.

For Brenda, the first entirely disability-centered course I taught was a junior-senior English major course, "Representations of (Dis)Ability in Literature and Film," under my department's grab-bag number, English 575, "Themes in Literature."[8] True to its number, the course was a grab bag, representing texts across multiple genres (drama, film, documentary, novels, poetry, and autobiography) and approaching disability from multiple—sometimes complementary, sometimes competing—perspectives. Thus, in approaching this rather unfamiliar subject, as well as employing a multi-textured generic approach and a pedagogical framework of setting texts in shifting relationships with each other, we grappled with a good amount of new and difficult material in ways that seemed new and difficult to many of the students. I had wanted to mix so much together quite deliberately and for several reasons. First, my intuition told me that introducing "disability"—as both a theme and a critical intervention—in reading literature and studying film would be the most successful way to attract junior-senior English majors to the class in the first place. I sensed that taking a multi-genre approach, with texts and authors who were both familiar and strange to students, as well as offering plenty of visual material (especially film), would help reel in enrollment. I needed to make the course accessible at the outset and interesting to our undergraduate body, regardless of the status of their own individual bodies.

Second, I ranged widely across genres and paired, sometimes tripled, texts in order to shake up norms surrounding notions of disability and disabled people. For example, we explored representations and issues around deafness in literature and film with a reading of Mark Medoff's Broadway-performed play *Children of a Lesser God* as compared to a screening of the Hollywood film by the same name, for which deaf actress Marlee Matlin won an Academy Award for best actress. Likewise, we considered several representations of John Merrick, the "Elephant Man," with a reading of Bernard Pomerance's play, *The Elephant Man,* a clip from David Bowie's production of Merrick's life, and some of the more "historical" records of Merrick and his condition (excerpted from Ashley Montagu's book about him). We also worked our way through interpretations of war veterans' experience and disability with a unit featuring Dalton Trumbo's classic manifesto-novel, *Johnny Got His Gun,* and the Jon Voight/Jane Fonda film *Coming Home.* We took on the classics, too, as we watched an A&E *Biography* about *The Hunchback of Notre Dame* and its multiple film representations. Then we read Hugo's novel itself (whose first French title had nothing to do with Quasimodo, the "hunchback," for only the later English printings of the novel began to focus on this disabled figure as the center of the story) and followed that reading with a double screening of the 1932 Lon Chaney version of the film (during the making of which Chaney, ironically, became disabled from performing with the heavy plaster-of-Paris hump on his back) and the new Disney animated version.

We engaged the tensions over parent-child relationships around disability, across gender and cultures, by reading several very different memoirs. First we encountered Paul West's 1970s' accounts of his deaf and brain-damaged daughter, rendered first in a kind of nonfiction meditation, *Words for a Deaf Daughter,* and then several years later in what West called his "wish fulfillment" novel, *Gala* (the two books are now printed together in one binding). Second we turned to Nobel prize-winning Japanese author Kenzaburo Ōe's account of life with his brain-damaged son, *A Healing Family*. This text also engaged us in multiple artistic representations since Hikari, the son, is himself a fairly gifted composer and pianist with two CDs to his credit (we listened to selections on those) and the wife/mother, Yukari, is a visual artist whose small sketches grace the book her husband wrote about her son. Finally, we closed out this set—and the class—with disabled author and mother Anne Finger's riveting and complex account of the birth of her (almost disabled) son, *Past Due: A Story of Disability, Pregnancy, and Birth*.

I wanted, in these ways and more, to keep the invocation and assignation of "disability" fluid, open, and unstable. By setting texts in conversations with each other, I thought we might best be able to explore literary representations in their plurality of bodies, minds, abilities, and disabilities. Employing Donna Haraway's version of feminism, which intentionally seeks out the "politics of interpretation, translation, stuttering, and the partly understood," I aimed to make the course about multiple subjects "with (at least) double vision . . . a critical vision consequent upon a critical positioning in inhomogenous gendered social space" (195). And although gender certainly figured heavily into the inhomogenous space in which I wanted to critically position the class, it was primarily in the larger inhomogenous space of "normalcy" that I hoped we would be roaming. I wanted to make a web of meaning for the way (dis)ability is employed in literature and film and, in so doing, to position disability as insight into reading literary and cultural representations of what bodies and minds can do and be. And I wanted that web to be strong yet supple, a thing that paradoxically traps and yet sustains—much as webs do.

To build the web, I opened with a preliminary lecture outlining some of the authors and characters luminous in "the canon" (ones they might already be familiar with) who also happened to be disabled: Homer, Tiresias, Captain Ahab, Alexander Pope, Samuel Johnson, Quasimodo, Benjy Compson, Flannery O'Connor, Richard III, and so on. With this introduction, students had already begun to ask critical questions about the politics of interpretation, translation, and the "partly understood" for these authors and characters; as junior and senior English majors, many thought they already knew these authors and characters, but now suddenly they were seeing them again, as multiple subjects through an at least double vision. "How did these characters and authors get to be 'that way'—disabled yet also often normalized in historical and literary interpretations? What does being 'that way' mean—in the context of their own time, for us now as their readers?" And then: "Is it possible for us to be 'that way,' too? In what ways are we like these characters and authors, and in what ways, too, do our own normalizing interpretations read us through them?" These are the questions we returned to repeatedly throughout the course.

With these questions and the multiply positioned texts, the students and I began to discover how truly difficult it was to locate the seemingly well-defined, oppositional positions between "disability" and "normalcy." We were in essence watching disability/normalcy deconstruct themselves, exploring how, as Derrida puts it, "an opposition of metaphysical concepts . . . is never the face-to-face of two terms, but a hierarchy and an order of subordination" (329). And we were discovering that disability identity, under deconstruction, "cannot limit itself or proceed immediately to a neutralization," but that, like the act of deconstruction we had placed it under, "it must, by means of a double gesture, a double science, a double writing, practice an *overturning* of the classical opposition [between 'normal' and 'disabled'] *and* a general *displacement* of the system" (329). Standing before the class—looking quite "normal" yet claiming "disability," engaging the double-hyphenated and doubly displaced (in both deaf and hearing worlds) position of "hard-of-hearing"—I myself deconstructed before their eyes. I went on writing, gesturing, speaking, questioning, and (re)positioning myself a little differently each day. I went on interpreting, translating, stuttering, and only partly understanding (and with my ears, this partial understanding is both literal and figurative)—even as I was probably only partly understood.

The risk of this partial understanding and the problems with overturning such classical oppositions and displacing systems like that of normalcy and the identity of (dis)ability means that things were not always so cozy in the courses I've taught around disability. In another course centered around the subject of disability a year after this first rather radiant experience with junior-senior English majors, things got considerably cloudier. Thunder and lightning and even some high winds stormed around us in my first graduate course on this subject, a three-department cross-listed course, "Representations of Disability in Culture, Science, and Literature." Two students in the course were visibly and actively "out" about their disabilities, acting out a bit, too. They spoke twice as much as the other students, and they made it increasingly risky for others, who were still in the process of outing their more hidden disabilities or who were out mostly by virtue of being *in* relationships with significant disabled others as children, spouses, parents, and even one as a personal aide. These two, and perhaps I as well in my role as (dis)abled instructor, engaged in the "crip-casteing"—the valued ordering of disabilities within the general category—I've seen in other similar places. At the Society for Disability Studies annual meeting, for example, it is always a band of very vocal and quite visibly out disabled scholars and activists who hold the microphones, who ask the questions, and who argue back and forth across the room with each other while a whole lot of the rest of us just hang back, look on, and listen in.

One of these onlookers in this particular course, a young graduate student who was the only student from a department outside the College of Humanities (where the course had been listed in English, Comparative Studies, and Women's Studies), wrote to me (but couldn't say in class, she felt) that she had never felt so afraid to speak up in class and that she had never before been so silent. Two other students were enrolled in the MFA creative writing program and, aside from the riskiness they felt they were engaged in just for taking a course that was heavy in critical theory and literary and rhetorical analysis, they were also acting out, exploring, and imagining ways to re-vision the stories they had been telling as fiction writers about more invisible kinds of disability—a mother's mental illness, a father's failing heart. They were looking for ways to carefully refashion into memoir, personal essays, and new journalism the heart disease and heartbreak of their mother, their father, and now their own physical and mental disabilities.

Another older graduate student—whose experience with disability was highly relational and slippery as the mother and wife of a disabled son and husband—bore the brunt of a lot of vicious attacks against mothers of disabled children. The two students who were out had very difficult relationships with their own mothers; this was something they wrote about with depth and frequency in many of their brief-response papers that we all shared with each other in class. Somehow the classroom space, the relational dynamics, and the subject matter—especially as we engaged a series of texts about able-mother/disabled-child relationships—made this particular real live mother too close and easy. They targeted her, but she didn't much want to be part of their practice. She fired back. And among these three, triangulated, I stood anything but still. As someone whose own relationship with her mother is targeted and treacherous, particularly around the unspoken subject of my "selective hearing" (as it is referred to in my family), and who is now the disabled mother of two "normal" children, I could see and sense the "logic"—both ethical and emotional—of *all* of their points, the rightness and righteousness of *all* of their positions.[9] My identity was slipping all over the place again, my understanding only partial in multiple ways.

One strategy I employed at this point was to sprinkle sawdust, so to speak, on our slippery classroom floor by situating the tensions over "bad mothers" more broadly. After one class when the (s)mothering issues around disabled adult children and their able-bodied mothers began to play out more personally, I worked to get the entire class to extract from other personal experiences as well as from their reading and knowledge in other arenas (women's studies, feminist theory, social work) what they knew about blaming mothers in our current cultural climate. I wanted to pull the discussion away from disability specifically in hopes of helping us achieve, if not some critical distance, at least a different angle on what had erupted in our previous class. First I had them write for themselves in response to a phrase written in big letters on the chalkboard, "Blaming Mothers." Then we worked together to fill the board with notes under smaller headings of "When/Where are mothers blamed?" "Who blames them?" "How are they blamed?" and most important, "Why are they blamed?" I pushed us all to counter, complicate, and contextualize any personal examples we might offer in working through these questions with what we had read, learned, and discussed from other texts and classrooms before we came to this one. At the end of this broader blaming discussion, I handed out two remarkable research pieces from Adrienne Asch and Michelle Fine's anthology, *Women with Disabilities*, where mothers specifically and women in general, as the caretakers of disabled people (their children, their parents, and institutionalized citizens), are subjected to societal scrutiny. The next class we returned to our regular reading, resumed following the syllabus, and although the subject of mothers in and around disability arose again, the air was a little less crackly, though still not clean. At least in this communal classroom space, the personal attacks on each other ceased after that point.

Our central point in these extended examples is that coming out in the way we do—presenting our identities as relational, fluid, conditional, and conditioned—seems to encourage students in our classes that are focused on sexuality or (dis)ability to embark on their own, sometimes difficult and often unfinished, search to understand their own desire, their own body, and their own identity. As a result they start to see the classroom as a place where the theoretical, the intellectual, the experiential, the personal, and the political all merge to shed meaning on their lives. As Rebecca Mark states, "De-emphasizing coming out in the classroom denies the epistemological and pedagogical power of the human presence and all that constitutes this presence—the body, the voice, the senses, the emotions. The desire to divorce [identity] from physical being ignores the simple fact that role models do change students' perceptions of themselves—that whom we learn from, how we learn, does help determine how and what we learn" (247).

RISKY PEDAGOGY IN (RELATIVELY) SAFE CLASSES

Without the context of sexuality or disability at the center of our classes—in other words, in the classes we teach that deal with regular subject matter—we still come out as we've described and we still end up as teachers whose bodies are constantly read and responded to by our students.[10] And our students still act out. However, there are some differences in these classes that we might characterize as having a lessened intensity. Because many of the students who take our desire-centered or disability-centered classes identify themselves as gay, lesbian, bisexual, and/or disabled, they bring a certain body of knowledge—and a knowledge of their own bodies—that students in our "standard" classes don't typically possess. They also bring an enthusiastic interest in exploring the issues of sexuality and (dis)ability, an interest that, as we've explained, gets complicated through our particular way of coming out. In our "normal" classes, our coming out is more contained because the discussion that surrounds it is not so concentrated or contested. In fact, students in these "ordinary" classes seem inclined to focus as much on the fact of our identity as on its slipperiness and on the question of what sexuality and (dis)ability have to do with literature and rhetoric. Often, when we come out in these classes, there is a moment of anxious silence, their muteness trying to shut off Brenda's mutability, their private desires trying to turn away from Debra's outed sexuality, their confusion seeking to restore our fluid identities to familiar categories.

Once the fact of our identities has registered with these students, questions often follow the silence. "What did your mother say when you came out as a lesbian?" "Are people born gay or is it a choice?" "Is it true that bisexuals are mistrusted by both gays and straights?" "How do you hear music?" "Do you use sign language at home?" "How do you lipread?" "Is it safe for you to drive?" And the questions are sometimes followed by confidences. "That was the bravest thing I've ever seen a teacher do." "I have a cousin who is gay and dying of AIDS." "My sister is a lesbian." "I'm bisexual." "I think I might be gay." "My grandmother has recently lost her hearing, and we worry about her because she now spends all her time alone." "My mother just had a stroke, and she can't talk, but they say she hears us." "I have a learning disability." "I know the sign language alphabet." "There was a deaf kid who lived down the block when I was growing up."

Besides the personal and experiential inquiries, the students also sometimes press us to explain how (dis)ability and sexuality are related to the subject matter of the course. To some extent, this is the same question that Eve Sedgwick writes about in *Epistemology of the Closet* when she concludes that, as a last resort, people dismiss the same-sex eroticism of an author by proclaiming, "The author or the author's important attachments may very well have been homosexual—but it would be provincial to let so insignificant a fact make any difference at all to our understanding of any serious project of life, writing, or thought" (53). Our response to this claim is to remind our students that literature has always served a normalizing as well as an imaginary function in our society, by which we mean that it reinforces yet also reinvents what it means to be human. Moreover, we remind students that literature typically deals with humans and the way their bodies experience the world and that these experiences are connected to epistemological, ontological, political, scientific, and economic frameworks through which our bodies are read and written. We point out that many of these frameworks have been built upon concepts of normalcy and abnormalcy, visibility and invisibility, the dominant and the marginalized. Part of our argument is that such concepts infiltrate the imaginations of authors, the actions of characters, and the responses of readers. We want our students to become more aware of these infiltrations and perhaps even to imagine other ways of conceiving, experiencing, and performing identity. So in the works that we read and study, we help our students pay attention not only to those bodies that are marked as "different" by virtue of their sexuality, disability, race, gender, or class but also to those bodies that are marked as "normal," and, even more, to the reasoning behind these markings and the spaces where the categories start to unravel, merge, or deconstruct.

For example, in a graduate course on the history of rhetoric, Brenda and her students pay a good bit of attention to how and why rhetoric—in both theory and practice—is so consumed with propriety, "taste," and prescribed ways of responding to situations, texts, audiences, and attacks. I point out that rhetoric serves and has served a normalizing and imaginary function in our culture—that it reinforces and reinvents what bodies can and can't do, whose body can and can't do it (rhetoric), and why bodies alone can or can't do it (why, as Plato insists, rhetoric is dangerous and we really need philosophy, dialectic, and truth). Throughout rhetoric's three-thousand-year history, treatises on taste, propriety, and the normal boundaries of speech and performance abound. Bodies are bound up in rhetoric's history everywhere. So, to illustrate, as we've just finished discussing rhetoric's "elocutionary movement," when prescriptions and descriptions of the range for a rhetor's normal delivery are abundant, I show a tape of sign language poetry performed by "Flying Words Project." Outside the typically assigned boundaries of speech and writing—beyond the common boundaries of rhetoric—a performance in sign language (where words do indeed fly) compels us all to rethink what rhetoric has long naturalized.

As another example, Debra often asks students to read romantic poems in which the gender of the speaker and/or of the listener is ambiguous. A number of Shakespeare sonnets will do. Students typically presume that the relationship is heterosexual, with Shakespeare speaking to a desired female partner. After they've pondered the complexities of each line, I then ask how they know the lover is female and whether there's any textual or even extratextual reason for that knowledge. For example, in *Sonnet 116,* the poet requests of himself that he not impede the marriage of true minds and determines that true love never alters. He then concludes with delightful ambiguity, "If this be error and upon me prov'd / I never writ, nor no man ever lov'd." With their perspective shifted, especially by noticing the ambiguity of the final line, some students will reconsider their initial presumption and even argue that the poem is written to a man;[11] some will adamantly defend their heterosexual reading, looking now for evidence that marks the lover as female, renaturalizing what has just been denaturalized; and a few will celebrate the ambiguity, proposing that such a poem enables everyone to project his or her own fantasies into it. I also remind them that the sex-gender system of Shakespeare's time differed from ours, not in an effort to support or exclude any of their interpretations but rather to further denaturalize our own way of thinking about sexuality.

Often by the end of the quarter in these typical classes, our students have stopped asking the question "What do disability and sexuality have to do with literature and rhetoric?" and are asking instead "Why have these identities and identity intersections been left out of literary and rhetorical study?" and "What other 'secrets' have been kept from us?" They have also begun to view the classroom as a place where the personal and the intellectual come together, for they will relate their own experiences (often a first-time realization that they even have such experiences) with disability, sexuality, race, class, and gender to the historical, literary, and rhetorical issues we discuss as a class. Of course, there are all sorts of reasons for these transformations in our students, but we believe that the process of reexamination is initiated by the process of performing our "secret," fluid, and intertwined identities and that their new engagement is enabled by our practice of coming out and passing.

RISKY REWARDS AND RELATIONS, OR, WHY DO IT THIS WAY?

Here, in conclusion, we can't neatly delineate the many effects and rewards of teaching about and through the slipperiness of identity. Perhaps the most significant result is that students begin to see that we relate to the subject matter we teach not simply on an intellectual plane but also in a personal space, or, more accurately, they begin to see that the lines between these areas—subject matter/self, intellectual/personal—are not easily drawn. This recognition inspires our students to explore the complex relations among us, the subject matter of the course, and themselves, an exploration that is enacted by their movement through the three questions we identified as prominent in their minds after we engage in this process of naming, claiming, contextualizing, and troubling our identities. First, they ask for more information about *us:* "How did you get to be that way?" This is apparently a question about origins that we transform into a discussion about social construction and the performance of identity. This move, in turn, encourages students to ask for more information about the *construction* of our own identities: "What does it mean to be that way?" A question about the effects of assigned and claimed identities on our lived experience, this inquiry moves us more deeply into conversations about the shaping effects of institutions (e.g., the family, medicine, law, religion, and education) and normalizing discourses on our identities. Finally, in many cases, our students want to know about *themselves:* "Is it possible for me to be that way too?" This question reveals their own understanding of the temporality and slipperiness of identity, especially sexual and disability identity, which—in our heterosexist, ableist society—can often be invisible or unreadable. Such identities are frequently fluid, contingent, and conditional. In short, we have opened up a space in our students' minds for imagining new ways of reading texts, bodies, and identities; for thinking about what can happen in a classroom and what teachers can be and do; and for reconsidering their own bodies, desires, and identities.

In the last few years, disability scholars and queer critics have begun to discuss the connections and crossovers between their lives and fields of study. In describing how we present historically discredited identities (lesbian and disabled) in the classroom, we hope that this chapter contributes to these conversations as well as to the larger conversation about how teachers might present their identity within a postmodern context. We think it is no accident that, independently, we first developed similar pedagogical approaches to both coming out and performing our identities and then only later began to understand—mostly because students we shared began to point it out to us—that we were enacting parallel pedagogies. After all, our fields (queer studies and disability studies) have worked passionately in the past decade to reorient identity away from medical and social models that label, fix, and often either castigate or attempt to cure (or alternatively to celebrate) "unfit" others toward a social constructionist model that seeks to account for the ways in which identity is constituted through "public practices and public property (namely, language)" (Caughie 14). Our understanding of our own identity has been profoundly altered by this work and has led both of us to reconfigure our identity presentations in the classroom from a simplistic liberal politics ("Come out and stay out") to a postmodern slipperiness that acknowledges the both the fluidity and the limits of identity.

Pamela Caughie notes that many critics writing on pedagogy today understand "risk taking in terms of the demands made on students. . . . Students do not choose to be at risk; rather, professors impose risk on students" (61). Although we believe that we ask our students to take risks—with their identities, their presumptions, and their understanding of the world—we also attempt to take those same risks as well. We take things personally, and so do our students, but, we hope, in the best sense of that phrase. By expressing and testing our own identifications, by relating them to the texts we read, and by making ourselves vulnerable to our students by letting them know who we are and what we are passionate about, we often feel at risk (but again in the best sense of that term). And we have found that by putting ourselves at risk, we provide room for students to do the same. The classroom doesn't always feel safe for any of us, but it almost always feels like important learning is taking place.

NOTES

1. Examples of such scholarship include Rebecca Mark, "Teaching from the Open Closet," *Listening to Silences: New Essays in Feminist Criticism,* ed. Elaine Hedges and Shelley Fisher Fishkin (New York: Oxford UP, 1994): 245–59; and Mary Elliott, "Coming Out in the Classroom: A Return to the Hard Place," *College English* 58.6 (1996): 693–708. Examples can also be found within the following works: *Coming Out of the Classroom Closet: Gay and Lesbian Students, Teachers, and Curricula,* ed. Karen

Harbeck (New York: Haworth, 1992); *Tilting the Tower: Lesbians, Teaching, Queer Subjects*, ed. Linda Garber (New York: Routledge, 1994); *Queer Words, Queer Images: Communication and the Construction of Homosexuality*, ed. R. Jeffrey Ringer (New York: New York UP, 1994); *Professions of Desire: Lesbian and Gay Studies in Literature*, ed. George Haggerty and Bonnie Zimmerman (New York: MLA, 1995); *Lesbians in Academia: Degrees of Freedom*, ed. Beth Mintz and Esther Rothblum (New York: Routledge, 1997); Karen Harbeck, *Gay and Lesbian Educators: Personal Freedoms, Public Constraints* (Malden, Mass.: Amethyst, 1997); *Out and about Campus: Personal Accounts by Lesbian, Gay, Bisexual and Transgendered College Students*, ed. Kim Howard and Annie Stevens (Los Angeles: Alyson, 2000).

2. Significantly, the scholarship about disabled teachers coming out in the classroom has only begun to emerge, and to our knowledge, this chapter is one of the first on the topic. We have heard speakers address this subject at various conferences, including the Enabling the Humanities Conference held at Ohio State in April 1998. However, the written work of these scholars is just starting to find its way into print. Other scholars working in disability studies have addressed their own identity as teachers or professionals in the field. For examples of this kind of work, see Simi Linton, *Claiming Disability: Knowledge and Identity* (New York UP, 1998); Lennard J. Davis, *Enforcing Normalcy: Disability, Deafness, and the Body* (London: Verso, 1995); and Ronald J. Anderson et al., *Enhancing Diversity: Educators with Disabilities* (Washington, D.C.: Gallaudet UP, 1998).

3. As we collaborated on this essay, we had long conversations about how to work with intersections of our identities and how to speak about our experiences without generalizing from or simplifying them. We want to make clear a few concerns that emerged from these conversations. First, by naming our identities as deaf and lesbian, respectively, we do not intend to suggest that one's (dis)ability identity and one's sexual identity are separate; quite the opposite, since one of the things we're trying to do here is to recognize some of the intersections of these identities as well as intersections along the lines of gender, race, and class. We are both acutely aware of the ways in which certain identities that we claim—for example, we are both white and middle-class, and Brenda identifies as heterosexual, Debra as able bodied—privilege us, and we attempt to account for some of those ways in this chapter. Second, in proposing that our identities are paradoxically conditional and permanent, imagined and real, we find that in the classroom we often have to dwell on experience: how we came to claim such an identity as well as why we view identity in this way. However, we are aware that not every gay, lesbian, and/or disabled teacher would feel comfortable or honest about making such claims—or that they would even consider their identity to be conditional or imagined. Our goal here is to present our approach and experiences as possibilities, not models.

4. See Lennard J. Davis, *Enforcing Normalcy: Disability, Deafness, and the Body* (London: Verso, 1995): 158–71.

5. Jyl Lynn Felman writes about her efforts when she teaches to "defy categorization. Identity in the postmodern classroom becomes the ultimate floating signifier" (144). Although our method differs from hers (she talks about herself as a kind of Puck-like performer who can become the student and enable the students to become the professor), we are working from a similar assumption about identity.

6. For example, Lorde suggests that white beauty standards in the 1950s made it hard for black lesbians to present themselves as "femme" (224).

7. Since this course, I've integrated the notion of queer and materials written by queer theorists more fully into my classes. Certainly the concept of queer—with its poststructural challenge to conventional understandings of sexual identity—is very much in line with the approach to identity that I take in my own coming out/passing practice and in my discussions of identity in the classroom. "Queer" has thus enabled many of my students to move beyond a simple gay/straight binary. However, the students always bring me back to the ways in which the gay/straight binary still informs and structures their lives. This real-world effect is one reason why I continue to tell my students that I identify as lesbian rather than name myself as queer.

8. Course description and syllabus are available through the following website: http://people.english.ohio-state.edu/Brueggemann.1/.

9. I learned my lesson from this tightrope experience, too: The next time I taught a similar graduate course around the subject of disability, a course called "Disability Discourses" under our department's "Seminar in Literacy Studies" number—I team-taught it with a colleague who was a leading folklorist, who was beginning to do disability studies-related work, and who was herself the mother of a multiply-disabled child. In this way, then, the mother position was complicated (between the two of us) as were the disciplinary angles and bodies of knowledge we could bring to bear on the subject.

10. In this section we invoke a variety of words (e.g., "standard," "regular") that echo the concept of "normalcy" in order to draw attention to the way in which our educational system participates in the normalizing of knowledge. Many of the courses we refer to in this section are part of the required curriculum at our university, whereas the courses referred to in the previous section are electives and are typically listed in the curriculum as special topics courses. We have found that the logic behind this classification contributes to the pedagogical conditions within which we perform our identities: By virtue of its classification as "special," the special topics courses make space for the performance of "deviant" identities, whereas the "normal" courses resist making such a space.

11. For information about the erotics of Shakespeare's sonnets, I draw upon Alan Sinfield, *Cultural Politics-Queer Reading* (Philadelphia: U of Pennsylvania P, 1994); Eve Sedgwick, *Between Men: English Literature and Male Homosocial Desire* (New York: Columbia UP, 1985); Bruce R. Smith, *Homosexual Desire in Shakespeare's England* (Chicago: U of Chicago P, 1991); and Kate Chedgzoy, *Shakespeare's Queer Children: Sexual Politics and Contemporary Culture* (New York: Manchester UP, 1995).

WORKS CITED

Anderson, Ronald J., Clayton E. Keller, and Joan M. Karp, eds. *Enhancing Diversity: Educators with Disabilities.* Washington, D.C.: Gallaudet UP, 1998.

Butler, Judith. *Bodies That Matter: On the Discursive Limits of "Sex."* New York: Routledge, 1993.

———. *Gender Trouble: Feminism and the Subversion of Identity.* New York: Routledge, 1990.

———. "Imitation and Gender Subordination." In *Inside/Out: Lesbian Theories, Gay Theories.* Ed. Diana Fuss. New York: Routledge, 1991. 13–31.

Caughie, Pamela L. *Passing and Pedagogy: The Dynamics of Responsibility.* Urbana: U of Illinois P, 1999.

Davis, Lennard J. *Enforcing Normalcy: Disability, Deafness, and the Body.* London: Verso, 1995.

Derrida, Jacques. *Margins of Philosophy.* Trans. Alan Bass. Chicago: U of Chicago P, 1982.

Elliott, Mary. "Coming Out in the Classroom: A Return to the Hard Place." *College English* 58.6 (1996): 693–708.

Felman, Jyl Lynn. *Never a Dull Moment: Teaching and the Art of Performance.* New York: Routledge, 2001.

Haraway, Donna. *Simians, Cyborgs, and Women: The Reinvention of Nature.* New York: Routledge, 1991.

hooks, bell. *Teaching to Transgress: Education as the Practice of Freedom.* New York: Routledge, 1994.

Linton, Simi. *Claiming Disability: Knowledge and Identity.* New York: New York UP, 1998.

Lorde, Audre. *Zami: A New Spelling of My Name.* Freedom, Calif.: Crossing, 1982.

Mark, Rebecca. "Teaching fom the Open Closet." In *Listening to Silences: New Essays in Feminist Criticism.* Ed. Elaine Hedges and Shelley Fisher Fishkin. New York: Oxford UP, 1994. 245–59.

Sedgwick, Eve Kosofsky. *Epistemology of the Closet.* Berkeley: U of California P, 1990.

Shakespeare, William. "Sonnet 116." *The Complete Works of Shakespeare.* Rev. ed. Ed. Hardin Craig and David Bevington. Glenview, Ill.: Scott, Foresman, 1973. 490.

Dangerous Responses

Michelle Cox
and
Katherine E. Tirabassi

> The decision to speak or write autobiographically must be made
> again and again. As each situation arises, we must ask: what is the
> nature of the constraint? What are the risks of speaking openly?
> Who benefits from my silence? Who benefits when I speak out?
> —Brenda Daly, in *Authoring a Life*

Composition teachers often talk about the way painful issues from the students' personal lives enter the classroom. We wonder where our responsibility lies in responding to the traumas students reveal in their writing. We wonder whether we are qualified to respond. But what do we do when the pain is on the teacher's side? Students can more easily break that boundary between the academic and the personal. The students are the ones doing the writing, and the act of writing, no matter what the topic, is always a vulnerable act. The students are the ones reading the assigned materials for the first time, and the assigned essays and short stories can often bring up painful memories. Though every member of a classroom helps create the general mood, students have less responsibility than the teacher does in this matter. Students often see composition teachers as mentors or even substitute parents and entrust them with secrets—through their writing, while conferencing, or even when trying to explain an absence or excuse a late essay. Teachers are usually protected from getting too personal by some of the reasons that allow students to be more vulnerable. The teachers' writing usually happens apart from the courses that they teach, creating a distance between the vulnerable space that the act of writing creates and the classroom space. The teacher is more familiar with the course materials, so the teacher is more aware of his or her own personal reactions to the pieces. And the teacher's role of responsibility in guiding the course as a whole is protecting in itself—this role takes the attention off the self and onto the students.

What are unknown about a composition course are the class makeup and the students' reactions to the course material and assignments. Sometimes a student's self-disclosure will spark a teacher's self-disclosure. For example, a student walks into a teacher's office and reads a draft about physical abuse by an ex-boyfriend. After she finishes reading, the student asks whether she should be writing about such a personal and painful topic—whether anyone would ever want to read it. The teacher self-discloses and tells the student that, as an abuse survivor herself, she values the student's work because her essay puts into words the feelings and experiences on which the teacher was still too afraid to dwell. She tells the student that her essay is helping her to heal—as it would for many other abuse survivors. In this situation the teacher's act of self-disclosure is well controlled. The teacher was probably mulling over the decision to self-disclose while the student read the draft, and the self-disclosure was contained—reaching the ears of only one student. The teacher also self-disclosed for a good reason—by discussing her own abuse, she validated the student's experiences and her act of writing about them. When the teacher self-discloses privately to one student, the justification is clearer than when the teacher self-discloses collectively to an entire classroom. How do we know when our self-disclosure to a whole class is justified, helpful, and in the best interest of our students and ourselves?

As composition teachers, we each asked ourselves this question during our second semester as teachers at the University of New Hampshire (UNH). We were each teaching freshman composition courses in a program called the "Christensen Hall Project" (C-Hall). In the C-Hall Project, the founders intended to create a learning community by assigning students involved in the project to the same residence hall and placing groups of twenty-four students in the same Freshman English course and health science lecture and lab. The teachers of the English and health science courses collaborated to make thematic and skills-based links between the two courses; what students learned in one class informed what they learned in the other.

Collaboration between English and science courses can be understandably difficult. At the end of our first semester of teaching, we discovered that we would each be taking part in the C-Hall project (and we each saw the project as a daunting task). Our Freshman English practicum professor Cinthia Gannett (who was one of the spearheads of the C-Hall Project) suggested that we collaborate on our Freshman English courses to ease the transition from the practicum to teaching in a learning community. During this semester we decided to write our syllabus and essay assignments collaboratively. We found that teaching the same curriculum served as an important assessment tool by helping us to continually evaluate our pedagogy and our assignments. Soon we discovered that this collaborative effort went much further than just being an assessment tool. Collaboration became an essential way for us to support each other as teachers, graduate students, colleagues, and friends. As David Bleich says in *Know and Tell: A Writing Pedagogy of Disclosure, Genre, and Membership*, "collaboration accompanies disclosure" (15), and when two teachers have collaborated as much as we have—by sitting at the computer together to put together new assignments, chatting in our shared office about how we plan on running a certain class, or checking in with each other over the phone to see how a class went—disclosure is inevitable. The very articulation of why we teach the way we do, which was the basis of most of those early collaboration conversations, was the beginning of that disclosure.

Paul Keegan's article, "Dangerous Parties," prompted more disclosures. When one of the English instructors handed us a copy of "Dangerous Parties" at the end of the first C-Hall staff meeting, she told us that her students connected strongly to this article because Keegan describes an incident that occurred in a residence hall at UNH. Her reason for using "Dangerous Parties" was to make a direct connection with the health science lecture on the dangers of alcohol consumption. She also pointed out that the article is a good example of a researched essay, an essay that Freshman English students write after midterm. We eventually decided to use the article but never expected the response it sparked in our students or in ourselves—a story we will tell in dialogue.

MICHELLE: I had forgotten about the article until Kate unburied it from her desk and suggested that we use it when we start teaching the researched essay. Kate told me that Keegan uses many interviews and thought it would be good for the students to analyze the ways he uses research. Without reading the article, I put it on the weekly class schedule.

I didn't read the article until after I had handed out the schedule. While my students were doing an in-class activity, I read the article at my desk the day before my students were assigned to read it. As I read, I became more and more uncomfortable. Keegan researches a 1987 incident that involves a UNH fresh-man, Sara, who had been out drinking at a fraternity party. By the time she came back to her residence hall, Stoke Hall, she had drunk so much that she was barely verbal. She was walking alone in Stoke when she was approached by Chris, a sophomore, who also lived in Stoke. Chris brought Sara into his room, had sex with her, then left and told his two friends, who, one by one, entered the room and also had sex with her. Chris and his friends felt that they weren't doing anything wrong. They felt that they were having sex with a will-ing partner. Sara did not remember what had happened until she began to hear rumors, and she did not call it rape until a therapist, whom she talked to three days later, gave it this name. In the article, Keegan asks whether the incident is a case of group sex or gang rape, vaguely implying that it is the latter. This inci-dent was clearly a case of gang rape. Why, then, did Keegan write the article so that the reader would question whether the incident was rape?

In the article Keegan also discusses the fallout after the incident. The word on what had happened spread through the campus like wildfire. Stu-dents hung banners on Hamilton Smith Hall saying "Beware, boys, rape will not be tolerated" and on Thompson Hall addressing UNH President Gordon Haaland, "Gordon, why do you allow rapists to stay on campus?" (154). The school held disciplinary hearings in Hamilton Smith, and the board decided that the boys were not guilty of sexual assault, but two of the boys were sus-pended for two semesters for "violating a university rule entitled 'Respect for Others'" (154). This sparked protests on campus. Two hundred students sur-rounded Thompson Hall, where the president's office is located, demanding that the school nullify the hearings, publicly apologize to Sara, and expel the three boys. Eventually the school complied. For the rest of the article Keegan interviews various students who were involved and explores fraternity parties and date rape in more detail.

I started our next class meeting by dividing the class into six groups and assigning each one a question that would cause students to analyze the article as a researched essay. I gave the students a few minutes to discuss the article in their groups and then had each group present on subjects such as voice, organization, thesis, interview, research, and interweaving personal materials. We did not have time to get to the last group on Wednesday, so I planned to use the beginning of Friday's class to continue our conversation. None of my students brought up the question of whether the incident was rape. The class ran without a hitch.

KATE: Before I taught on Wednesday morning, I talked with Michelle about her students' reactions to the article. She told me that her class did a great job analyzing the article and offered to give me the questions she used with her work groups. I copied them down, but I had decided to tackle the essay's con-tent before moving on to the author's stylistic choices. Because I had been a residence hall director for four years before I became a teacher, I was familiar with the myths students carry about rape, and I anticipated a divided class, one that would debate whether Sara was raped.

What I had not anticipated was an undivided class. The first person to speak about the article was "Sally," a vocal student who had expressed strong feminist views earlier in the semester and who I believed would argue that Sara had been raped. Yet I was surprised to hear Sally place responsibility for the rape on the victim. Sally argued that since Sara had gotten drunk, Sara was at fault for getting into the "situation" she did. The discussion then spiraled quickly away from the rape question and toward the irresponsibility of one's actions while intoxicated. I heard students say that Sara should've known better and that if she was determined to get drunk, then she should've realized that she was going to do "something stupid." Students jumped on Sally's bandwagon, many making the argument that since Sara was drunk and could not remember what happened, she was to blame. One student even argued that since Sara consented to one hug and one kiss from Jon (one of the men involved), she was engaging in sexual foreplay with him. Only one student argued that Sara was raped, suggesting that because Sara was intoxicated, she could not have been thinking clearly and therefore could not consent to having sex with one man, let alone three.

As a teacher I felt the responsibility to allow students to express their opinions, yet I also felt a responsibility to make my students aware that they had dangerous misconceptions about rape. In her book *Authoring a Life,* Brenda Daly talks about her struggle with interjecting her own beliefs into class discussion, stating, "I consciously avoid exerting too much control over discussions but, rather, encourage students to raise questions" (162). Usually I would agree with Daly's approach to class discussions; however, I felt caught between my pedagogical philosophies and my personal reactions to the discussion. I could feel the residence life training churning inside of me while the students talked. I wanted to scream all of the current rape statistics and facts I knew at my students. I wanted to tell them stories that would scare them into being more careful—stories about bringing "Kerri," a freshman woman visiting my residence hall, to the hospital for a rape examination just hours after three men had raped her. I wanted to tell them that I had sat and listened while Kerri told the Utah State University Police what she could remember—she told the story three times to three different officers, her voice a monotone and emotionless each time. As I listened to my students blame Sara for her rape, I felt as though I were betraying all rape survivors, allowing the discussion to blame rape victims for getting raped. I began to understand why Brenda Daly questions whether her approach to class discussion is at times too laissez-faire. As my students repeated rape myth after rape myth, I asked myself: "When should I step in? When has this freedom of expression gone too far? Have I abandoned rape survivors completely?"

At the end of class I collected my students' reader responses and walked to my office, feeling shocked and drained. Later that day, during a student conference, a female student expressed her disappointment with the women of our class. She said that she was sad that so many of the women were convinced that Sara was not raped. Her sadness and her willingness to express it gave me the confidence I needed. At that moment I resolved to revisit the content of the article on Friday, feeling that I owed this student a safe forum for her voice.

MICHELLE: When Kate told me about her students' responses to the article, I felt fortunate that I did not have to face the same controversy in my class. On Friday, however, after the last group presented and I was getting ready to move on to a writing exercise, one student announced that she did not believe that Sara was raped. Thinking back to Kate's class discussion, I asked, "Does anyone else feel this way?" Many students nodded. Five or six students started talking at once, raising their voices to be heard. They repeated many of the myths that Kate had told me her students had expressed. I jumped in to defend Sara. A couple of students timidly followed my lead. Then the student who first asserted that Sara was not raped said loudly, in frustration, "*Come on, guys, this girl was not being responsible. She obviously set herself up for this.*"

The more we talked, the less comfortable I became. I realized that the students weren't very educated on rape. In his article Keegan cites that one in eight women are raped before they leave college. The students didn't think that he could be right. One student said that she thought the number was more like one in a hundred, while another said, "No, I would think it's something more like one in fifty." I told them that I thought that the number was higher now, more like one in four, and then asked for a volunteer to look up the current statistics for the next class. I also told them that I have known about nine women who have been raped, one of whom had been raped in a dorm here at UNH.

One woman said that the fact that Sara took so long to report the rape proved that she had decided to call it rape in order to save her reputation. I asked whether anyone else had friends who had been raped, and a few students raised their hands. I asked them how long it took their friends to report the rape. One student said that it took her friend close to a year because her friend hadn't known whether she should call what had happened to her rape for a long time and then felt ashamed to tell anyone. The women in the class pointed out again and again that Sarah should have been more responsible, that she should not have drunk so much, and that she should party with friends that would watch out for her. I said that we all at certain times drink too much. I said that I have definitely drunk too much at times, and had I been raped during these times, would I have been to blame? I also pointed out that in their reader responses, many students acknowledged that they don't go to parties with their good friends, the friends they talk to and do homework with, but with their drinking buddies or party friends, people who are not there to watch their backs, but to get drunk with.

The class discussion swirled around and around. During the discussion many of us got visibly upset. One student, who was arguing that Sara was not raped, shook as she talked. Students leaned forward when they argued, speaking directly to the last person who spoke. I was shaking and felt my face turn red when I spoke about the time my close friend Caitlin got raped in the dorm. And during the whole discussion, I felt myself on the edge of self-disclosure. I was raped when I was fifteen, after drinking, by an acquaintance. My students' comments brought back too many memories. I hadn't talked about my rape in years.

KATE: Early Friday morning, as I read my students' reader responses, I discovered that seven of my students believed that Sara was raped. In the class discussion, some of these same students had proclaimed that Sara had engaged in consensual sex. Why was there such a gap between what these students expressed in the public forum of the classroom and what they had expressed during the private act of writing? Had peer pressure during Wednesday's class silenced some students? In their reader responses, some of these students shared stories about friends who had recently been raped while intoxicated. Perhaps their fear of publicly disclosing their friends' stories stopped them from defending Sara in the class discussion, a fear that could have been heightened by the fact that these students all lived in the same residence hall and knew many of the same people. Or perhaps these students didn't want to publicly admit their feelings about Sara's rape so that they could continue to feel safe when they go to fraternity parties.

I would be teaching this class in five hours. How could I draw out the voices of those students who had been silenced? As a composition teacher, how far could I go in educating my students about rape? I began to think proactively. I created a handout entitled "Dangerous Parties: Anonymous Responses from English 401," where I synthesized comments from the students' reader responses. In the handout I included two sections: "Voices you heard in class" and "Voices you didn't hear." In the second section I quoted students who said things such as "[Sara's case is] a perfect example of why rape happens over and over again, the guys get away with it" and "the only fault of [Sara's] was going to the fraternity and getting drunk but that doesn't make it right for three boys to rape her." After quickly typing the handout, I called the Director of the Sexual Harassment and Rape Prevention Program (SHARPP), and we discussed some possible strategies. She liked my handout idea, and she put together a packet of information that I could give to my students. I then called a former student, whom I knew had become a SHARPP advocate, and asked if he could attend my class.

I started class by having the students read the handout. The room fell silent, except for a few shuffling feet. When I asked for reactions to the handout, students said that, given our discussion on Wednesday, they were surprised that so many students believed Sara was raped. The discussion began, some students sticking to their beliefs, and others asking the SHARPP advocate questions, as though they were trying to make up their minds. I thought that I had done a great job. I had provided the students with the statistics they needed, I provided them with a trained expert on sexual assault, and I had provided a forum for the silenced voices to surface. I was in control of the situation.

But inside, I was not in control. Some of my students argued that Sara couldn't have been raped because the residents (and even the R.A.) who were standing in the hallway would have heard a struggle; they would have heard Sara trying to fight off her attacker. I could see TV rape scenes running through the eyes of all of my students. Did they truly believe that Sara, as drunk as she was, could have had the coordination to put up such a fight? Did they really think that every woman being raped tried to fight off her attacker? Didn't they know that some women freeze when they are attacked? I no longer wanted to listen to this discussion. I stopped focusing on their words and let my mind wander.

MICHELLE: The day after class, the word "rape" seemed to hang before my eyes. When I shut my eyes to it, the word went to the tip of my tongue, threatening to be voiced. I couldn't talk to my husband because I know he feels upset when he hears about the rape. I couldn't talk to my mother because the pain of the rape still hangs between us. I wasn't sure that I wanted to share this story with Kate yet. In an Autobiographical Criticism course I was taking with Diane Freedman, we were discussing self-disclosure in the writing classroom and in academia. Diane had offered to let us write "running writing"—short pieces throughout the semester rather than a long essay at the end of the semester. I needed to write. I stayed up late Saturday night and wrote about how the discussion in my Freshman English course had brought me to the edge of disclosing that I had been raped. I wrote about how I felt stuck at that edge. I E-mailed the essay to my professor with a short note about how my Freshman English course was connecting to our class discussion. At the last minute I copied Kate into the message.

KATE: When I read Michelle's E-mail, I was shocked. Michelle had prefaced it with these words: "Hi, Kate, I wrote some running writing to Diane and would like to share it with you. Thanks, Michelle." The beginning of her essay recounted her past week teaching Freshman English. I admired her willingness to write about the struggle she was having educating her students about rape. Near the end of the essay, I read the words, "I was raped . . ."—and my stomach turned cold. I stopped reading to recover and to let her words sink in. The fact that she was raped meant that she was feeling as helpless as I was about our students' misconceptions about rape. I was raped when I was eighteen. In our office the following day I had no idea what to say to Michelle. We made small talk about this and that, and, after a long enough pause Michelle asked, "Did you get my E-mail?" Silence. "Yes," I told her. "And we need to talk."

Interlude: That night we shared the details of our stories with one another. We will pause here to share our stories in dialogue.

MICHELLE: *When I was fifteen, I was raped.*

KATE: *When I was eighteen, I was raped.*

MICHELLE: *I was sixteen when I put a name to what happened to me. I told my best friend, Tammy. She didn't believe me—she accused me of trying to save my reputation.*

KATE: *I was a freshman in college when I was raped. I didn't call it rape until the beginning of my junior year. I was in Residence Life Training, preparing for my second year as a Resident Assistant (R.A.). After doing a session on date rape, my friend Cassie began to remember that she had been raped five years earlier. While she told me her story, flashbacks began to haunt me. With Cassie's help, I began to piece together my story.*

MICHELLE: *I told Tammy about the rape in response to her accusation that I was a slut. I was a sophomore in high school when I was raped. Tammy had seen me later that night, blood streaking down my pants, and she congratulated me on finally having sex. I remember nodding blankly, giving what happened to me the name sex, and not changing that name to rape until Tammy was screaming "slut" at me during an argument a year later.*

KATE: *Soon after I remembered my rape, I told Maggie, a close friend of mine. She had a long-time crush on Joe, my rapist, and she didn't want to believe my story. She told me that I couldn't have been raped by Joe, that he was "too nice of a guy." After talking to Maggie, I tried to shut my story out of my mind. Cassie asked me how my meeting with Maggie went. I told her that I now doubted my own memory. Telling me that I had to believe myself, Cassie told me that she was beginning counseling and that I should go, too. I took her advice. When my counselor Linda listened to my story, she said that I had been raped. I didn't believe her until she repeated the story to me, emphasizing Joe's premeditation. Nor did I believe her when she told me that the rape wasn't my fault. She urged me to repeat "It wasn't my fault" over and over until I believed myself.*

MICHELLE: I thought about disclosing to my students, but I remembered a scene described by Ruth Behar in her book *The Vulnerable Observer*. She tells about the "terrible silence, like a dark storm" that enveloped a conference room after one of her colleagues self-disclosed about being abused (17). I could imagine myself as standing in the center of that silence, waiting for my students' next move, no longer in control of my classroom. Part of me says that I was the wrong person to teach this article. A person with more distance would be better equipped. But part of me says that my closeness to the subject should make me the perfect person and should make me an authority. But without self-disclosing, how could I be an authority? A line from a They Might Be Giants song played again and again in my mind: *I was caught in the middle like a bird without a beak.* Like a bird, I felt the pressure of my song, my story, at the back of my throat, but I could not sing this song. I had to get out of that middle space.

KATE: I now know that my mind wandered during class discussions because my students were invalidating my own response to being raped, and I refused to listen. In my mind's eye, an old movie began to flicker. I could see the pale cinderblock wall, the closed door, the loft bed strangely placed on the floor. I could feel the panic beginning to rise in my throat. I remember saying "No" and then telling him that he was hurting me. My limbs felt numb. I couldn't move. Then his gruff voice, "It's ok . . . you'll be all right in a second." Through the cinderblock wall I could hear one student's voice saying that some women feel trapped, panicked, and unable to move; they "freeze." Freezing, like I did. When the SHARPP advocate began to make an analogy that seemed safe enough, I let myself tune back into the discussion.

Until my students unknowingly grazed the edges of my own experience, I didn't know that I could still react so emotionally to my own rape. I realized that I could use my personal experience to refute their claim, but my self-disclosure would be risky. Maybe my students wouldn't believe me just as Maggie had not. I worried that my self-disclosure would invalidate my authority to speak or that my students would see me as being on a crusade of sorts. I wondered whether my self-disclosure would have broken through the hypothetical layer of the discussion. I wanted to be real, but like Michelle, I was afraid of the silence that Behar describes. Brenda Daly talks about the dilemma of self-disclosure for a scholar: "In my view, if a female teacher discloses a history of sexual abuse, some students might infer that she lacks detachment and neutrality" (185). I decided that I couldn't trust my students to accept my experience as a valid one. I didn't want to risk finding out that I had become another Sara in their eyes.

MICHELLE: I felt the impulse to go out and do research. Cloaked with information, I could act the authority without self-disclosing. But I chose not to disclose to my class, nor did I do the research. Instead I asked for volunteers to do research on issues concerning rape and report their findings to the class over the next week. One student looked up current statistics of rape, another looked up the definition of sexual assault in the UNH student handbook, another looked up definitions of consent, and another looked up the history of SHARPP. We didn't do much with this information in class. After each report was given, I asked how the students related this information to our conversation about "Dangerous Parties." One of these small conversations was illuminating. The student reporting on current statistics said that only six percent of rape survivors report the rape, and that very few rapes that get reported actually end in prosecution—only about two percent. I asked, "Why do you think so few women report a rape?" One student, the same one who had reported on the research that day, answered, "Maybe they feel that no one would believe them." The class fell silent at this moment. I felt that the students were recognizing their own reactions to Sara. I nodded and said quietly, "Judging from the feedback that Sara received, I think this could be the case."

A LOOK BACKWARD

KATE: I thought that the paralyzing fear connected with my rape was behind me. I am happily married and haven't had any flashbacks in years. Yet, since that class discussion, I find myself looking over my shoulder when I'm walking home, even at dusk. Sometimes, as I quicken my steps, I clutch my keys (my only devices for self-defense); I'm ready to kick and scream and fight for my right not to be violated again. Sometimes the fear overtakes me. On the verge of screaming, I run to my car, fumble with my keys, hands shaking, and fling my bag onto the passenger's seat. As I get in the car, slam the door, and lock myself in, I have to catch my breath. As I wait, the terror begins to subside, my breathing slows, and I calm down. *Nothing has happened to me. I'm OK. . . . This time.*

MICHELLE: I had thought that I had gotten over the rape. After all, it happened twelve years ago. I never did get therapy for it. Since no one believed me, I feared that I had fabricated the whole thing or that it really was just sex that I was trying to escape responsibility for. A part of me still believes that I fabricated my rape and that someday someone will catch me in my lie.

I was fifteen. Tammy and I were walking barefoot down Simpson Road, the road on which we grew up. A truck full of guys drove by. We heard the gravel of the Smith farm driveway crunch and watched the truck reappear around the bend. The truck stopped, and one of the three men invited us to drink beer with them, motioning to a red-and-white cooler in the back. I didn't want to go, but Tammy was always looking for adventure, always trying to catch men's eyes. She often criticized me for not wearing makeup and for caring more about books than men. So we got into their truck. They drove us down a trail that led into the woods. They had been on their way home from a construction job. After we drank a few cans of beer, one of the men took off with the truck to go "find a chick"; another, Paul, walked to a different part of the woods with Tammy; and I was left behind with the third, a blond man who looked like he was in his thirties. For so long, I have blamed myself for what happened that night. Only now, through the class conversation around "Dangerous Parties" and long talks with Kate, do I *know* that what happened that night was rape. I may not have self-disclosed to my students, but I have found a way out of that middle space.

FINAL REFLECTIONS . . .

As we think back now, we stand by our decision not to self-disclose to our students. As Daly says, "personal confession, especially by a teacher, would inappropriately shift the focus of discussion from the text to the teacher." Rather than choosing to self-disclose to our students, we both chose to keep the students' attention on the text, and, as Daly says, "this focus on the text . . . allows us, both teachers and students, to place emotion-laden topics at a distance where they can be more effectively analyzed" (192). In our case, we needed that distance in order have a constructive conversation with our students and maintain control of our classrooms.

Our collaboration provided an appropriate space for self-disclosure. In his book *Know and Tell*, David Bleich states that "classroom and research collaboration . . . change the underlying assumptions of academic life, which are individualism, apprentice learning, and academic integrity achieved through isolated research, study, and writing [and we would add teaching]." Had we not been collaborating on our teaching that semester, each of us would have been alone in our struggle to educate our students about rape and to wade through our own traumatic memories. Bleich continues, "As practices that are bound together, disclosure and collaboration work toward uniting teaching and research" (15). That semester we were involved in many rings of collaboration: the C-Hall learning community, the health science teacher that we were linked with, and each other through our teaching. By writing about that semester, we are bringing that research and teaching together.

Writing also provided an appropriate space for self-disclosure, from the first short piece of running writing by Michelle, to our E-mail dialogues, to this collaborative essay. As Brenda Daly says, "I have not overcome the powerful taboo against bringing personal (and emotional) issues into the classroom. I fear that, if I become emotional, I might lose my 'professional' composure, my authority. For that reason, disclosing my personal history in the classroom remains far more difficult for me than writing about it" (191). We agree. We chose not to disclose to our students, but we did choose to disclose to each other, our professor, and now, through writing, to a wider audience.

Though a vulnerable act, self-disclosure through writing is always more controllable (and revisable) than self-disclosure through speech in the classroom setting. For this chapter, we have taken the time to sift through our emotions, choose our words carefully, and reconstruct our layers of memory. Self-disclosure through writing becomes crafted, not spontaneous, creating a safer space for self-disclosure.

As Louise DeSalvo writes in *Writing as a Way of Healing: How Telling Our Stories Transforms Our Lives*, "Writing about difficulties enables us to discover the wholeness of things, the connectedness of human experience. We understand that our greatest shocks do not separate us from humankind. Instead, through expressing ourselves, we establish our connection with others and with the world" (43). As we see it, writing is always transactional and therefore collaborative. Our collaboration, through both conversation and writing, helped us make sense of the chaotic emotions and responses in the classroom. Our responses to our students could have become dangerous. We could have become defensive—shutting down the classroom discussion to assert what we knew personally about rape and using our authority to silence the voices we did not want to hear. By talking and writing with each other, we were able to create the distance we needed to remain effective educators—to keep our attention on the learning process of the students. Through our experiences, collaboration in teaching, writing, and teacher-research provides an essential human connection among teachers—a connection that can help us assess our pedagogy, create effective learning communities, and heal the collaborators in the process.

WORKS CITED

Behar, Ruth. *The Vulnerable Observer: Anthropology That Breaks Your Heart*. Boston: Beacon, 1996.

Bleich, David. *Know and Tell: A Writing Pedagogy of Disclosure, Genre, and Membership*. Portsmouth, N.H.: Boynton/Cook, 1998.

Daly, Brenda. *Authoring a Life: A Woman's Survival in and through Literary Studies*. Albany: SUNY P, 1998.

DeSalvo, Louise. *Writing as a Way of Healing: How Telling Our Stories Transforms Our Lives*. New York: Harper, 1999.

Keegan, Paul. "Dangerous Parties." *New England Monthly* (Feb. 1988): 144–57.

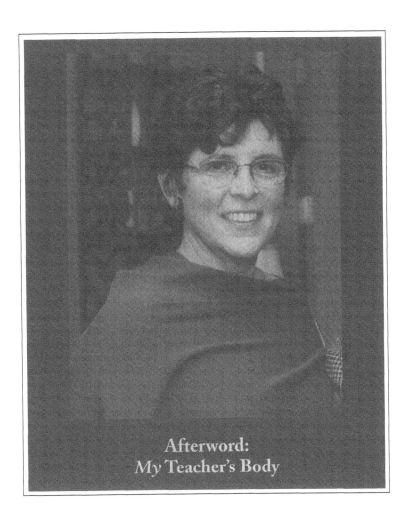

Afterword:
My Teacher's Body

Madeleine R. Grumet

That is the improvisation that I offer to this collection of essays. What I gain by the insertion of the personal pronoun is an assertion that in this discourse about the embodied experiences of teaching, every body is simultaneously a subject and an object. *My* teacher's body points simultaneously to my own body and to that of the person who teaches me. If this move adds particularity and relation, it also complements the categorical effect of *the* teacher's body and its important suggestion that teaching is embedded in cultural meanings, sedimented in history, and reinforced by ideology and emotion.

Our bodies are simultaneously both subject and object. This was the ambiguity that Sartre struggled with in *Being and Nothingness* as he described the way we are frozen in the gaze of another, a gaze that in Lacan's ontology freezes us in another's appraisal. Standing in front of the room, receiving the gaze of students, teachers risk that objectification and often cope with it by assuming stereotyped costumes, the rumpled absent-minded professor, or the Soho aesthete. In *Bitter Milk: Women and Teaching*, I suggest that the teacher's inclination to lecture was a way of avoiding the gaze, distracting students with verbal stimuli. But my body is not only material and the object of another's gaze, it is also my contact with the world, and through it runs a stream of responses and meanings that escapes the channels that culture has constructed to contain it. For Merleau-Ponty it is the precondition of our consciousness, reversing the Cartesian order that would make being contingent on thought, to maintain "I am, therefore I think":

> [W]hen I reflect on the essence of subjectivity, I find it bound up with that of the body and that of the world, this is because my existence as subjectivity is merely one with my existence as a body and with the existence of the world, and because the subject that I am, when taken concretely, is inseparable from this body and this world. The ontological world and body which we find at the core of the subject are not the world or body as idea, but on the one hand the world itself contracted into a comprehensive grasp, and on the other the body itself as a knowing-body. (408)

I want to have it both ways and shall, as I move in this afterword back and forth between the teacher's body and my teacher's body, simultaneously subject and object. Here I echo many of the authors in this volume, as I argue that the exploration of the tension between object and subject is pedagogically important. This drama of subject and object is played out on three planes: the experience of one's own body; the relationship of the knower to the known, informed by phenomenology's study of how the world appears to consciousness; and the study of intersubjectivity, a discourse of psychoanalysis and object relations theory. The performance of pedagogy takes place on each of these three stages simultaneously. The authors in this volume have not used this subject/object terminology, but they are very aware of the objectification they experience in the gaze of their students and in these reflections assert their subjectivity. They address the phenomenology of knowing as they consider how their particular perspectives can and should influence those of their students—and vice versa. And they consider the struggles of intersubjectivity as they address their desire to establish mutual recognition in their classrooms that allows them to communicate meaningfully with their students without relinquishing their own independence or undermining that of their students.[1]

Imagine this as a volley of pedagogy. The thing to be known—the object—is the ball. As it passes from teacher to student and back again, each swing and follow-through expresses the subjectivity that keeps the ball in the air. In this game, however, the ball cannot stay the same, for each exchange that reveals subjectivity reveals as well the stance and perception that constitute the object and thus change it.

This alternation of subject and object echoes the transactions that have constituted our own egos as well as our sense of the world. As our figure/ground perception develops, offering us a meaningful world, what was once completely distant from us, perhaps not even perceived, becomes an object that receives our attention. And then if attention leads to interest, we become engaged with this object. We may handle it, push it away, take it home, eat it, or dream about it. And each of these acts is saturated with our situation and feelings. Our intentionality does the handling, pushing, taking, eating, and dreaming. Once accomplished, these actions enlarge our consciousness of the world and make other actions—poking, stroking, giving, and speaking—possible.

This mixture of curiosity and desire that orients us toward all of those creatures and all of that stuff outside of ourselves erupts at the beginning of our knowing. In *The Transcendence of the Ego* Sartre portrayed intentionality as an empty wind blowing toward objects, and Merleau-Ponty pulled it into human experience by naming the world as the answer to the body's question. Nevertheless, often the empty wind, the body's questions, are directed by someone else. "Look," instructs a mother as her finger leads a baby's gaze to an approaching grandparent, a gliding plane, or a new toy. This primordial pedagogy that directs an infant's attention to the things in the world that its mother cares about is also connected to the infant's intentionality because it relies on the body ties that link mother and infant. The link between subject and object is forged by relation: an infant's capacity to love and be loved by its parents.

These terms, subject and object, organize epistemology—and in psychoanalytic theory, object relations—but they are displaced onto students and curriculum in education. When they appear in educational discourse, *subject* no longer indicates consciousness; it refers to topics for study, more appropriately objects for our attention. And *object* is a term for goals, as in "what is the object of this lesson?" When the subjects and objects of intentional consciousness are extended to pedagogy, they erase the teacher's subjectivity. Her intentionality, rooted in her idiosyncratic experience in the world, is drawn into the word for the material that our society has chosen to train our minds: subject matter. The object of the teacher's intentionality is ignored and transferred to the students as it denotes a strategy for the manipulation of students' consciousness as they realize the object of the lesson.

There are many cultural moments and themes that have contributed to this effacement of the teacher's subjectivity. Sometimes in the chapters of this book, you can hear the writers' recognition that when they write about themselves, about their experience of the classroom, and about how *they* feel, they are violating the convention that teachers are transparent: "sans teeth, sans eyes, sans taste, sans everything" (Shakespeare, *As You Like It* II.vii).

There are many reasons, some good, many just old and familiar, for this effacement. They are found in Philippe Ariès's argument that the ideology of childhood innocence was constructed during the Renaissance, when parents were moving from rural villages to larger and more complex urban settings and projecting their fears of a complex society onto their offspring. They are found in the history of the feminization of teaching that accompanied the growth of the common schools and flourished in the era of industrialization. They are found in the recognition that real teaching involves intense communication and relation, often leading to the abjection that denies eros in order to honor the vulnerability and freedom of the student. They are found in the desire of the community to control what children experience, foisting them onto teachers for care while attempting to control the teacher's influence and expression.

In this heterogeneous place, a nation whose authors were all descended from immigrants, nation building employed a national discourse that claimed to be public, accessible to all who could read. Michael Warner has argued that the invention and proliferation of print, erasing the bodies of its authors from their expression, was necessary to the development of the public sphere:

> The bourgeois public sphere claimed to have no relation to the body image at all. Public issues were depersonalized so that, in theory, any person would have the ability to offer an opinion about them and submit that opinion to the impersonal test of public debate without personal hazard. Yet the bourgeois public sphere continued to rely on features of certain bodies. Access to the public came in the whiteness and maleness that were then denied as forms of positivity, since the white male qua public person was only abstract rather than white and male. (382)

Nevertheless, despite this linguistic eclipse of subjectivity, in the classroom, "behind the classroom door," the teacher's embodied intentionality and the students' meet. Whatever we have noticed, touched, and grabbed probably becomes part of our intuitive sense of the world. But it does not become knowledge until it is resymbolized in reflection that gathers up the intentional moment and tags it. The tag may be verbal or visual; it may be a smell or texture. But as soon as it is tagged and entered into our system of memories and associations, it becomes part of our subjectivity—part of the equipment and interest that will travel with us the next time we encounter something that smells like a pear or feels like satin. And so the objects of intentionality, the otherness that surrounds and beckons us, get coded and filed in a linguistic system saturated with history and culture. Intentionality and reflexivity turn objects into a subjectivity that is always expanding and noticing more of the world.

This subjective intentionality is grounded in our bodies. What teachers and their students notice and care about may differ; yet here they are, gathered in the same space and time, day out and day in, looking at the same object.

Paulo Freire used to talk about curriculum as an object to be known.[2] He said we needed to place it in the middle of the table and then approach it, each from our own perspective, history, and interest. Nevertheless, this table setting has not been customary in most classrooms. More likely is Foucault's portrayal, in *Discipline and Punish*, of the Panopticon, whose center is held by a surveying authority, fixing those on the perimeter with its normative gaze: surveillance.

Many teachers in this volume have brought their students to Freire's table by asking them to think and write about their own experiences. These are body-texts, narratives that take place in space and time, remembered and anchored in sense memory as well as logical associations. The use of autobiographical writing in many of the courses described in the preceding chapters should not be attributed to a motivational ploy. Students are not asked to talk about their experience just so that they get interested and then don't notice that the subject has been switched to the assigned text.

The mixing of autobiographical texts with the assigned readings of a course, theoretical, classical, or literary, provides an intertextuality that anchors abstractions in lived, sensuous experience. Autobiographical writings can provide the questions and perspectives that students bring to their study of texts. They can provide the lived details that confirm or challenge a text's claims. They can be read using the text as an interpretive scheme, so that the assumptions that have organized the autobiographical narrative can themselves be challenged.

The teachers in this text also challenge the illusion that meanings inhere in subject matter and lessons. They understand that teaching is not only about socialization to the codes and meanings of our ever-expanding culture. The abstentions that pull the classroom out from the press and preoccupations of domesticity and the marketplace also create a space that permits cultural norms and assumptions to be identified, investigated, challenged, and changed. This is the aesthetic dimension of teaching that improvises on everyday perceptions, creating ways of seeing our shared meanings that simultaneously offer critique of the status quo and visions of a new version.

By admitting that we have bodies, these teachers prevent their aesthetic process from sliding into idealism. Too often the liminal space of the classroom claims the distinction of critique or vision by refusing to acknowledge the material, embodied day-to-day experience that an alternative view must negotiate. My body throws a horizon around my imagination. It does not reduce my subjectivity to my arthritic knee; it does not erase my mortality because my hair is still brown. But it tethers my imagination to a set of possibilities, which, although it is protean, is not limitless. This aesthetic reveals the reciprocity of subjectivity and objectivity by recognizing that the object of study, whether it is literature, sociology, field biology, or composition, is constituted by an inquiring subjectivity: We see what we look for, and what we look for is constituted not only by what my body can do, but also what it cannot do. Every stance, near or far, still or running like the wind, is a point of presence from which we may know the world.

It is this kind of pedagogy that the authors of these essays describe, worry over, and at times celebrate. All teaching involves complex and sensitive decisions. But because these teachers are willing to acknowledge their power and their vulnerability, as well as that of their students, their narratives of teaching interrogate the ethics of their choices.

I think of ethics as the rules for intimate relationships with people I don't really know, for we rarely use the term *ethics* to describe the behavior of lovers, of parents and their children, or even of neighbors. We refer to ethics to describe the actions and judgments of some people (often called professionals) who have the power and legal permission to relate to other people in ways that are intimate: judging them, healing them, representing them, or teaching them.

Teachers who disclose perspectives and understandings that they have drawn from their lived, embodied experience in the world are profoundly challenging their students' own frames for action and judgment. The challenge is subtle but compelling. If my life experience diverges from that of my students or that of the cultural norm—mid-forties, able bodied, heterosexual, slim, Caucasian, upper middle class—and I acknowledge my own "take," my students are challenged in two ways: They are provoked to acknowledge their own difference from the norm, and they are invited to entertain and acknowledge the possibility that they may indeed be like me, someone whom they had assumed was different from them.

Young people, anxious about their futures, their safety, and their capacity to engage society successfully, are often resistant to these invitations. Even though they know in their heart of hearts that the hero and heroines of popular culture are fictions and rarely correspond to any real people, living or dead, they collude with their peers to sustain the ideal and to reach for it themselves. It is a guide, an icon of cultural approval and success, and it is a disguise that conceals their particular bodies, class status, life histories, and anxieties.

Furthermore, and here they are like their elders, students excuse themselves from empathy toward people whom they perceive to be vulnerable by differentiating themselves from people whom they perceive as weak or marginalized. We all, as Kristeva has pointed out, tend to deny the difference within ourselves—the desires we don't act on, the fears or angers we don't express—projecting those refused characteristics onto others who appear different from us. So, at the heart of every bias that derogates otherness, is the fear that the stigmatized characteristic resides within us. Now imagine the turmoil that can emerge if the person bearing that stigma is my teacher, and if my experience of her warmth, or intelligence, or power diminishes my capacity to ignore or dismiss the issues that she represents and that I wish to evade.

Here is where these author/teachers are both thoughtful and generous. Their chapters remind us that we have passed through the era of identity politics, when members of oppressed and marginalized groups, in an effort to declare specificity and be witnessed, collapsed subjectivity—which edges away from any objectification—into identity. But their essays do not flee identity politics by returning to the putative neutrality that denies the specificity of the body and the sedimentations of history or posits a learning consciousness, sans teeth, sans taste, sans eyes, sans everything.

It is possible to evade these issues. Again, if the subject is subject matter, and the object belongs to the lesson rather than my intentionality, we, students and teachers, can pretend to ignore each other and ourselves as we participate in the performance of teaching and learning. The categories of student, female, Asian, deaf, teacher, gay, or old—even if dressed up as identity politics—distract us from imagining the subjectivity that animates every identity without completely coinciding with it. But if these categories are claimed, interpreted through our practice, and elaborated in our stories, then we cannot continue to gather together in classrooms behaving as if each of us is there alone.

These teachers tolerate the generative tension of pedagogy, recognizing their own subjectivity as well as that of their students, and inviting their students to reciprocate. It is a delicate and ethical invitation; it has required these teachers to imagine their students' worlds and feelings so that as they disclose their own, they do not overwhelm their students or repudiate lived understandings.

Scott Smith:

No student, in my eight years of being on that table at the head of the class, has ever asked me to explain the paragraphs of my legs or the argument of my dwarfism. No one has yet to break that membrane of silence. As I walk into three new classrooms and into the academic lives of sixty new students this semester, I wonder whether the question will ever be asked or whether it is even something that is appropriate.

Kate Tirabassi:

Until my students unknowingly grazed the edges of my own experience, I didn't know that I could still react so emotionally to my own rape. I realized that I could use my personal experience to refute their claim, but my self-disclosure would be risky. Maybe my students wouldn't believe me just as Maggie and my mother had not. I worried that my self-disclosure would invalidate my authority to speak and that my students would see me as being on a crusade of sorts.

Brenda Brueggemann and Debra Moddelmog:

First, they ask for more information about *us:* "How did you get to be that way?" This is apparently a question about origins that we transform into a discussion about social construction and the performance of identity. This move, in turn, encourages students to ask for more information about the *construction* of our own identities: "What does it mean to be that way?" A question about the effects of assigned and claimed identities on our lived experience, this inquiry moves us more deeply into conversations about the shaping effects of institutions (e.g., the family, medicine, law, religion, and education) and normalizing discourses on our identities. Finally, in many cases, our students want to know about *themselves:* "Is it possible for me to be that way too?"

Amy Gerald:

Perhaps my students really wanted to see me as whole person, especially when evidence of my life away from the university was so apparent. I felt uneasy about sharing information and experiences about my pregnancy with my students because I thought it was an inappropriate subject to bring into a writing classroom. How hypocritical is that attitude, when I assign journal entries and paper assignments that ask students how they *feel* about race, gender, family, and other personal subjects?

Carolyn DiPalma:

The group in the corner turned to face me, surprising me by walking forward together and presenting me with a dish on top of which rested a "bald" cake—an angel food cake without icing—to celebrate and support my decision for baldness. It was a moving and lovely gesture, and again I was quite touched. But it was also more than that. Sharing that cake was a way for us to all share the complicated and dynamic tensions of that classroom. It was a way for the students to speak out and participate in my experience and for me to join them in their experience. The cake marked a recognition that we were going through an ill-defined and important process together—one at which we were all willing to work. I recognized the moment not as sentimental, but as political, an ironic moment of classroom power in which action, support, awakening, investment, coalition building, and recognition of mortality became political practices of the day. I understood that for students, too, coming to terms with serious illness meant, in part, facing such a possibility for themselves. Likewise, witnessing and celebrating my recovery also implied the possibility of their own.
From that day on I taught brazenly bald.

It is not easy to give up the idealization that teaching offers. We stand before our students, older, credentialed, and endowed with the power to judge them. Ah, the lure of mimesis. We want them to be like us, to confirm our choices, admire our achievements, and share our interests. The capacity to read and write and speak like us, to manipulate numbers, stethoscopes, or paint brushes as we do may indeed move them along the path to material, social, and intellectual success. So the temptation is to be present just so much but not enough to risk their alienation. And if we keep the curriculum idealized or always pointing to a reality that no one in the room owns, we can pleasantly agree on what is interesting, important, right, and good.

But our bodies give us away. We express our specificity in the torn tendon, the blushing cheek. Shortness of breath undermines emphatic ideas; a clenched fist belies a cheerful acquiescence. And in this volume these teachers do not turn away from what they have seen, and felt, and heard in their classrooms. They are carefully measuring and adjusting the space between themselves and their students. They are imaginatively trying to see themselves in their students' eyes, and they make a mighty effort to stave off the defensiveness that can pop up when those students are dismissive, impatient, or insulting. They engage a dialectical pedagogy that challenges idealized language and text with embodied experience and confronts easy retreats to determinism by invoking the contrary and limitless possibilities of human subjectivity.

Finally, by acknowledging the specificity of their embodied lives and histories, these teachers admit specificity and particularity into the conversations of their classrooms. In this nation haunted by its origin as a frontier outpost peopled by immigrants who fled the towns, villages, and cities of Europe, we have always embedded a nostalgia for those forsaken places in the curriculum where we glorify their culture. Although we encouraged the study of the cosmopolitan culture of other places—world history, foreign languages, and philosophy—we discouraged attention to whatever was familiar, current, and part of the everyday experience of our students. That preference for the distant and exotic has been modified as curriculum embraces the relatively new fields of social history and popular culture, but it is still our tendency to step over the campus, the neighborhood, or the county when we are looking for suitable objects of knowledge. I am not advocating a solely current and proximate curriculum, but I am celebrating a curriculum at every level of education that acknowledges the existential realities of its teachers and students. These teachers make themselves present so that their students may be present as well and in that presence integrate their anxious, sweaty, sublime ideas and feelings with the stuff of texts and theories. That is how they all get smart.

NOTES

1. In *The Bonds of Love*, Jessica Benjamin brings Hegel's thought and object relations theory to explore mutual recognition as an alternative to domination/submission.

2. Personal communication.

WORKS CITED

Ariès, Philippe. *Centuries of Childhood*. Trans. Robert Baldick. New York: Random, 1965.

Benjamin, Jessica. *The Bonds of Love*. New York: Pantheon, 1988.

Foucault, Michel. *Discipline and Punish*. Trans. Alan Sheridan. New York: Random, 1979.

Grumet, Madeleine, R. *Bitter Milk: Women and Teaching*. Amherst: U of Massachusetts P, 1988.

Kristeva, Julia. "Women's Time." Trans. Alice Jardine and Harry Blake. *Feminist Theory: A Critique of Ideology*. Ed. Nannerl O. Keohane, Michelle Z. Rosaldo, and Barbara C. Gelpi. Chicago: U of Chicago P, 1981. 31–53.

Lacan, Jacques. "The Eye and the Gaze." Trans. Alain Sheridan. *The Four Fundamental Concepts of Psycho-analysis*. Ed. Jacques-Alain Miller. New York: Norton, 1981.

Merleau-Ponty, Maurice. *Phenomenology of Perception*. Trans. Colin Wilson. New York: Humanities, 1964.

Sartre, Jean-Paul. "The Look." *Being and Nothingness*. Trans. Hazel Barnes. New York: Washington Square, 1966.

———. *The Transcendence of the Ego*. Trans. Forrest Williams and Robert Kilpatrick. New York: Octagon, 1972.

Shakespeare, William. *As You Like It*. 1599.

Warner, Michael. "The Mass Public and the Mass Subject." *Habermas and the Public Sphere*. Ed. Craig Calhoun. Boston: MIT P, 1993.

Epilogue

Diane P. Freedman
and
Martha Stoddard Holmes

After issuing a call for papers for a proposed MLA special session on "The Teacher's Body," Martha realized she was already on the docket too many times to serve as the session organizer, so she asked Diane whether she would like to evaluate the submissions and put together the panel proposal. Diane readily agreed and was amazed at the richness of the materials that kept arriving. After proposing the session to MLA, only to have it be rejected, Diane convinced Martha that the stories they'd so far received in paper or abstract form had to be told to the academic profession at large; we would just have to expand the call, ask for follow-up essays to the abstracts, and put together what we knew would be an important volume. The gift we didn't anticipate was a network of new and renewed relationships with our contributors, who are diverse in ages, disciplines, institutions, geographical regions, and, of course, bodies.

We are thrilled that the essays in this volume consistently confront professional and pedagogical issues rarely articulated in academic life or discourse even in the era of a "memoir boom" and the putative post-diversity environment in which all manner of utterances—and identities—are supposedly possible. We are certain that these honest and critically framed stories need to circulate and instigate the exploration of other such stories. *The Teacher's Body* demonstrates that even though a teacher cannot be dismissed simply for being married, disabled, pregnant, queer, old, or ill—in short, for having a body—

teachers, students, and administrators are still unsure of how to talk through, around, and about the bodies that lie between us. Our greater institutional openness about what identities can be claimed and affirmed in the classroom and what marginal or private topics can be central to our intellectual conversations may have raised more complex questions about the teacher's body and obscured the fact that we haven't found a satisfactory mode for talking through the embodied dynamics in any academic setting.

Having loudly articulated our commitment to conceptual and statistical diversity, as many of our campuses have, we have often not stopped to think on a local level about what the daily praxis of the inclusive classroom really involves or had satisfying conversations about how to work through the problems that arise when we let our bodies into the academy.

Drawing on the increasing awareness that teaching and research in the academy are inevitably shaped by one's individual and collective life experiences and vice versa, this volume provides the pathways for those conversations, just as the process itself of putting it together generated remarkable interchanges among contributors and editors. We thank them—and each other—and wait breathlessly for the next round of the conversation.

Contributors

JONATHAN ALEXANDER is Associate Professor of English and Women's Studies at the University of Cincinnati, where he teaches writing, lesbian and gay studies, and Web literacy. He has published in *Feminist Teacher; Radical Teacher; The Journal of Bisexuality; The Journal of Gay, Lesbian, and Bisexual Identity; Computers and Composition;* and *The International Journal of Gender and Sexuality Studies,* among others. A book, *Queer Composition(s): Queer Theory in the Writing Classroom,* coedited with Michelle Gibson, is forthcoming.

SIMONE A. JAMES ALEXANDER, Assistant Professor of African American Studies at Seton Hall University, has also taught at the Pratt Institute; Rutgers University, where she received her Ph.D.; Borough of Manhattan Community College; and the University of Peoples' Friendship in Moscow. She is the author of *Mother Imagery in the Novels of Afro-Caribbean Women* and articles on Jamaica Kincaid, Paule Marshall, and others.

BRENDA JO BRUEGGEMANN is Associate Professor of English at Ohio State University, where she also directs the first-year writing program. She is the author of *Lend Me Your Ear: Rhetorical Constructions of Deafness;* articles in journals and collections on disability studies, deaf studies, literacy studies, qualitative research, pedagogy, and professional issues for English studies; and several published literary essays. She is coeditor of *Disability Studies: Enabling the Humanities,* and editor of a forthcoming collection, *Perspectives on Literacy, Deafness, and Culture.*

MICHELLE COX is a Ph.D. student in composition/rhetoric at the University of New Hampshire. She has been a freshman English instructor and a writing fellow and has worked as a writing and curriculum design consultant. Her other research interests include writing in the disciplines, second language writing, and genre systems.

BRENDA DALY, Professor of English at Iowa State University, teaches courses such as "Trauma, Memory, Healing, and Contemporary Women's Narratives." Her most recent book, *Authoring a Life*, is an autobiographical-scholarly account of how, within the context of the women's movement, reading and writing enabled her to overcome the trauma of sexual abuse.

CORTNEY DAVIS, nurse practitioner at Danbury Hospital, Danbury, Connecticut, is the author of *I Knew a Woman: The Experience of the Female Body* and of two volumes of poetry, *The Body Flute* and *Details of Flesh*. She is coeditor of the volumes *Between the Heartbeats: Poetry and Prose by Nurses* and *Intensive Care: More Poetry and Prose by Nurses*. Cortney often gives readings and teaches creative writing workshops for healthcare professionals.

CAROLYN DIPALMA is Assistant Professor of Women's Studies at the University of South Florida. She is coeditor of *Teaching Introduction to Women's Studies: Expectations and Strategies*. She has published essays in *Configurations: A Journal of Literature, Science and Technology; Asian Journal of Women's Studies; Intertexts;* and *The Reader's Guide to Women's Studies*, as well as reviews in *Hypatia* and *Theory and Event*. She teaches feminist theory, political theory, body politics, women's health, and the introductory course to women's studies. She is especially interested in body politics.

BETTY SMITH FRANKLIN is Associate Professor of Curriculum, Foundations, and Research at Georgia Southern University in Statesboro. With her students and colleagues she has just completed a huge art installation, "Imagining Education."

DIANE P. FREEDMAN, Associate Professor of English and core faculty member in Women's Studies at the University of New Hampshire, teaches courses in American literature and theory, nature writing, poetry, and memoir. Her publications include *An Alchemy of Genres: Cross-Genre Writing by American Feminist Poet-Critics; Millay at 100: A Critical Reappraisal; The Intimate Critique: Autobiographical Literary Criticism*, coedited with Olivia Frey and Frances Murphy Zauhar; and essays in *Confessions of the Critics; Personal Effects; "Turning the Century": Feminist Theory in the 1990s; Anxious Power: Reading, Writing, and Ambivalence in Narrative by Women; Constructing and Reconstructing Gender; ISLE; Teaching Prose; College Literature;* and *Personal Effects*, among others. Her next book is a collection titled *Autobiographical Writing across the Disciplines: A Critical Reader*, coedited with Olivia Frey. She is also at work on a collection of nature essays.

ROSEMARIE GARLAND-THOMSON is Associate Professor of Women's Studies at Emory University. She is the author of *Extraordinary Bodies: Figuring Physical Disability in American Literature and Culture;* the editor of *Freakery: Cultural Spectacles of the Extraordinary Body;* and coeditor of *Disability Studies: Enabling the Humanities.*

AMY SPANGLER GERALD is a graduate teaching assistant at the University of North Carolina at Greensboro, where she teaches composition, literature, and women's studies courses. She is currently writing her dissertation affirming the importance of personal voice and narrative in feminist pedagogy. Her daughter Abby is now an active toddler who loves to read and talk, like her mom.

ALLISON GIFFEN is Assistant Professor in the English department at Western Washington University. Her fields of interest are early and nineteenth-century American women writers, and she has published works on gender, genre, and teaching in *Genre and Writing: Issues, Arguments and Alternatives.* Some of her recent work considers what it means to be figured as a daughter when building a professional career, an essay of which appears in *American Transcendental Quarterly.* She has coedited a forthcoming collection, *"Jewish First Wife, Divorced": The Selected Letters and Papers of Ethel Gross and Harry Hopkins,* and is currently at work on a study titled *Till Grief melodious grow: Early American Women Poets and the Discursive Formation of Poetic Identity.*

MADELEINE R. GRUMET is Dean of the School of Education at the University of North Carolina, Chapel Hill, and the author of *Bitter Milk: Women and Teaching* as well as numerous publications about teaching, gender, and the body.

DIANE PRICE HERNDL is Associate Professor of English at Iowa State University, the author of *Invalid Women: Figuring Feminine Illness in American Fiction and Culture, 1840–1940,* and the coeditor of *Feminisms: An Anthology of Literary Criticism and Theory.* She is at work on a new book, *Thinking through Breast Cancer.*

MARTHA STODDARD HOLMES is Assistant Professor and Graduate Coordinator, Literature and Writing Studies, California State University, San Marcos, and Assistant Clinical Professor, Voluntary, Department of Family Medicine, School of Medicine, University of California, San Diego. She has published essays on disability in Victorian popular theatre and in the writing of Wilkie Collins, Charles Dickens, and Henry Mayhew. Her book *Fictions of Affliction: Physical Disability in Victorian Culture* is forthcoming. Current projects include an essay on Victorian ideologies of pain and palliative care and a special issue of the *Journal of Medical Humanities,* "Disability and Medicine beyond the Medical Model," coedited with Rosemarie Garland-Thomson.

PETRA KUPPERS is a disabled community artist, Artistic Director of The Olimpias (http://www.olimpias.net), which investigates identity politics, community arts, performance, and (new) media. She is also an assistant professor at Bryant College, Smithfield, Rhode Island, who publishes on disability and performance. The Olimpias give workshops, create performances, and set up installations in the United States and Europe.

ROD MICHALKO is Associate Professor of Sociology at St. Francis Xavier University in Antigonish, Nova Scotia. He is author of *The Mystery of the Eye and the Shadow of Blindness; The Two in One: Walking with Smokie, Walking with Blindness;* and *The Difference That Disability Makes*, forthcoming. In all of his work, Rod Michalko makes use of contemporary social theory as a way to articulate his lived experience of blindness in particular and disability in general.

DEBRA A. MODDELMOG is Professor of English and an associated faculty member of both the Women's Studies Department and the Comparative Studies Department at Ohio State University. Her most recent book is *Reading Desire: In Pursuit of Ernest Hemingway*. She is also the author of essays on Ernest Hemingway, Katherine Anne Porter, William Faulkner, Thomas Pynchon, and multiculturalism.

RAY PENCE is a Ph.D. student in American studies at the University of Kansas. He is in his eighth year as a graduate teaching assistant and is currently working on his dissertation, which addresses the Rehabilitation Act of 1973.

RICHARD L. RADTKE is Full Research Professor in Fisheries Oceanography in the School of Ocean and Earth Sciences and Technology at the University of Hawaii. He has over seventy publications and numerous scientific meeting presentations. In the past two years, Dr. Radtke has traveled for research to Alaska, China, Indonesia, Canada, and Greenland. For his career accomplishments and community service, he has been honored as one of Hawaii's Three Outstanding Young Persons of 1990 and disabled person of the year for 1990 and received the University of Hawaii's highest award for community service, the Robert W. Clopton Award. Dr. Radtke also received a U.S. Presidential Award for Excellence in Science, Mathematics, and Engineering Mentoring (one of ten in the nation).

JAMES R. SKOUGE is Assistant Professor at the University of Hawaii, specializing in assistive technology and media in special education. He collaborates with Richard Radtke on many post-secondary transition activities for youths with and without disabilities, notably a youth television production, *Through the Viewfinder*.

SCOTT ANDREW SMITH received his Ph.D. from Kent State University in the summer of 2000. He currently teaches advanced writing at the University of Southern California and has taught both composition and creative writing for nine years. He taught at Kansas State and Kent State before moving to Los Angeles to teach and live by the ocean.

KATHERINE E. TIRABASSI is a Ph.D. student in composition/rhetoric at the University of New Hampshire. She has taught freshman composition and creative nonfiction and is currently the assistant director for the Robert J. Connors Writing Center at the University of New Hampshire. Her other research interests include writing across the curriculum, writing centers, and literacy studies.

KIMBERLY WALLACE-SANDERS is Assistant Professor in the Institutes of Liberal Arts and Women's Studies at Emory University. She teaches courses on cultural representations of the female body, representations of race and gender in American culture, women and American identity, nineteenth-century African American popular culture, and African American material culture. Her work appears in *American Quarterly, Initiatives, SAGE: A Scholarly Black Woman's Journal, Oxford Companion to African American Literature*, and *Burning Down the House: Recycling Domesticity*. She is completing a book, *Motherlove Supreme: Maternal Obsessions and the Black Mammy Figure in America*.

PAM WHITFIELD is a doctoral student at the University of North Carolina at Greensboro, where she teaches composition, rhetoric, and technical communication. She has published academic articles and personal essays in China, Hong Kong, and the United States. Marrying a Chinese citizen has allowed her to maintain ties to her "second culture."

Index

37113549R00160

Made in the USA
Lexington, KY
21 April 2019